THE COUNTRY
GUESTHOUSE

This Large Print Book carries the
Seal of Approval of N.A.V.H.

A SULLIVAN'S CROSSING NOVEL

THE COUNTRY GUESTHOUSE

ROBYN CARR

WHEELER PUBLISHING
A part of Gale, a Cengage Company

GALE
A Cengage Company

LIBRARY OF CONGRESS CIP DATA ON FILE.
CATALOGUING IN PUBLICATION FOR THIS BOOK
IS AVAILABLE FROM THE LIBRARY OF CONGRESS

ISBN-13: 978-1-4328-7241-0 (hardcover alk. paper)

Published in 2020 by arrangement with Harlequin Books S.A.

Printed in the United States of America
1 2 3 4 5 6 7 24 23 22 21 20

For Mariah Stewart, who is always ready with a fortifying, insightful, funny and powerful pep talk. Thank you, my friend.

Forever — is composed of nows.
      — EMILY DICKINSON

PROLOGUE

Hannah Russell loved the rented cabin she and her colleagues were staying in — it was exquisite. The upscale, relatively new five bedroom/five bath house was in the woods on a lake and had a huge deck from which there was an amazing view of the Rockies. Well, during the day when the sun was out. Just now it was raining. Make that sleeting. By morning there might be nothing but a sheet of ice covering everything. For tonight, there was a blazing fire, and a mixture of rain and ice pelting against the roof and windows.

The cabin was the only part of this retreat she loved. It was her company's leadership training and team building retreat. Her third one. And she was *over* it.

Hannah's boss was really into organizing these professional growth retreats off campus, far away from their daily grind. Of course, *he* didn't attend — but he sent his executives and their teams. Their cell phones and laptops were collected upon arrival, the TVs were not turned on, no radios allowed, no contact with the outside world. They were forced to communicate face-to-face and leave their workaday worlds behind. Dave, director of marketing, said, "I had less withdrawal in drug treatment." Then there were a series of group sessions and exercises. *Hannah, you're going to fold your hands over your chest and let yourself fall backward, trusting Tim to catch you.* This was quite challenging as she didn't trust Tim to respond to an email in a timely manner. And when he finally did, it would lack accurate information. The only thing about Tim she was sure of was that he would take her job if he had an opportunity.

Of course, Tim didn't catch Hannah. "I think I broke my tailbone," she said, rubbing her behind. "I'll need an ambulance. Someone call an ambulance."

"We're not allowed to use our phones," Tim said.

There had been a time or two she had to admit she actually got something out of one of the retreats, but it was usually no more than she could get out of a book, blog or TED Talk. It usually depended on the effectiveness of the moderator. If the moderator was motivating, inventive, experienced and encouraging, there could be some bonding and a few principles to take back to the job, helping them work together more efficiently. That was almost a bad thing — if their sales numbers went up, Peter, the CEO, thought the retreat made the difference and would instruct HR to schedule another one. But if their moderator was a thirty-year-old former beauty contestant in tight jeans who flirted with all of the male employees, like this one did, it was doomed.

This particular retreat was scheduled to last five nights. Hannah and the moderator, the only women, each had their own bedrooms while the men doubled up. The large two-story house with a loft also had a library, a bar and a wine cellar. The bar and wine cellar were locked. On the second night, Todd, Wayne and Dave were in one of the bedrooms passing around a couple of joints while Tim quite noisily banged the moderator in the master suite.

The timing of this retreat wasn't good. Not only did Hannah have a lot of work she'd like to catch up on, her relationship with her fiancé had been strained lately. Wyatt was a little prickly for unknown reasons. They were planning a wedding that would take place in six months and seemed to disagree on everything. She was starting to wonder how couples survived wedding planning. But right now if she had a free weekend, she should spend it with Wyatt, injecting their relationship with a little love and attention, see if she could find out what was irritating him so much. If she had to travel for work, which she frequently did, she would at least be able to talk to Wyatt on the phone. This trip pissed her off. She'd told Peter it was a bad time. Peter told her to take one for the team.

The team appeared to be getting high and getting laid while Hannah was becoming increasingly annoyed.

She decided to pick the lock on the hall closet door to find her laptop and phone. She packed up her things. Now would come the challenging part — aside from some hiking they had planned that the weather had ruined, they weren't going on outings. A van had brought them from the Denver airport and would return to pick them up at the end of the retreat. She wasn't going to be walking anywhere. But she now had a phone. And a computer, though no Wi-Fi password. Tim and the moderator were still going at it and the other guys were killing the Doritos and potato chips, after which they would sleep the sleep of the stoned.

She looked at her old itinerary on her cell phone, called the car service that had provided the van and arranged to be picked up at 6:00 a.m.

She didn't leave a note. Let them think a bear had gotten her.

She sighed a big sigh as she made her escape. She instructed the driver to take her straight to the airport. A few miles into the drive she saw a campground with a store, on the other side of the big lake. The campground looked vacant but there was a light on in the general store. She said to the driver, "Stop over there and if they have coffee, I'll buy you a cup."

"You'll be charged for a stop," he said pleasantly.

"It'll be worth it," she said. "How do you like your coffee?"

"Just black, ma'am."

The sign on the door said the hours of operation were from nine to five, but the door was unlocked and a bell jingled when she swung it open. "Hello? Anybody home?" she called out.

"Well, what have we here?" a man said. "Only the ducks are out in this weather."

She walked toward the back. "It seems to have stopped raining," Hannah said. "Are you open? The sign says . . ."

13

"Barely, but I lit the stove and I have the coffee ready. I was worried about the trees — that was some ice storm last night. If they're covered with freezing rain they can break off in big chunks — it's awful. Where you coming from at the crack of dawn?"

"Oh, I was at an Airbnb on the other side of the lake and I'm running away, but I won't get far without coffee. I hired a car to take me back to the Denver airport."

"What's the matter, girl? Didn't that air thing work out?"

She laughed and said, "The place is beautiful and comfortable and the views are stunning, but I was with a bunch of men at a corporate retreat. They confiscated our laptops and phones and forced us to play psychological games aimed at making us better corporate team members. A worthy thought, but next time I think some of my staff should have a retreat teaching them how to get their work done. That would be so much more helpful."

"Cream or sugar?"

"I think both. I'm celebrating my escape. And one black for my driver."

"If you're celebrating, you should have a sweet roll or muffin," he said.

The door opened and a woman rushed in. "Sully! There's a big black SUV parked out

— Oh," she said. She patted down her hair and pulled her hoodie closed. She seemed to be wearing her pajamas and boots.

"We were just getting acquainted, sweetheart. I'm Sully," he said, sticking out a hand to Hannah. "This here is Helen, who I left asleep when I snuck out."

"I'm Hannah. I was telling your husband, I was at an Airbnb on the other side of the lake for a corporate retreat — me and a flirty female moderator and a bunch of men. And I decided last night, I've had enough."

"Was it dreadful?" Helen asked.

"Yes," she said. "Plus, I have a fiancé at home. I'd rather spend my time with him than four men who all think they should have my job."

"And if you don't mind — what is your job?" Helen asked, pouring herself a cup of coffee.

"Don't take offense at Helen, girl. She's particularly nosy. If you'd rather not —"

"I sell hospital equipment for a major distributor. Not bandages or bedpans — more like everything from MRIs to prosthetic joints. I'm a sales manager, which means I have a team working for me."

"I bet you were at Owen's place," Helen said. "He must be traveling again."

"I honestly don't know whose house it is.

15

But I'd love to stay in that place when there aren't any work-related people on the premises. What a great place it would be to recharge."

"Let me ask you — were there a lot of stunning, artsy photographs and lithographs on display?" Helen said.

"Yes! You know the owner?"

"Well, he's a neighbor. A well-known photographer. He's won awards for his work, but he travels so often he finally found a way to make his trips slightly less economically painful — he rents out the house. Look him up sometime — his name is Owen Abrams and he does astonishing work."

"The house is stunning," Hannah said.

Sully provided two coffees in to-go cups. "Now, you want a little pastry to go with that?" he asked.

"A couple of muffins, please. It was very nice meeting you both. What do I owe you?"

"Consider it a treat, it's so nice to meet you. Come back and see us in your leisure time," Helen said. "Sully has cabins for people not inclined to camp or rent a big house."

But Hannah was thinking about that house — that lovely, large, beautiful house. The best thing in the world would be to convince Wyatt to take some time off and rent that house for a couple of weeks. It might help mend their relationship. Or failing that, she had girlfriends . . . Hannah had been working so hard the last several years. Wyatt had as well, but his job as a pharmaceutical sales rep was considerably less stressful than hers as a sales manager. He had only himself and his accounts to worry about while Hannah had to worry about her entire team. He made less money, but he seemed more carefree. Maybe because he was living in Hannah's house, rent-free.

Hannah had been climbing the corporate ladder for years and was a little burned-out, yet she made too much money to quit. Wyatt's suggestion was that she see someone about her depression. She hadn't thought of herself as depressed just because she wished they could be alone together and talk the way they used to.

Then she got home. She hadn't called Wyatt. She expected him to be home — it was Saturday and it was still early. She heard voices and scuffling. She left her bag and purse near the door from the garage and walked down the hall to the master bedroom. And in her bedroom she found Wyatt and Stephanie frantically scrambling to grab their clothes.

"Seriously?" was all Hannah could say.

Wyatt was sleeping with Hannah's assistant while Hannah was at a retreat with her colleagues. Rich.

Stephanie looked at Wyatt in a panic and burst into tears. "How am I going to get home? Are you going to take me home?"

"Get an Uber," Hannah said. "Oh, and you're fired."

To climb steep hills
requires slow pace at first.
— WILLIAM SHAKESPEARE

1

Owen and his Great Dane, Romeo, walked around the lake and up the road to Sully's store. Sully was sitting on the porch with his son-in-law, Cal Jones. His little grand-daughter was sitting on the porch steps. The moment three-year-old Elizabeth saw them, she clapped her hands and yelled, "Wo-meo!" The Great Dane paused, turned his big head to look up at Owen. "Okay," Owen said. Romeo took off at a gallop, looking like a pony, loping across the yard to his welcome party. Sully's yellow Lab, Beau, met Romeo at the porch steps and the two dogs treated themselves to a trot around the yard.

Owen leaned his walking stick against the porch, doffed his backpack and ruffled Elizabeth's hair as he took the steps.

"Hey, neighbor," Sully said. "How's the shootin' today?"

"I only see the good stuff if I leave the

camera at home," Owen said. He shook Sully's hand, then Cal's. "Looks like the campground's filling up."

"It's always spring break somewhere," Sully said. "At least I get the outdoorsy types instead of the drink-till-you-puke types."

Owen laughed. "Good planning, Sully. Is it too early for a beer?" he asked, looking at Cal's beer.

"I hope not," Cal said. "Maggie's in Denver. I'm holding down the fort with Elizabeth's help."

"Your secret is safe with me," Owen said.

"That's nice, but unnecessary. Now that Elizabeth can actually talk, nothing is sacred."

"What's a sacwed, Daddy?"

"I'll tell you later," Cal said.

Owen got himself a cold bottle of beer from the cooler inside, left a few dollars on the counter and wandered back onto the porch. He sat down, stretched out his very long legs and took a long pull on his beer. Romeo and Beau wandered back to the store porch. Romeo treated Elizabeth to a full face wash, cleaning her off with a few hearty licks. She squealed with delight and said, "Oh-oh-oh-oh, Womeo! I love you, too."

The men all laughed. "Why can't the weather be like this all year?" Owen asked.

"Because we need that snowpack," Sully said. "Don't need those summer fires, though. You just coming home or you getting ready to go away again?"

"I've been back a week," Owen said. "Next is Taiwan in about a month, but they've been having some serious weather issues right where I plan to shoot. I'm keeping an eye on that."

Owen, a photographer, was a freelancer. When he was younger he did a lot of portraits, school pictures, weddings, family Christmas cards, that sort of thing. When he was in his thirties he began doing more artistic photographs and sometimes more political photos — war-ravaged villages, citizens of impoverished countries, the poverty or decadence in his own country, as well as interesting or beautiful landscapes, mountains, wildlife. Then he wrote accompanying essays or blogs for his photos and became something of a travel writer, with a twist. He would expose the blunders, chaos, humor and turmoil in his own little world of professional photography, and he became famous — reluctantly. He snuck into the kitchens of five-star hotels, backstage at concerts, into locker rooms at sporting events and behind the scenes at dog shows — anything that seemed interesting and where he could potentially expose a secret or insight or revelation. A few books of his collected photos and essays were published and, for some crazy reason, people bought them.

What he was most interested in was art and travel, experiencing other cultures. And solitude — he always traveled alone.

"I'm spending a couple of weeks in Vietnam in July. I love Vietnam," Owen said.

"I can't remember loving it," Sully said.

"Exactly what my dad said." Owen laughed.

"It's so polite of you to remind me I'm old enough to be your father," Sully said.

"Old enough to be mine, too," Cal said. "Oh, that's right, you kind of are. By marriage."

"Where's Helen?" Owen asked.

"Some kind of writing convention in New York."

"And you never go along?"

"Not to these book things," Sully said. "She's better off without me. She and the writer friends whoop it up. I don't have the wanderlust like you and Helen. And someone has to be around here to mind the store.

I can't see renting out my place like you do yours."

"That doesn't always work out so great," Owen said. "There are times it's a little awkward. Sometimes a trip gets canceled and I end up being on the property. But that's only happened twice. The Realtor who manages the rentals around here always contacts the guests and offers a refund or another place, but if they want the house, I just stay in the barn and they mostly ignore me." He took a drink of his beer. "I should probably sell the house and move into the barn. It's really all I need."

"Why'd you build that big house, then?" Sully asked.

"I like that house," Owen said. "I also like the barn."

The barn had been converted into a studio and guesthouse. There was a bedroom and kitchenette behind the studio. The light was good. He had all his camera equipment set up there, plus shelves for his favorite books. There was a bigger library in the main house — Owen loved books. He took people in very small doses and liked his own company. He was drawn to nature, travel, reading, quiet and his work. He blew up and transferred his pictures onto canvases, mounted them himself, carted them around to a variety of galleries and gift shops, and the last few years he had been contracted to provide his photos to hotels, restaurants and private buyers.

"You know I live in a barn," Cal reminded Owen.

"My barn isn't as fancy as your barn. It's a shop. With a bed in it. But my house trumps your house." Then he grinned.

"What do you do with all those bedrooms?" Sully asked.

"Nothing except when I rent it out. In a few years I might sell it. I don't know. I like the location. And sometimes my sister and her kids come. Plus, I have friends . . ."

"You do?" Sully asked.

"Well, yeah. Some. Not too many. I don't want too many. How many have you got?"

"About six," Sully said, smiling. "And a town. Plus the Jones clan intermarried with some of my friends so now I have a big family, and I never saw that coming."

"Neither did the Jones clan," Cal said.

"Is your whole family here now?" Owen asked Cal.

"All but my parents and my sister Sedona — she's still back east, but she turns up regularly for visits. Sierra and Connie are neighbors now. Dakota just took a teaching job right smack between Boulder and Timberlake, so we see him and Sid a lot. Sid's brother and his wife live in town. It's a complicated web. I could make you up a chart."

"Is there going to be a test?" Owen asked. But he was thinking he had far fewer connections, and he wondered if they found him odd. But of course they found him odd — he was six foot five and thin, seen wandering around the trails with his backpack full of cameras and his giant dog named Romeo. His big house was full of unused bedrooms that he let strangers borrow. He explained away his solitary ways as a life of art when the truth was he was afraid of close relationships and he distracted himself with travel. Women hit on him a lot. They probably suspected he was rich. From time to time he let them catch him, just not for long. He was only a little rich. He made a very respectable living.

"If you met the right woman you could have a mess of kids," Sully said.

"You think there's any chance of that now?" Owen asked. "I'm forty-five and dull."

"I didn't know you were only forty-five," Cal said, grinning.

"Another twenty years and you'll be a cranky old man and fit right in," Sully said.

"Then again, I only met Helen about a year ago. I still can't figure out what she sees in me." Then he laughed wickedly.

Owen was crazy about Helen. She and Sully were living together. Helen wrote mystery novels that Sully said were filled with gore and dead bodies. He claimed to sleep with one eye open. Owen thought they were the cutest couple anywhere. "Maybe when I'm seventy, I'll meet the right one. You're a good example — if you can find a perfect woman, anyone can."

"Well, good luck to you," Sully said. "But that ain't gonna help use all those bedrooms much by then."

The few weeks after finding her fiancé with her assistant turned into a complete nightmare for Hannah. She faced some very unpleasant and immediate chores: get Wyatt out of her house, hire some temporary admin help at the office and try to ignore the never-ending gossip about how Hannah came home from a business trip to find her fiancé and assistant knocking boots. Everyone but Hannah was quite entertained by the tantalizing story.

Hannah and Wyatt had been together for three years. They'd dated for a year, lived together for a year and been engaged for a year. Hannah was thirty-five; he was not her first boyfriend. He wasn't her first fiancé, for that matter. She overheard one of the gossips say, "Maybe three's the charm."

She had to tell her friends who were supposed to be bridesmaids. Except Stephanie, who had also been a designated bridesmaid. That was irrelevant now, though Hannah did wonder if they were still seeing each other. Maybe Wyatt could marry her since he already had the tux ordered.

Hannah also had to cancel everything that had been reserved ahead of the wedding date — reception hall, caterer, photographer, flowers, band. The wedding was barely planned and yet there was all this detritus. The last time she'd broken up with a fiancé, they hadn't gotten this far into the planning — all she'd had to do was give back the ring. Wyatt was not getting the ring back — she'd sell it to pay for a vacation for herself.

All that cleanup took a full week. She then called the Realtor in Colorado and booked the house near Sullivan's Crossing for the first available two-week rental. She wanted a quiet, beautiful place to get her head together. It wouldn't be available for several weeks, but that gave her something to look forward to. Spring in the Rockies.

And then, just as she was starting to feel

like herself again, the world came to an end. Her college roommate and best friend, Erin Waters, was consoling her on the phone, telling her it wasn't her fault, that no, she didn't attract losers, that everything was going to work out for the best — and all the while she was coughing relentlessly.

"You are going to see a doctor about that, aren't you?" Hannah asked.

"Absolutely," Erin said. "I feel like shit. I've been trying to sleep it off. But I guess I need drugs. I can't remember ever being this sick."

"And is Noah all right?" Hannah asked, speaking of Erin's five-year-old son.

"He's fine. I'm giving him extra vitamin C just in case. I have a doctor's appointment this afternoon and he'll be with Linda." Linda was Noah's regular babysitter, and Noah and Erin were very close to Linda and her family.

"Then you better stay home and rest."

"You know I will. I'm no martyr."

"Call me when you're back from the doctor. Let me know how it went, what he said."

"Sure," she said. Then she coughed hard and they ended the call.

Erin didn't call back. Instead, it was Linda who called a few days later. She explained that as soon as she examined Erin, the doctor called an emergency transport. She was taken to the hospital and admitted to the ICU with an advanced case of pneumonia, and in a very short period of time, she had passed away. Just slipped away. They resuscitated her twice and had her on life support for about twenty-four hours.

Devastated and in shock, Hannah headed for Madison at Linda's first call, as did their other two best friends, Sharon and Kate. They all stayed with Noah at Erin's house and made the funeral arrangements. They not only made all the arrangements, they paid for everything, as well. According to Erin's wishes, she preferred to be cremated and have a celebration of life. You wouldn't think a thirty-five-year-old woman would have articulated such desires, but she had a child, was estranged from her family, worked as a paralegal and had spelled out her wishes in a very precise will. The four women had been very close since college, kept in touch, saw each other regularly even though three of them lived in Minneapolis and Erin had moved to Madison after college.

It was a very complicated and unpleasant situation. Erin and her mother had always had a strained relationship and hadn't spoken in years. The main cause seemed to

31

be a half brother who had been a delinquent since he was quite young. Erin said he was abusive and her mother had always stood up for him, even when she witnessed his horrible treatment of Erin. There was a time shortly after Hannah met Erin that Erin's brother had beat her, though he was five years younger. The police had been called. Erin wasn't too badly hurt but her mother pleaded with her to say it hadn't happened, claim she'd fallen so Roger wouldn't be arrested. He had only been fifteen at the time and had already been in lots of trouble. Erin refused and mother and daughter, being on opposite sides, withdrew from each other. Their communication from that point on was spotty and never friendly.

In fact, something Hannah and Erin had in common, something that had bonded them in college and later, was their difficulty with their mothers. Hannah's mother had passed away a couple of years ago but Erin's was still going strong, still protecting her son, regularly asking Erin to help Roger. Erin finally took a job in Madison when she was about twenty-six mainly to put distance between herself and her family.

Despite her troubled relationship with her mother, Erin was a wonderful, loving, happy person and had many good friends in and

around Madison. Erin's mother was noti-
fied of her daughter's death but it wasn't
really a surprise that no family members at-
tended the celebration of life. The place was
throbbing with people, all stunned and
grieving, for she had always been a healthy
and vibrant young woman, so active and
positive. There hadn't been a man in her
life at the moment, but a couple of exes
turned up to pay their respects and to check
on Noah, though none were Noah's father.

And that was where things got really
complicated. Erin's will indicated that she
didn't want Noah to be raised by her mother
or her brother. She was afraid her mother
would allow Roger near and that he'd be
abusive to Noah. Her will was very clear.
Calling on a years-old promise, Noah was
to go into Hannah's custody. Hannah, who
wondered if she'd ever marry, wondered if
she even wanted to anymore, and who was
slowly getting used to the idea that she'd
never have children. Hannah, who had
called off not one but two weddings.

Sharon and Kate were also named as
alternates but both were married. Sharon
was expecting her second child and Kate
was the mother of two children and three
stepchildren. Both women were nurses, one
married to a teacher and one to an aircraft

mechanic. They were working mothers with very full and busy lives. And Erin had made it clear she wanted it to be Hannah.

"I have no idea how to raise a child," Hannah said.

"Neither did we," Kate said. "I feel your pain. I inherited three stepchildren who hated me on sight. At least Noah loves you."

"We've lived in different towns. We haven't spent that much time together. He knows us all mostly because his mom was close to us." Because as young women will do, when they did get together, they tried to leave the kids behind. There were the occasional holiday gatherings, kids included, but as Hannah didn't have kids for Noah to play with, she felt they hadn't really bonded yet. And Noah had a couple of health issues that Hannah wasn't up to speed on because, while she paid attention when Erin talked, she wasn't dealing with his condition every day. He had a very mild case of cerebral palsy that caused weakness in his legs and for that he wore leg braces, used forearm crutches and spent a lot of time in physical therapy. Fortunately he was otherwise healthy. She knew there was every possibility those legs would strengthen and he'd reach his full mobility potential with the proper care. But not only was Hannah not a nurse like her other two friends, she was also not a mother.

"And yet, when she asked you, you said yes," Sharon reminded her.

"The first time it came up, we were in college!" Hannah said. "We were talking about our mothers — both of them were terrible mothers! And she said, 'If I ever have a family, will you take my children if anything should happen to me and my husband? And I promise to do the same for you!' And then five years ago when she decided to have a baby alone, she asked me again. Five years ago when I was thirty and I thought I was getting married in less than a year. I thought I'd get married and have a family. I didn't ever expect it to really happen or that I'd be on my own when it did. Oh God, I love Noah, but what if I fail him?"

That was when she remembered Erin had said the same thing when she was expecting — and she was the best mom Noah could have asked for.

"Sometimes those physical and health problems are easier to deal with than the emotional ones," Kate said. "My kids are all physically healthy but they have one emotional crisis after another. At least Erin and Noah had a plan and he was being treated. The last time we talked, Erin said he was improving steadily and she was confident that Noah was going to be strong and able in every way."

"And grieving his mother," Hannah said. "What if I fail him there?"

"All of us are at risk for that," Kate said. "We'll help you as much as we can. I think she was depending on all of us."

In the end the three women stayed with Noah for a week, accomplished a very lovely service, packed up his belongings and closed up Erin's house, putting it in the hands of a Realtor. Burying his mother and leaving his beloved babysitter was hard on him, but Hannah promised him they would be visiting Linda and her children, who had become his friends. Hannah, along with Sharon and Kate, met with Noah's doctors and physical therapists, collected his medical records and headed back to Minneapolis. There was a trust and insurance money, though it would take a while for all of that to be settled, but Noah was medically insured, thanks to Erin's diligence, and Hannah could look at a list of good practitioners that his Madison doctors and therapists had recommended.

But it had taken her the better part of a half hour to get his leg braces on the first time. And Noah had to help her.

Hannah immediately took family leave. She planned to cancel her Colorado getaway, though that was low on her list of priorities. It was already April and she wanted to get Noah registered for school in the fall so they could spend the next few months getting to know each other before he started his life with a new school. She also needed to find a new babysitter so she could work, figure out how she was going to travel for business, set him up with new doctors . . .

And then Noah said the words that broke her heart. "Hannah, is my mom happy?"

It took every cell in her body to keep from crumbling. "She is safe and happy and living the life of an angel among angels who laugh and sing and watch over us. She's happy and she's always near. She lives in our hearts because when we remember her, we know she's close to us. She loves us and we love her. Okay?"

"Okay," he said. "It would be better for me if she was here."

"I know, buddy. I know." She hugged him close. "You know what? Screw work and responsibility. We have a vacation coming up. I rented us a huge cabin, a beautiful cabin on a beautiful lake in the Rocky Mountains, and it's amazing. There are lots of elk. I mean lots. What do you say? Should we take a vacation before we do all this work of settling in? We need time together, you and me."

"Okay. Hannah, but is *screw* one of those words you're not supposed to say?"

"Probably. I'll have to read up on that."

*Be sure you put your feet in the
right place, then stand firm.*
— ABRAHAM LINCOLN

2

It had taken a lot of planning and organization to move Noah to Hannah's Minneapolis house. All his clothes and toys were transferred and Hannah held on to a few of Erin's things — some everyday dishes, a few books, a couple of cozy sweaters, some quilts and blankets and her journal. The entries were few and spotty, but one day she would share it with Noah. They had to see new doctors and meet with her lawyer to establish her as his legal guardian. They met with a physical therapist, who gave her a pamphlet that showed the at-home exercises they could do to strengthen his legs. During that time they spent several weekend days and evenings with Sharon and Kate and their families to help Noah get a sense of belonging, to ease his loneliness. Sharon's and Kate's kids were wonderful with him.

Some nights were hard. The first time she heard him crying for his mom, she went to his room, scooped him up and carried him to her bed. They cuddled each other to sleep. But Noah could barely walk without his leg braces and crutches, so if he wanted to get up in the night, Hannah had to carry him. And if he wanted to wander to her room, he put on his braces to get there, then nearly broke her shins with his heavy shoes when he crawled into bed. Sometimes they cried together and sometimes they laughed, and they talked a lot about Erin.

There was nothing on earth better able to drive the thought of Wyatt and a failed relationship from her mind and heart like the company of a little boy. It was only days before she thought she wouldn't be able to live without him.

Hannah was emotionally and physically exhausted and worried about a lot of things she couldn't control, but she was so happy to be packing for a real retreat. She was grateful she'd been too busy to cancel that rental. She thought she'd be going alone, using the time to heal from her breakup with Wyatt, but now she and Noah would have each other. They could explore, read, watch movies, go fishing, get to know each other better. Then the phone rang and the Realtor who had booked the beautiful house said the owner's trip had been canceled and he would be staying in his studio on the property. If that was not acceptable to Hannah, she could look around for another place.

"He'll be there?" Hannah asked.

"Yes, this has happened a couple of times. He has a spacious shop and guesthouse, where he works, and says he has no problem with renting you the house. He won't access the house while you're there. He won't be a bother. On the other hand, if you have a problem, you can knock on his door. He'll be right across the yard. But it's entirely up to you."

"I feel awkward taking his house," she said.

The Realtor laughed. "Oh, Ms. Russell, you're paying top dollar for that beautiful house. The owner doesn't mind, but the final decision is yours. I can try to find you an alternate residence. Or I'd be happy to give you a refund."

She had longed for that space, and now she had Noah and a need to escape to help them heal and bond. "I have a five-year-old son," Hannah said. It was the first time she had claimed him thusly. "Can you vouch for his character?"

"Absolutely. Owen Abrams is a fine man. He's well-known around the lake and town.

If this worries you, remember you can call my cell day or night, but I don't think you'll have a single problem. In fact, if you do have a question or problem, like the Wi-Fi is out or you can't find the remote for the TV, he's right on the property. Owen is very hospitable."

"Owen," she repeated. Yes, that was the man Helen mentioned. She pictured an older person, maybe around Sully and Helen's age. Maybe Owen would be grandfatherly toward Noah, which would be so welcome, since he didn't have any experience with a grandparent. Erin's mother had never spent any time with Noah; Hannah wasn't sure if Noah even knew she existed. At the thought of seeing Sully and Helen again, her decision was made.

"Am I going to school from your house?" Noah asked Hannah.

"Eventually, but we have the whole summer first and we have so many things to see and do."

"It's okay if we don't do anything," he said.

That's probably what depression or grief sounds like in a five-year-old, Hannah thought. "We're going to do all kinds of stuff," she said. She knew the fresh air and sunshine and lake would be good for both of them. "First, let's get our clothes packed, and then we can decide what toys and electronics to take. The house has TVs all over the place, but we're not going to sit in front of the TV. And there's Wi-Fi but no computer so we'll take my laptop and tablet. We're going to want to buy fishing stuff when we get there. We should buy new bathing suits before we go!" She made a face. "I suppose I'm going to have to learn how to put a worm on a hook." Then she shivered all over, making a terrible face. And Noah laughed.

So there was the lesson. Just look like a ridiculous fool and it would tickle him.

She sighed. It was going to be a very long summer.

They packed everything up and started off in the car. If it were just Hannah or Hannah and a girlfriend, they'd push it, make it in a day and a half or less, but with a five-year-old, there were many stops. If it were just Hannah, the radio would be blasting out the latest tunes, but instead she kept the volume down and played an audiobook or podcast. Noah put on his headphones and watched a movie or two. They ate ice cream in the car.

"My mom never let me eat in the car," he said.

"We're on vacay," she replied with a big smile.

Sharon called during the drive and Hannah answered with, "You're on speaker."

"How is the trip going so far? Noah?"

"It's okay. We eat ice cream in the car."

"Fabulous! Are you seeing anything interesting?"

"No. It's only cornfields. Cornfields forever."

It was toward the end of the first day of driving that Noah said, "Hannah, will you tell me things about my mom?"

"What kinds of things, honey?"

"I don't know," he said. "The regular stuff. Just how she was. So I don't forget the regular stuff. You know?"

She did know. He might not be able to articulate it but he wanted to be reminded of her, the woman who was his mom and her best friend. The ordinary things that made her a whole person.

"Hmm. She always smelled so good — a little like flowers and soap and maybe some lotion. Purple was her favorite color. There was so much purple in your house! She was left-handed. Do you remember that? So sometimes when she was chopping up stuff

45

for dinner she was terrifying — it looked like she was about to cut her fingers off. She ate tomatoes like apples — she'd lick the outside skin, sprinkle a little salt on the wet spot and go after it. Lick, sprinkle, bite. I remember when she decided to knit a sweater," Hannah said with a laugh. "Oh God, that was hilarious! She had the biggest knotty mess going on there and she was so determined, she actually finished it. One sleeve was three inches longer than the other! Horrible!" Hannah giggled and Noah joined her. "Now that I think of it, she had a number of half-done crafts around the house. She hooked half a rug. She did half a crewel picture, a couple of petit points that would never become throw pillows, and she collected a lot of fabric for a quilt that she just didn't get around to. She liked to read, talk on the phone, always had her laptop open on the coffee table. She sat on the floor a lot. I hate the floor. I want something soft under me, a nice soft couch. And she was a girlie girl — she liked ruffles and lace and flowers and lipstick. She always got her nails done — fingers and toes . . ."

"She said people at work noticed her hands because she was at the desk, moving papers around," he put in.

"That's right, because she worked in an

office, gestured with her hands while she talked . . ."

"She had a cowlick," he said. "In front. I have a cowlick in back." He pointed to his crown.

"I didn't know that," Hannah said.

"Did you know about the tattoo?" he asked.

"I did!" she said with a laugh. "I thought she was crazy to do that."

"She was gonna do one more," he informed her. "One you could see without pulling her pants down. It was gonna be for me."

"Awesome," Hannah said. "Just knowing that she wanted to do that is almost as good as if she did."

"Almost," he said quietly.

"She read all the time, late into the night. She didn't watch too much TV. If it was a good book, she would read at stoplights. She would tell me about every book she was reading and she couldn't fall asleep until she did one more page, one more page, one more page. I do that, too. Do you love to read?"

He shrugged his shoulders as she watched his reflection in the rearview mirror. "My mom used to read to me."

"We're going to do some reading together

this summer, okay? We'll find amazing, wonderful books about adventures and stuff and we'll read together. We could go to the nearest library. Maybe you'll catch the bug. But for right now, watch for a McDonald's. I'm thinking fries."

"Yeah, I could think that," he said.

And Hannah said a silent prayer. *Oh, please, God, help me with this. I am not good enough for this boy, at least not now. He deserves better.*

Their first day of driving was long, and the second day they got up early, had a big breakfast and hit the road running. Noah spent a lot of time with his headphones on, watching movies or falling asleep, and they didn't stop as many times as they had the first day. When they were within an hour of the house, Hannah pulled into a grocery store lot. "Almost done for the day, kiddo," she said. "We'll need some groceries. And I need your help because I'm not sure what all your favorite foods are."

"'Kay," he said, unstrapping himself from his safety seat.

She went around to help him out of the SUV's back seat but he brushed her hands away and managed to get out on his own. He might be slow and stiff-legged, given the braces, but he was confident and self-sufficient. They loaded up on groceries and headed for the house. "I hope you like this place," she said, buckling him in. "It's beautiful. It has lots of books. And we have Netflix so maybe tonight we can watch a movie."

"'Kay," he said.

"You pretty tired, buddy?"

"Yeah," he said. "I was wishing Mom could come."

"Me, too," Hannah said. "But we'll have fun, I think. There's a campground on the other side of the lake and I met the people who run it. We'll check it out. Maybe there will be kids there, camping with their parents. Maybe you'll make friends."

"Maybe," he said. "Usually I just have Linda's kids or the teachers because . . ." He stopped and shrugged.

"Because?" she pushed.

"I'm not very fast," he said.

"You're getting stronger and better every day. We'll work at it, Noah. Your mother said you wouldn't have to wear the braces forever. She said your condition is mild, that you'll be walking without braces before you know it."

"I'll know it," he said.

"Let's buy all of our supplies and then

we'll get set up at the house and plan our adventures," she said.

It wasn't long until they pulled into the clearing and she watched Noah's reaction to the majestic cabin. "Look at that," he said, straightening. "It's like a castle! Made of logs!"

"Isn't it beautiful?" she asked, thrilled to her very marrow that she had somehow pleased Noah. There it sat atop a long lot that sloped ever so slightly toward a crystalline blue lake, a wooden dock stretching out from the shore. There was a small building that looked a little like a stable that she guessed it was the owner's shop and guesthouse. "Wait till you see it inside!"

"And look at that lake!" he said. "Are there horses in that barn?"

"I'm afraid not," she said. "That's where the owner works." But at that moment she'd cash in her retirement for horses for Noah.

She came around to his side in case he wanted help to get out. But, once again, he brushed her aside. He was happy and excited to be done with the drive. And just as Noah was getting out, a very large dark brown dog appeared. His ears were upright and pointed, his legs spindly, and his head was square with a wet pink tongue hanging out of his mouth.

"Whoa!" Noah said, hanging on to Hannah so he wouldn't fall. "Hey, look at you," he said, just as the Great Dane stuck his wet nose into Noah's face. "You're bigger than me!"

There was a whistle and a shout. "Romeo!"

The dog backed away, looking for all the world like he might be embarrassed.

"Hi. Ms. Russell?" a very tall man asked. "I'm Owen Abrams."

"Oh, hello," she said. "I didn't know I'd see you today."

"What kind of dog is that?" Noah asked.

"This is Romeo. He's a Great Dane," Owen said. "He's very nice and extremely friendly but you have to watch out — he can be clumsy and he's so big it can be a catastrophe. He loves kids and sometimes he loves them too much." Right on cue, Romeo almost licked Noah's face off. But Noah laughed wildly and immediately put his arms around Romeo's neck.

"And your name is?" Owen asked.

"Noah," he said, hanging on to Romeo. "I didn't never have a dog."

He's a good dog," Owen said. "He's a rescue. He's been with me five years now and he's almost six years old. That's his full adult height and he's off the charts, but he's gentle. And sweet. It's just that he's clumsy, like I said. He sometimes knocks people over just saying hello." Then he said to Hannah, "Let me help you get your stuff inside, and then I'll leave you to your vacation."

"You're living in that barn there?" Noah asked.

"Yes, it's nice inside and I have everything I need. I love the house but I admit, sometimes it just swallows me up." He pulled a couple of grocery sacks out of the back of the SUV.

"Come on, Noah, let's get you up the stairs onto the porch while I unload," Hannah said. "You can call Romeo to come with you if it's all right with Owen. Once you're up the stairs." Then she handed him the crutches.

Glancing over her shoulder, she saw Owen was frozen, watching Noah walk stiff-legged toward the stairs. He frowned and met her eyes. She smiled at him.

"It's all right with me and I am sure it will be fine with Romeo," Owen said.

Hannah got Noah situated on a deck chair. Then she clicked her tongue against her teeth to call the dog. He lumbered up the stairs and slowly went to Noah, sitting down politely beside him, patiently accepting the boy's petting.

Hannah tried the door to the house. It was unlocked, probably because Owen was home. She'd been told the key would be under the mat — great security system. Then she went down the steps to unload their groceries and luggage. "Don't let that big dog eat you," she told Noah on the fly.

It took a few trips, even with Owen's help, to get everything out of the SUV and into the house. She left the bags near the master bedroom door and began putting away the groceries. "Thank you for your help, Owen. Can I call you Owen or would you prefer Mr. Abrams?"

"Owen is great."

"And I'm Hannah. I appreciate the help and the use of your very beautiful home. Just what the doctor ordered."

"Do you mind me asking about your son's —"

"He's not my son," she said in a whisper. "Not yet. He's my best friend's son. She passed away a few weeks ago. It's been very hard on both of us, Noah and me. And on Erin's other close friends. It was sudden and unexpected — complications from the flu. I guess that's the best way to explain it. It was a bad flu and went downhill from there. As for Noah's condition, the leg braces. He has cerebral palsy, a very mild case, and with good medical care and therapy he will overcome most if not all of the problems associated with it. He's getting stronger every year. He's the best kid. Right now we're really missing his mom."

"I'm sorry for your loss," he said. "Is there anything more I can do to help you settle in?"

Hannah grinned. "Can we borrow the dog for a couple of weeks? That's the biggest smile I've seen on Noah's face in weeks."

"I'll be around," he said. "And when I'm around, Romeo is around. Just be careful because he's —"

"I know. Clumsy."

He pushed his shaggy hair back with a big hand and smiled shyly. The man was so tall, Hannah was staring into his chest. "I can relate to the poor guy's problem. I'm a little clumsy, too," he said.

One of the issues with having a trauma buried in your past was obsession. Owen was at his computer for hours while Hannah and Noah settled into the house. He researched her car license, her name, and while he didn't know Noah's last name, he soon found it. Erin Waters of Madison had been survived by her son, Noah, her mother, Victoria Addison, her half brother, Roger

Addison, many friends . . . Hannah's name and Noah's turned up in the obituary. It also turned up on LinkedIn. Hannah's name popped up here and there in business-related stories and while there was no media coverage of her taking custody of a little boy, he became comfortable with the idea that she was legit and he was not dealing with a kidnapping.

But he'd watch the situation closely. He had that undercover agent, Romeo. If anyone could make a kid talk it was a big Great Dane.

Then he read for a couple of hours about cerebral palsy and what appeared to be diplegia — he read about physical therapy, about prognosis. It was quite hopeful.

The next thing he knew, Romeo was whining to go out in the early morning before it was even entirely light. Owen held him off as long as possible. When he did open the door, Romeo ran barking onto the lawn and chased a couple of does. When he came back a moment later, he looked like he was grinning.

"That was just plain rude, Romeo," Owen said. "They were girls, for one thing. And they weren't bothering you."

"And one of them looked very preggers," came a voice from across the yard.

There sat Hannah on the porch, a cup of coffee balanced on the arm of her chair. He walked over to her. "She was pretty quick, though, wasn't she?"

"Oh, she skedaddled. Would you like a coffee?"

"You've got a pot on?"

"I've been up awhile. How do you take it?"

"Black. Thanks. That's very neighborly of you. Especially since you weren't expecting me to be hanging around."

"That dog is going to save my life," she said. Romeo came up on the porch and nudged her. "Yes, you are a handsome dude." Then she went inside to fetch the coffee.

"I take it Noah is sleeping in," Owen said, accepting the cup.

"He had a restless night and now he's fallen back to sleep. Sometimes there are things like muscle spasms or contractures— tightening. Sometimes his legs hurt and jerk. A little massage helps." She sipped her coffee. "It helped more when his mom did it but he's stuck with me."

"This must be such a hard transition. For both of you."

"It's going to take a lot of getting used to. But he's so brave and good-natured. If I toss and turn I wake up mean as a bear."

Owen grinned. "Were you ever married?" he asked. "No, wait, that was personal. I apologize."

"You're okay. No. I was engaged. Twice. I'm glad I discovered it wasn't a good idea before the vows. You?"

"I went through a divorce ten years ago, but I'm still on friendly terms with my ex, though she remarried."

"That must be a little awkward . . ."

"Nah, it's okay. We didn't want any of the same things but she's a very good person. A good friend. We rarely see each other but she checks in sometimes, asks me where I've been lately. I check on her sometimes, less often. I'm not as outgoing or social as she is. She married a man who loves being around lots of people and I live on a lake in the mountains and travel alone."

"You're not that antisocial," she said. "You're sitting on the porch with me and it's not even seven. We're having a coffee klatch." She pulled her feet up and held her cup with both hands. "And while you didn't intend to impose, I'm very happy for the company."

"If you ever need space, just say so," he said.

"Oh, I will. I'm not some withering flower.

But honestly, with the situation as it is right now, having another adult to talk to is . . . I don't know . . . Fortifying. A little later today I'm going to run over to the Crossing and say hello. As I was leaving your place last time I stopped there for coffee and met the owner and his wife. Nice people."

"Helen and Sully are a couple but not married. Wonderful folks. You said something last night about your girlfriends? About Noah and your girlfriends? I'm not sure I got that reference right . . ."

"We went to college together, four of us. Me, Erin — that's Noah's mom — Sharon and Kate. We met freshman year and hit it off. We were actually a few of the poor kids — we couldn't afford to live on campus or join sororities. We all had jobs and as many credits as we could carry, not to mention loans. By our second year we could afford to share a crappy off-campus duplex because none of us could stand living at home another minute. We helped each other study, find jobs and boyfriends, became each other's therapists and confidantes, and I swear, without each other, we would not have gotten degrees. Sharon and Kate are both married with kids and Erin and I were in their weddings. Erin never did get married. And I had to call off two weddings. I am not planning a third."

"But Noah . . . ?"

"Suffice it to say, there was no man in the picture." And she closed the door on that topic.

But Owen was stubborn. "Where's his male influence? Grandpa? Uncle?"

"Erin had many good friends and if you'd known her you wouldn't be at all surprised to learn that there were even a couple of really nice ex-boyfriends at her memorial. She was close with a lot of people from work, from her neighborhood. She was active in the community. She was involved with the Cerebral Palsy Foundation and a couple of other support groups. Noah had been with the same babysitter for a long time and she has a lovely husband and a few kids. Saying goodbye to her was almost as hard as saying goodbye to his mom. But at least we can Skype and visit Linda and her family." She glanced over her shoulder and lowered her voice. "Noah's grandpa is dead and his uncle is a bad person. Erin was very clear in her will and to her friends, her half brother is not to be part of Noah's life. Erin and her mother have been estranged for years. That's all I have to say about that."

"I didn't mean to pry," he said uncomfortably.

She lifted one corner of her mouth in a sly smile. "I wouldn't want you to think I kidnapped him."

"I'm sure you didn't," he said. Then he grinned. And he could see in her eyes that she knew he had probably checked her out as much as possible.

"Good for you," she said. A bit of a ruckus behind her caused her to turn and see Noah struggling out the door, using his crutches. "Good morning, cowboy," she said, getting up. "Oh, good for you, using just the crutches. You feeling kind of strong today?" She looked at Owen. "The braces give him more independence and freedom but the crutches help him with the balance. He's building muscle strength in his legs. It's taxing, though."

Noah completely ignored her as he went straight for the dog. Romeo sat up and gave Noah a good-morning kiss.

"If you'd been up a little earlier, you would have seen Romeo chase off a couple of deer," Hannah said.

"It was very rude of him," Owen said. "Those ladies were just grazing, not bothering anyone."

"How'd you know they were ladies?"

Noah asked. "You look under 'em?"

Owen laughed. "I didn't have to go to that much trouble. The bucks have antlers and the does don't. Same with the elk. The guys get the headgear and they use it to fight each other. Or to defend themselves and their does. You're going to learn a lot on this vacation, aren't you?"

"I guess," he said, not taking his hands off Romeo. And then the big dog flipped over on his back, making his belly available. "What are you gonna do today?" he asked.

"Well, I'll take Romeo for a hike, I'll work in my shop a little while, I might fish. You like to fish?"

"I only did it once," he said.

"If you're not busy later, we can go out on the dock. About that dock — you have to be with Hannah or me. The water is pretty deep. If you lost your balance and fell in with your braces on, you'd sink. A life jacket would be a good precaution but even that might not be enough. You can't flap your feet with the braces. You have to be with an adult who can swim. Noah, did you get that?"

"Uh-huh," he said, scratching Romeo's belly.

"What did I say?" Owen pushed.

"I can't go on the dock without you or

Hannah because I could sink and drown."

"That's good enough," Owen said.

"Want some breakfast, buddy?" Hannah asked.

"Can Romeo have some breakfast?"

"He eats only dog food," Owen said. "I've got it at the barn. He doesn't look like he's starving."

"I'm going to mess up some eggs," Hannah said. "Would you like to join us, Owen? In your house," she added with a laugh.

"Now, it's not my house for two weeks. I don't want to get in the way. But okay, I could eat. Then we can start our days."

What lies behind us and
what lies before us are
but tiny matters compared
to what lies within us.
— RALPH WALDO EMERSON

3

Noah did not seem at all intrigued by the possibility of going to a campground until they got there. Hannah had completely forgotten about Beau, Sully's yellow Lab.

"Well, howdy do," Sully said when he saw Hannah. "I heard you were coming back, without the executive team this time. Nice to see you again."

"Good to see you, Sully. Sully, this is my best guy, Noah. We're a team now. Noah, this gentleman, Mr. Sullivan, owns this campground and this is Beau, his dog."

Noah was immediately rubbing the dog behind his ears. "Does everybody here got a dog?"

"Nearly," he said. "How do you like my lake?"

"Is that whole lake yours?" Noah asked.

"Nope, but I claim the part of it that's up against my land and have the use of the whole thing. Would you like to throw the ball for Beau? Or would you like a cold drink or something to eat? Or would you like to be left alone?"

"Can I throw the ball, please?" Noah said.

"You bet." Sully stuck a hand under the counter at the cash register and pulled out a tennis ball. The second he did that, Beau started to prance. "My advice is throw the ball into the yard before you go down the porch steps. Beau sometimes gets ahead of himself and knocks people down."

"I will," Noah said.

Silence hung in the air while Noah and Beau went outdoors. Noah clip-clopped in his heavy shoes that held the braces, and Beau's nails against the wooden floors went *tickety-tickety-tickety.* Then they heard Noah yell, "Go get it!"

"I didn't know you had a child," Sully said.

"I didn't," she said, keeping her voice down. "Right after I met you my best friend passed away. She got sick, had complications and in just a matter of days she was gone. Noah was her son. Years ago she asked me to be the guardian to her children if she was ever lucky enough to have them and I said yes. Of course, I said yes. And I asked the same of her. Neither of us had family to do that. So here I am, a few weeks later.

Noah has always known me as Aunt Hannah, a girlfriend auntie he saw a few times a year. I woke up one morning and my whole life had changed."

"Damn near that same thing happened to Helen," he said.

"Really?"

"She is Aunt Helen, raised her niece from the age of four. Her niece is Leigh Shandon, the town doctor at the urgent care, so it all worked out in the end. I'll get her to come over on her break. She's writing on the porch." He pulled his cell phone out of his pocket and texted Helen.

"Want to get a drink and sit on the porch, where we can keep an eye on the boy and his dog?"

"Excellent idea," Hannah said. She reached in the cooler for a diet cola and followed Sully. By the time she was sitting at a table with him, Noah was working that dog like a trainer. When Beau returned the ball, Noah had him sit, stay, fetch. Then Beau returned the ball again and Noah rewarded him with many hugs and petting.

"What's up with the braces?" Sully asked.

She explained Noah's condition, his limitations but good prognosis. "The hardest part for him right now is that he's growing and suffers some muscle contractures and

66

pain, but he's getting stronger all the time. This might be a setback, losing his mom. She was his best cheerleader."

Helen walked over from the house to the store and joined them on the porch and chatted for a while, listening to Hannah's story, then briefly telling her own.

"It was so similar, except it was my little sister, pregnant at eighteen, then a routine surgery when she was twenty-two went awry and we lost her. From that point on, it was the two of us, just me and Leigh. It was both the hardest and best part of my life. I am grateful for every day of it. As you will be, I'm sure."

"It's a gift," Hannah said. Then in a whisper she added, "I'm so afraid I'll screw it up."

"I know," Helen said. "Every parent says that."

"Well, I did screw it up," Sully said. "But Maggie turned out great in spite of me. You want a sandwich, sweetheart?"

"Oh, thank you, Sully," Helen said. "That would be so nice. Hannah, how about a sandwich for you two? It's probably break time."

"You guys," Hannah said. "You make me feel like a visiting relative!"

"Locals turn into family around here,"

Helen said. "That's how Sully made me love him. He wooed me with lunch. And other things."

When Sully brought a plate of sandwiches out, Hannah called Noah to come.

"Just a little while longer, Hannah! Please."

"Come and eat," Sully said. "Bring Beau with you. You can play again after lunch. I can't have you wear out my dog."

"'Kay," he said. As they were walking toward the porch, Beau was jumping at the ball and Noah just gave it to him. When he got to the porch, he said, "It's better if Beau carries the ball, I guess. I'm not going to make him fall down."

By the time they got back to Owen's house, Owen was on the dock, sitting in a canvas deck chair. A couple of fishing rods were standing up, balanced in the slats, their lines out. Noah went nearly running to the dock and Romeo got up, wagging in anticipation.

"Owen, whatcha got there?" Noah said.

"I'm doing a little fishing. You want to try?"

"Is it okay?"

"Of course. I invited you."

Noah fished for an hour before he caught anything and giggled at the way Romeo barked at the fish. About a half hour later, Noah got up to go ask Hannah for some drinks. Romeo jumped up with excitement and accidentally knocked him off the dock and into the water. With lightning speed, Owen reached those long arms down into the water, grabbed Noah's collar and hauled him up onto the dock before he could sink.

Hannah, hearing the commotion, came running, her feet pounding on the dock. But what she saw was a soaking-wet Noah, sitting on the dock, laughing so hard he snorted.

"Oh, Noah, did you fall in?"

"I wouldn't say that," Noah said between giggles. "More like some big horse knocked me in."

"I told you he's a little clumsy."

"You need dry clothes right away. I don't want you getting a chill."

"I'm not getting a chill. And I only got one fish so far and Owen threw him back!"

"I have an idea," Owen said. "It's after four. Get cleaned up and dried off and I'll take you out for dinner. We'll go to town to Shandon's. They have the best burgers in Colorado and the biggest ice-cream sundaes I've ever seen."

"Owen, you don't have to do that," Hannah said.

"It's the least I can do! Romeo tried to dunk my fishing buddy! I haven't had anyone to fish with for a long time. What do you say, Noah? Want to go out to dinner?"

"Can we, Hannah?"

"If you'd like. But let's please get you dried off and warmed up."

Noah squished and laughed all the way back to the house. Hannah made him take a warm bath and helped him get into dry clothes, as much as he would let her help. She had to use the blow-dryer on his shoes and muttered, "First thing we're going to do is get another pair of these shoes . . ."

"They cost a million dollars, my mom said."

"Then I'll have to get a loan," she said.

In an hour Hannah and Noah were sitting politely on the porch, patiently waiting. "I could go get him," Noah said.

"It's only five. Let's not be overanxious."

But just about then, Owen came out of the barn. He walked across the yard and said, "I see you're ready to do the town. Can we take your SUV, Hannah? You've got Noah's booster all hooked in."

Owen drove, the seat pushed all the way back, Noah laughing at how Owen had to fold up his long legs and his knees still hit the steering wheel. It was as if Noah had

70

never been out to dinner before — he yam-
mered the whole way. *Does Romeo ever get
to go in the truck? Can Romeo fetch? Are you
gonna have a hamburger and ice cream? How
long you been fishing? How long you been
here? Your whole life?*

Hannah sighed and just chuckled. Once
at the pub and seated in a booth, they
looked at menus and Hannah said, "I think
the burgers are huge. Do you want a kid's
size or do you want to tell me what you
want on your burger and share it with me?
Because I won't be able to eat a whole one
anyway."

Noah chose to share and in no time their
table was filled with the most beautiful food.
And it should not have surprised her that
Owen knew a lot of people, but then,
anyone who lived around here for a while
would be well acquainted. A few local
firefighters were there and stopped by to
say hello, which thrilled Noah. They even
invited him to drop by the firehouse sometime to sit on the big engine. The pub's
owner, Rob Shandon, introduced himself to
Hannah and Noah. Owen introduced them
as his rental guests.

"Aren't you usually out of town when the
place has guests?" Rob asked.

Owen explained his trip had been canceled

but he was glad of that because he now had a fishing buddy. Anyone who stopped by the booth to say hello to Owen was introduced to Hannah and Noah.

Noah had barely put a dent in his burger when it was time for ice-cream sundaes. When they came to the table, Noah actually sighed, making Hannah and Owen laugh.

On the way home, the sunset still an hour away, Noah was nodding off in the back seat.

"Someone had a big day," Hannah said.

"Need me to carry him in for you?"

"Nah," she said. "I'm getting some pretty good upper body muscles."

"I'm going to let Romeo out for his evening romp. If you're not too tired, would you like to sit on the porch for a while?"

"I'm not the tired one," she said, giving a grunt as she hoisted Noah into her arms.

When she got him inside, he flopped back on the bed, his arms and legs totally limp. She got rid of those heavy shoes first, then the braces, the socks, then tried to sit him up to pull his shirt over his head. He put his head on her shoulder and didn't help a bit. "Give me a hand here, buddy. We'll get your pants off and you can just wear your T-shirt and some flannel bottoms, in case you get cold in the night."

"Hannah," he said in his tiny voice. "I knew we were having a vacation. But I didn't know I was gonna like it."

"We're just getting started, honey." She kissed his brow. "Snuggle under, snug as a bug. I love you, Noah."

"Love you, too, Mama."

For just a moment, Hannah nearly crumbled in tears. And quickly, Noah began to snore softly. He'd been with her for just a moment, his mother. She found herself hoping he would remember that in the morning. "Hold him tight, Erin," she whispered.

Owen leaned back and put his feet up on the porch rail, admiring the moon glistening on the lake. When Hannah stepped onto the porch, she was looking somehow bedraggled. He should have insisted on carrying Noah.

She sat down with a sniff.

"Uh-oh," he said. "Something's wrong."

"It's just one of those things that I suppose could happen a lot. He just said, 'I love you, too, Mama.'" She inhaled a jagged breath. "Poor guy. And I miss her so much, too."

"Of course you do," he said. "You know what would be good? We should raid the landlord's liquor closet and wine cellar." He stood.

"Oh, that's locked," she said absently. He tilted his head and gave her a sly smile. "Oh, right, you probably have the key."

"What's your pleasure? Wine? Cocktail? Brandy? Liqueur?"

"A glass of wine. Any red would be lovely, thank you."

He went slowly, giving her a chance to cry a little if that was what she wanted or needed. He returned with a bottle, a corkscrew and two glasses. He showed her the label and she said, "Whoa. I don't know much about wine but whoever bought that does. Bordeaux '82."

"Let's see if it lives up to its reputation. There are a lot of counterfeits running around and I'm no expert." He pulled the cork and smelled it. "I think we'll be okay."

Romeo came to the porch and lay down right beside Hannah. She casually gave that big head a massage. "Good old boy, you did a good deed today. You made a little boy happy. We'll work on your gracefulness."

Owen poured a small amount in a glass for Hannah to taste. She swirled and sniffed and tasted. "Oh, Owen," she said. "This is so nice."

He smiled and added to her glass. Then

he poured his and put the bottle on the deck. "You know, the melancholy way the day came to an end notwithstanding, we all had a very nice day. Noah had some big fun!" Then he brought the wine to his lips. "Damn, that's actually wonderful. And I didn't even let it breathe."

"Owen, I really don't know what to say. You've been so generous with your time, your house, spoiling us. I know you have to work and this is so unexpected."

"Looked like the two of you could use a little spoiling. You've both been through quite an upheaval. And selfishly, I had a great time, except for about three seconds when I was really hoping I could grab Noah before he went under." He laughed. "I didn't want to go in — that lake is *cold*. I think we need wet suits. There's an idea. That might be my best idea yet."

"You know I'm not expecting you to entertain us while we're here . . ."

"Make your own plans," he said. "I'm flexible. If you two have time, maybe we'll knock around. If not, I know how to keep busy. I like my own company, dim-witted as I am. But I also like kids. And you could use some adult company."

"It's a shame you and your wife didn't have kids. You're so good with them."

"It's pretty easy to be good with a kid like Noah. He's dealing with what can be a disabling medical condition and just suffered an enormous loss, and yet . . ." He shook his head. "He's a bright spot."

"I guess we're going to have to get a dog," she said weakly. "I've always traveled so much for work, I couldn't manage a dog even though I love them."

"I travel all the time but I have a sister in Denver. On my way to the airport, Romeo goes to play with his cousins — two nephews, a niece and two canines — a golden and a poodle."

"Well, that's convenient. Kudos to you for thinking ahead."

"I wasn't thinking ahead," he said with a laugh. "I saw some jackass dump a dog by the side of the road. Chained him to a tree, left a bowl of water and sped away. It was all I could do to keep from chasing him down and punching him in the face, but instead I loaded this hair bag into the back seat. I wondered what kind of dog this was — I thought he was full grown. The vet pronounced him a five-month-old Great Dane who would double in size. He probably ate his first owner's house. He tried to eat mine! But it took me about two days to know I'd never give him up. Romeo has a good soul. He's talked me through many a rough patch."

"He's so sweet," she said, her hand on his big head.

"So, your job . . .?"

"It seems so long ago already. I'm in sales for a medical equipment and supply company. It's highly competitive and fast-paced and I was getting a little burned-out. The last time I was at your house it was with a few salesmen. It was a team-building retreat that went south fast. We failed at team building and I defected. I went home to a breakup with my fiancé. I had barely cleared him out of my house and canceled all the wedding plans when we lost Erin. Inheriting a five-year-old involves a lot of reorganizing, moving, legal paperwork . . ."

"And you've been off work this whole time?"

"I took family leave. It was my only option. I may not have given birth but I did become a mother."

"How much time do you get?"

"Up to three months paid, up to three more months without pay. If I need it, I can push that to six months. Our other two best friends have offered to keep Noah when I have to leave town, but there's a lot of other stuff to figure out. They're working mothers. A vacation is one thing but we have to get established with a new medical team and physical therapists. And school will be a challenge — I want to be available for him if I'm needed. Am I going to have to go the private school route? So, I'm thinking about what kind of career adjustment I can make so I don't travel as often. The future still looks pretty foggy."

Owen leaned forward. "I have a feeling you're the kind of person who can figure things like that out pretty easily. Efficiently."

She laughed. "Efficiency — the bane of my existence. I find myself thinking things like 'I better eat something now so I don't forget later.' Or 'I should hurry and fall asleep so I can get up and start working again. That would be efficient.' "

"You never leave work on your desk?" he asked.

"And you know what that usually gets you? More work. They give it to the person who can get it done. And that's not always synonymous with who gets the promotion."

"That's old news," he said. "It's always been that way."

"Do you have a boss, Owen?" she asked.

"I have obligations," he said. "I've signed contracts for which I have to produce work on a schedule. But I'm a lot like you — I do the work that has to be done. I'm not driven but I'm motivated. And my only boss is me, if you don't count Romeo. He has needs." Romeo, relaxed, had sprawled on the deck, rolled onto his back, feet in the air. A huff of laughter came out of Owen. "He leads a very stressful life."

"I bet when you have your room, he sleeps on the bed with you."

Owen stiffened. "Was your comforter dirty or hairy?"

"No," she laughed. "Everything is perfectly clean. Sterile."

"That's Mrs. Bourne. She and her daughter and daughter-in-law do the cleaning. They're amazing. Except they have no concept of time zones. Even though I tell them where I'll be, it isn't unusual for Mrs. Bourne to call me at three in the morning to ask me if I'm ready to have the duvet washed or the refrigerator emptied out for the next round of guests. They could call the Realtor who manages the rental schedule, but no."

"They sure do a great job on the house. Do you ever live in it?"

"Oh, yes, for weeks or months at a time. I only rent it out about twelve weeks a year, when I'm away. Mrs. Bourne takes care of the barn, too. I have become an extremely lazy man."

"I bet you're not," she said. "Tell me what you're working on now."

"I'll show you tomorrow if you have time."

"If I have time?" she asked with a laugh. "I'm here to do nothing and I'm already exhausted. Tell me about it."

"I'm working on a few things. I love collections. Sometimes they become books with accompanying essays. I did one on trees. Who cares about trees? It turns out a lot of people. And in chasing them down, I've learned of cultural regard for trees, mystical beliefs, spiritual relationships with trees, trees that covered ten generations with their branches, trees that were murdered for money and the land beneath them died and went fallow. There are places in Mexico where maidens marry trees to fight back deforestation and to protest illegal logging. Who knew?

"Right now I'm collecting pictures of homecomings—military homecomings, refugee reunions, people returning home after incarceration, even people reunited with their pets. I think it's going to be a wonderful collection. It will make people cry, and have you noticed people love to cry? As long as they're not in pain. If they cry at reunions, those are happy tears. And every reunion has a story." He laughed. "I hated every writing assignment I ever got in school because I wanted to see pictures! And now the writing that accompanies the picture is so much fun for me."

"Do you cry while you're finding the pictures and writing the essays?" she asked.

He laughed quietly. "I'm a softie. I'll cry at the drop of a hat. It's embarrassing."

"I think it's wonderful," she said. Then she lifted her empty glass toward him. "Just half," she said.

They talked through the entire bottle of wine. Owen told her about beginning to take pictures in junior high and high school, studying photography and other things in college before quitting so he could concentrate on pictures, then taking any job that included a camera, until about ten years ago, finding surprising success in the mountains of Colorado, shooting his travels, his collections, writing his essays.

She started to tell him about her college days and ended up telling him about breaking up with two fiancés, both apparently in need of more than one partner. One when she was thirty, the next at thirty-five.

"Was your heart badly broken?" he asked.

"It was bruised. My pride was broken. But before I could wallow, Erin died and there was a little boy with a broken heart, putting all my problems in their proper place. He had a good life in Madison and I had to take him away. The one bright spot is that Noah knows us — me, Sharon and Kate — and we're all in the Minneapolis area. Kate's kids are a little older and they're very sweet to Noah. That will help. And I pray I can find a babysitter or nanny half as good as his Linda was. Linda was like a grandmother to him. Her whole family embraced Noah."

"You said Noah's mother's family is not good," Owen said. "I'm trying not to think about what that might mean . . ."

"One of the things that made Erin and me close was our similar family situations. We had kind of hard childhoods. Not hungry or homeless hard, but emotionally difficult. We were both abandoned by our fathers and were left with mothers who seemed to resent us. In my case, I was adopted. I'm told I was a terrible baby, cried all the time. Or maybe I had a mother who wanted a baby but was unprepared for what that meant. My father left, my mother remarried and had two daughters in that marriage. And I knew that I was not the favorite child. There was even a time in my teenage years when one of my sisters pointed out that they weren't really related to me in any way. When I went to college, I didn't get any help from my family and it was obvious they didn't miss me. The only time they called was when they wanted something. I made a new family with my friends.

"Erin's situation was worse. She never knew her father. Her mother remarried after being deserted by Erin's father and immediately had a son, who she worshipped. He was five years younger than Erin but he was a terrible brat. He was constantly in trouble and eventually served time for robbery, theft, assault, and he was accused of far more that he wasn't convicted of. Erin stopped speaking to her mother years ago and it was over her brother. Erin had loaned him money that, of course, he didn't repay. Then Erin's mother wanted Erin to come up with bail money and when Erin refused, that was last straw. They were estranged long before Noah came along. In fact, Victoria didn't even come to Erin's celebration of life. I was relieved, to tell the truth. All of Erin's friends and especially Linda, the babysitter, knew that Noah was to be protected from the Addisons at all cost, probably because of her brother. Erin's will is very clear about that. Erin was a paralegal and her boss was also her lawyer — he knew the facts. And not only do I have a lawyer representing me in this matter, Noah has an attorney ad litem. Roger Addison is a bad seed and his mother has a blind eye. Roger has had problems with addiction and crime. Erin didn't trust her mother to keep Noah and his estate safe. It's going to take a while to settle everything, from the sale of Erin's house and other estate matters, but I've been granted legal guardianship. When Noah's had a little breathing room and has had time to grieve, I'll talk to him about adoption."

The information about Roger made the hairs on the back of Owen's neck stand up. He hated hearing that. "Where do they live?"

"I have no idea where Roger is but his mother is in Minneapolis. I've met her exactly once, for maybe ten minutes. We all grew up there but didn't know each other until college."

"You have to be diligent, Hannah. It sounds terrible."

"I know. But it's not just me — Kate and Sharon are also on high alert. We'll keep Noah safe. Whatever that takes."

"Your friend was smart to put him in your hands."

She laughed. "I hope I'm up to your

praise. What about your childhood, Owen? Was it tainted by trouble like ours?"

"My childhood," he said with a sigh. "My childhood was perfect. Ideal. My parents were happy people who not only loved each other, they liked each other. They were courteous to each other, helpful and funny and kind. We laughed. My younger sister and I had those days we were horrid and it didn't throw them at all. I remember having a tantrum and trying to destroy my room and I overheard my mother say to my father, 'He's going to have so much to clean up — try not to laugh.' Even in the worst crises of my young life, they were calm and encouraging. I'm sure if not for them, I'd be destitute and miserable now. I mean, what kind of parents encourage their son's love for photography when he's quitting college to pursue it?"

"They must be so proud of you," she said.

"My mother is. She brags. I hope she's not giving out my address. She always has someone who needs to talk to me about professional photography and publishing. But . . . I lost my father about ten years ago. I really miss him. He passed too young. He was sixty. He'd never had any retirement. My mom is now seventy, living on her own, driving herself everywhere, is in fantastic health, active in the community. After my father died, she moved to Denver to be close to my sister." He thought for a minute. "I better visit her pretty soon."

"Do you stay in touch?"

"Oh, sure. We call and text and FaceTime. She hates that, but I want to see her when we talk, as if it will tell me something about how she's getting along. My sister sees her every week. Sometimes more often."

They talked until it was pitch-dark.

"You should get some sleep," Owen said. "Noah's going to be recharged by morning."

"I know," she said with a laugh. "I'm thinking of trying to find horses. He so loves animals. He'd be so thrilled to have a ride."

"I'll help you find horses," Owen said.

"My God, I think you are my prince! Don't get any ideas, Owen," she teased. "I'm not planning any more weddings! It's just me and Noah now."

Owen puttered around the barn for a little while before going to bed. He would have company tomorrow, of that he had no doubt. He tidied up, not that it needed much. He put things that had run astray in neat piles or in their proper places. He put his few dishes and cups in the dishwasher, clothes he had dropped or draped in the laundry basket. He gave the bathroom a quick wipe. It didn't take him long. He was by nature tidy. But he could get a little distracted sometimes . . .

He was honest with Hannah when he said he'd had a perfect childhood. But he hadn't mentioned the painful fact that his son hadn't.

He didn't ever talk about it. Sometimes people managed to find out, he supposed because of his ex-wife's notoriety. She still worked under the name Abrams, though she'd remarried and had two more children. But he didn't like telling people because the tragedy of it was so overpowering that the look of shock and pity in their eyes was just plain unbearable.

His seven-year-old boy, Brayden, was playing in the front yard one minute, gone the next. Owen had been putting out trash and straightening up in the garage while Brayden was riding his skateboard up and down the driveway, up and down the sidewalk — he had a three-house distance limit. Owen was organizing because the mess on the workbench and shelves, tools and photography equipment, was all his. It moved around as he slept, he told Sheila.

It couldn't have been more than five

minutes. He had not heard a car. He came out of the garage and there was the skateboard and no Brayden.

He'd heard other parents who'd experienced such travesty talk about how everything was a blur, a haze. Not so for Owen. He remembered every detail. Since Owen had been working in the garage and Brayden had not passed by to enter the house, he went in search and found the skateboard a couple of doors down. He called out to Brayden and there no response. Then he knocked on a few doors. Only one family had kids Brayden's age and they weren't home, but none of the other neighbors had seen him. He checked, yelling into the house, but his wife said he hadn't come in. Sheila was making dinner so he raced up and down the street, calling Brayden's name. It only took a short block and half for him to know — this was not going to be okay.

The police were called. There were hours of questioning while they assured Owen and Sheila that other officers were looking everywhere: playgrounds, schoolyards, strip malls, empty lots. They gave the police a picture; there was an Amber Alert. Days passed, days of not sleeping, days of crying, trying to comfort his wife, hearing about small leads that went nowhere. At first, Owen and Sheila were treated like suspects. The FBI was called. There was no ransom call. Owen's parents offered a hundred-thousand-dollar reward for information that led to the discovery of their grandson — money Owen couldn't imagine them actually having.

They all lived in constant fear and pain — Owen and Sheila, their parents, their siblings, the neighborhood, the school. The city. Owen and Sheila made public pleas for information, for help. Volunteers manned phone banks and knocked on doors and walked through nearby fields.

Days and then weeks and then months passed. All the while the police and FBI had certain ideas of suspects but no trace of Brayden could be found. Owen and Sheila couldn't hold it together. He withdrew into himself, single-minded about finding his son but just not up to any public scrutiny. Sheila, on the other hand, became a PR genius overnight and turned to all the help agencies and organizations that advocated for lost and missing and abducted children. She became vocal about trafficking and abuse and was making speeches and televised public service announcements. She was interviewed on all the major talk shows.

Even before Brayden's remains were found Owen knew they weren't going to be able to keep the marriage together. And then they discovered that Brayden had been buried in the desert outside LA in a place that could have been seen from the road, had anyone been connecting the dots. He'd been dead eighteen months. His kidnapper was one of the police's prime suspects and was identified and convicted through DNA testing. That brought a whole nightmare of images that threatened to rip Owen's guts out.

Sheila took to the public to stir up the outrage and to work to protect innocent children from this kind of trafficking and to make the requirements of convicted pedophiles even stricter, she'd brand their foreheads if she could. She left her law practice and became a full-time advocate. She began getting offers from everywhere, from lobbying groups to commercial television. She made the rounds of talk shows again and spoke to larger and larger audiences.

Owen couldn't do it. He needed to be alone. He needed to grieve. He didn't have any problem with Sheila going that route, making her grief not only public but useful. But he couldn't. He went to his sister's house in Denver. He walked through the Rockies and other ranges for a year, his camera in his backpack. He talked to Sheila every few days, cried with her, comforted her and took her comfort.

And then one day she said, "You're not coming back to LA, are you?"

And he had said, "No. I'm sorry, I can't."

"I understand," she said. "As long as you don't blame me."

"Blame *you?* God, if it's anyone's fault, it's mine! I was watching him!"

"Here's what we know," she said so calmly, so sanely. "The monster who took him knew that all the conditions were perfect — no cars, no pedestrians, no one looking out of windows, a tall hedge, a van. He needed ten seconds or less. And since no one on God's green earth can promise never to look away for ten seconds, I'm going to do everything in my power to make it harder for the predators. To keep at least a few children from going through this."

"And a few parents," he said. He admired her so much. "Please tell me you can forgive me that I can't go on this crusade with you."

"Owen, I love you and I'm going to do this with or without you, but understand something — I never thought I had this in me. But I do. And it matters. It can do good things."

"It matters," he repeated. "It will do good

things. Thank you. I'm proud of you."

There was one more casualty before life could move forward. Owen's father, Ben Abrams, died of a heart attack. Brayden had not been gone two years, his remains barely found, and Ben's heart had been in tatters. From the time Ben's firstborn grandchild, Brayden, went missing, the victim of a violent crime, Ben had been suffering. His tears had been harder on Owen than his own. Ben had been the sweetest man to ever live; never a temper, rarely a frown. He had been married to his wife for almost forty years and in that time there had been so much love and laughter. Until a monster with no conscience had interrupted their lives.

Owen held his mother tight and said, "Please don't leave me. I need you. You have to be strong. You have to live. I think one more loss will kill me."

"We will live, Owen. We will live the way Ben and Brayden would want us to live. We will sleep peacefully knowing that they're together, waiting for us to join them. And they'll be happy to wait a long time."

So it was that twelve years after losing his son, the joy of his life, the great rains and floods of Taiwan kept him home from his trip where he met a pretty and funny woman and her little boy, the boy in leg braces who needed a man and his dog because they were also suffering a terrible loss. It would not be a life-changing event for him — his life was not changeable. But he had a couple of weeks to make their lives a little better.

Love comes to those who still hope
even though they have been
disappointed,
to those who still believe even
though they
have been betrayed, to those who
still love
even though they have been hurt before.
— AUTHOR UNKNOWN

4

It was not yet seven when Hannah sat on the porch with a cup of hot coffee and watched as Noah moved across the yard to the barn. She had told him very sternly that Owen and Romeo might not be awake and he was not to knock! No knocking! And he'd said, "Okay. I can be really quiet." Noah crept up to the door and pressed his ear against it and was completely still. Listening. Then he shouted across the yard, "I think they might be awake in there!" And Hannah laughed so hard she was surprised she didn't slide off the chair.

Within moments Owen opened the door. He was wearing his sweatpants, a long-sleeved T-shirt and slippers. Yes, old-man slippers, the leather kind that grandfathers on television wore. He held a cup of coffee. Romeo almost knocked Noah over in his happiness to have a visitor.

"Let him take a minute to go to the

bathroom, Noah," Owen said. "He's probably about to explode."

"Okay! Romeo, do your business!" Noah raised a crutch and gestured at the yard. As if he understood, Romeo walked out there, sniffing, looking for just the right spot.

"Did you sleep well?" Owen asked.

"I did," he said. "Hannah said I was worn to a nub."

"You did have a pretty big day," Owen said, ruffling his hair. "You ready for another one?"

"Okay. Without the getting knocked in the lake part."

"I feel ya, buddy," he said. He walked up onto the porch and smiled at Hannah.

"I'm sorry," she said, but her eyes were full of glee. "I told him to be very quiet."

He sat down on the porch chair. "That's what happens when you make friends with a five-year-old. Did you sleep well?"

"Oh, yes," she said. "And Noah slept through the night for the first time in a long time. I think all that activity is good for his muscles."

"Have you had breakfast?" Owen asked.

"I could make us some. Noah has already had cereal. As you probably witnessed, keeping him in till a reasonable hour was pretty tough. You want some eggs?"

"Since Noah has eaten, we can have another cup of coffee, comb our hair, lock up Romeo and go to town to the diner. Best breakfast anywhere."

"Is that what you normally do?" she asked.

"I'm known to make an appearance now and then. But after breakfast I'd like to go to an aquatic shop in Colorado Springs. We're going to get wet suits, me and Noah. I was reading about diplegia. Swimming is great. We could find a pool but look out there, we have the best pool."

She was speechless.

He leaned toward her. "That lake doesn't warm up until July, I swear. And we can't get in there and learn swimming and come out with nuts. Well, I suppose you can." Then he smiled boyishly.

"Sounds like another very big day," she said. "When are we going to see your pictures? And what you're working on?"

"After a little breakfast and a shopping trip," he said.

She stood. "Ready for a little more coffee? And incidentally, my hair is combed."

"It looks beautiful," he said. "I meant to add that." When she brought back the coffee, he asked, "Did you think about what kinds of things you wanted to do while you're here?"

"Besides bond with my new partner? I'd love to do a little hiking but that might not be feasible. I'm not sure Noah is up to a lot of hiking."

"The trails are sometimes uneven terrain," he said. "But we can pick some easy ones and I can piggyback him when he gets tired. If you'll carry my backpack."

"What's in the backpack?"

"Guess," he said with a grin.

"Of course. You never go anywhere without a camera."

"Everything looks like the shot of a lifetime when you don't have your camera."

"I had visions of reading in a hammock . . ."

"I'll put up the hammock," he said.

"What made you come here? Build here?"

"I was visiting my sister and I did a lot of hiking and some camping, though not so much of the latter. Poor woman, I told her I wanted to come for a couple of weeks and I never left. But I had taken over her basement game room — I needed a shop. I stumbled on this land for sale. It was a nice plot with a barn on it. The barn was still in decent shape and I thought I could make it an apartment. It was perfect. Then three years later I built the house, don't ask me why. Because I could. It's an investment. I should probably live in the barn and sell the house but I just can't."

"Why?" she asked.

"Well, I like it a lot. But the bigger question is, what if I sell it and don't like my neighbors?"

She just shook her head. "You're a very strange man."

"I know it," he said. "I'm going to go put some jeans on. I'm hungry. Does Noah have to change?"

"No, but I do. I'll be right with you."

Before they left, Owen put Romeo in the barn. "I'll be back in about four hours." Then he closed the door. Noah was standing there, openmouthed. "Romeo can tell time," Owen said. "Know how I know?" Noah shook his head. "If I'm late he gives me the cold shoulder, like he's mad about something."

"Really?"

"That's what I think," Owen said. "Let's get going — I shouldn't be late getting back."

Breakfast at the diner was very successful. Hannah was stuffed. It was so good she kept eating long past the need. She had some kind of breakfast sandwich — eggs, cheese, peppers, onions and sausage inside thick bread that was grilled. It was amazing and she moaned for a half hour afterward.

The trip to the aquatic supply store was not quite as successful. Owen, at six foot five, was not able to find a wet suit in his size, and Noah, at five years old, could not find one. Only Hannah, who had not been convinced she should have one, found a wet suit that fit. But the manager measured them and said he could find wet suits and have them shipped to Owen's address. "Priority, please," Owen said. "We only have a little over a week left before Noah and Hannah leave and we want to get in some serious swimming before that."

Then they were off to Owen's barn to see his pictures. Some of them anyway.

Hannah didn't mention that before dropping off to sleep the night before, she had raided Owen's library. She'd had a hunch there would be samplings of his work and she was right, though they were hardly prominently displayed. Owen's house had a very small library, possibly eight by ten feet. There were floor- to-ceiling shelves and one overstuffed leather chair and ottoman with a standing lamp behind it and a small table at the right hand. But it was chockablock full of books and she found his lovely narrated photo books tucked neatly into one corner. Trees, flowers, exotic food, native costumes, weddings around the world and, of course, the landscape and wildlife of Colorado. She carried them off to the bedroom to page through them.

The library had one small sign on a shelf that said "Be so kind as to return books to the shelves and not to your suitcase so that the next guest might enjoy them."

The books were beautiful but even more beautiful was Owen's voice. She could hear him on the page, telling each picture's story. *Nothing serves as a greater illustration of our own existence than the tree, boughs spread wide and curiously reaching, roots deep and firm.* There were pictures of lush, healthy forests as well as brutal logging and fires that left hillsides bare. There were images of Mexican maidens who'd married trees in Oaxaca as well as tree huggers chained to trees to protest illegal logging in the Pacific Northwest. People across the globe planted, chopped, destroyed, replanted. Birth, death, rejuvenation. *Conservationists rail about the killing of the planet as if they don't know — the planet will survive. It always has; it always will. Left alone, it will scrub the poison out of its air; vegetation will replace the death of an assaulted earth; animals will breed and populate. It is we who will die. And disappear.*

There was a melancholy in that voice. A

sweet, soft vulnerability that probably wooed women everywhere, just as that narrative voice wooed her. She suspected a deep wound. His failed marriage, perhaps. He said they were still good friends, that they stayed in touch.

When Noah woke her in the morning, she was sprawled out on the king-size bed, lying atop books and dreams. She quickly gathered them up and put them away. Noah had no concept of discretion — he told everything he saw.

But that visit with Owen's amazing talent made her even more anxious for an afternoon spent in his shop, looking at his pictures and learning his process.

The barn wasn't huge. Half was his shop — computers, large wide-screen monitors, cupboards, shelves, countertop, easels, storyboards, reams of photo paper, cutters, tools of all types. An archway led to a small one-room apartment behind his shop. He had a bed, sofa, shelves with books, a table and two chairs, a galley kitchen and a large bathroom with a big shower. In his walk-in closet there were drawers as well as rods for hanging clothes and a small stacked washer and dryer.

"This is amazing. From outside it looks like a small barn, not much more than an oversize shed," Hannah said.

"It once held a tack room, supply closet and four horse stalls. Cal Jones has a barn. Huge barn. He gutted it and turned it into a big, beautiful house — five bedrooms and an office, four- and-a-half baths. He works out of his home. If I can think of an excuse, I'll take you to see it. Amazing remodel."

"You could live here comfortably forever."

"I know. That's why I flirt with the idea of selling the house. It feels so self-indulgent for one man."

"Noah! Honey, don't touch that," she said, noticing Noah's hands curiously checking out some big lenses.

"You're okay, Noah. That's a telescope. One night when we have a clear sky we'll get it out and look at the moon and stars."

"Really?" he asked.

"Really. How'd you like to take some pictures?"

"Huh? Can I?"

"Sure. Let's find a camera more your size."

And the hours were eaten up by browsing through pictures, both printed and matted in oversize file drawers and on his monitors, and with Owen showing Noah how to point, focus and snap pictures. Noah's favorite model was Romeo, big surprise. Then Noah asked if Owen had any peanut butter and jelly.

"Oh, Noah, it's after four!" Hannah said. She'd been sitting on the floor near the bookcase, paging through some of Owen's books — his and those of other photographers. "Good thing you had two breakfasts! We missed lunch. Oh, I'm a terrible mother! Come on, let's go over to the big house and I'll make you something."

"I have a better idea," Owen said. "Let's all go and throw together some dinner. I think it's almost wine time."

"What can I make?" she asked, trying to think of what she had.

"Let's have a look through your refrigerator and see what's there. I'll cook," Owen said.

It turned out a little help was needed from Owen's kitchen in the barn. He concocted some chicken and pasta dish with a creamy pesto sauce, spinach, sun-dried tomatoes and mushrooms. Hannah was nearly drooling but she was sure she'd have to make Noah a grilled cheese.

But, of course, Noah loved it because Owen made it. And he told them, "My mom used to put spinach and other vegetables in everything. This is so good. It's reminding me of her."

After dinner Noah played with Romeo in the yard while the May sun hovered just above the Rockies. Owen and Hannah sat on the porch, trying to digest another wonderful meal. Then Noah came up on the porch and slumped against Hannah, yawning.

"Oh, no, you don't, young man! You're not falling asleep without a bath again. Let's get you cleaned up, teeth brushed and in your pajamas . . ."

"I can't," he said with a whine.

"We're getting it done even if I have to hold the toothbrush!" she said, lifting him. "You gained weight today!"

"I'll clean up the kitchen while you get bedtime rolling," Owen said.

Noah was so tired Hannah had to practically hold his head out of the bath to keep him from drowning. She did have to hold the toothbrush, but she got him into clean jammies and into bed. He was yawning big before she kissed him. "I love you, Noah," she whispered.

"I love you, too, Hannah," he said. Then he was out.

When she got back to the porch, Owen held up a bottle of wine. "It's not your bedtime yet, is it?"

■ ■ ■ ■

Late that night, much too late, she texted Kate asking if she was awake. Her cell phone rang immediately.

"Everything okay?" Kate asked.

"Oh, Kate, this is the best thing I've ever done. Noah is so happy, completely worn-out, his cheeks pink from sunshine, his laughter is quick and crazy. There is this wonderful man here with a big lovable dog named Romeo who adores Noah — the dog, I mean. Although Owen loves him, too. He took us to get wet suits today because swimming will be good for Noah and the lake is too cold and . . . and he's so nice."

"Oh, boy," Kate said.

"I'm okay," Hannah said. "It's not romantic. But I've never met anyone like him in my life. I can't wait to tell you about him. He's sort of famous. Also, he's kind of shy. He's published these books. Wonderful, amazing books. I never imagined Noah and I would run into someone like this . . ."

The days became a kind of fluid beauty for Hannah. Noah rarely woke up during the night and when he did, he was able to go back to sleep. He cuddled a lot, especially if he was a little tired. He woke up each morning filled with excitement, anxious to get his playmates across the yard moving. A couple of mornings Romeo found deer in the yard and chased them. Once there was a buck and he briefly turned on the Great Dane, though he didn't get too near, but Romeo yelped and ran as though he'd been gored, causing Noah and Owen to laugh wildly.

The wet suits arrived and Noah and Owen got right into them. They donned their rubber shoes, waded into the lake, and within a half hour Noah was swimming! They didn't wear flippers because Owen had read that learning to kick using the power of his ankles was better for building strength and stretching out tendons. Hannah couldn't get Noah out for two hours, and then only long enough for a brief rest and a lunch break, and then he was begging to go back in.

In the afternoons, Hannah read to Noah in the hammock. What she learned right away was that Noah had some powerful reading skills. When she asked him how long he'd been reading he couldn't exactly remember. "I didn't play outside as much as the other kids," he said.

On an early-May morning they woke up to a gentle rain and Noah begged and begged to go swimming. Hannah was firm that he could wait at least until the sun came out. Since Owen had explained about Helen Culver's occupation as a writer and since Hannah already knew about Helen's experience "inheriting" her niece, she thought maybe that rainy morning might be a good time to pay a visit to the Crossing. "Let's go to Sully's and you can say hello to Beau," she suggested. "Owen, do you want to come along? I'll just stay an hour or two if Helen isn't too busy."

Owen decided that the time would give him a chance to concentrate on some of his work. Hannah stuffed her backpack with diversions for Noah — his tablet, a couple of games, crayons and pens.

"Well, look here, the rain brings you out again," Sully said when she walked into the store. "How's the vacation going, young man?"

"We have wet suits and we can swim in them without freezing our nuts off," he said.

Hannah put her hand over her mouth. "I'll, ah, speak to Owen about his choice of words."

"Sounds like it's accurate enough," Sully said. "We men tend to speak our minds around these parts."

"Can I play with Beau?" Noah asked.

"As long as you don't let him out. There's no dog I know who loves rain and mud like this one and I'm not in the mood to wash him. I have an idea. You want to brush him for me? Unload about ten pounds of hair?"

"I could maybe do that," he said.

"On the porch, then," Sully said. "And don't you let him in the yard."

"Do you think I could interrupt Helen's writing?" Hannah asked. "I've been wanting to talk with her."

"She'd prolly welcome it," Sully said. "At least the people she's killing off in that book will be grateful."

"Do you mind if Noah stays with you and Beau for just a little while?"

"I'd be real happy about that," he said. Hannah shrugged out of her backpack, handing it to Sully. "Well, now, I know there's no bottles or diapers in here, so what've we got?"

"Games and stuff," Noah said with a little giggle. "To keep me busy."

"I see," Sully said. "If you brush the dog, then you can maybe teach me one of these games."

"I could do that," he said.

Helen looked up from her computer and smiled at Hannah. "I was hoping you were coming for a visit."

"Are you in the thick of it? Your story?"

"Ach, it's the most boring story I've ever written. At the moment, at least. How is your vacation so far?" Helen closed her laptop and indicated the other chair at her small table.

Hannah sat down. "Magic," she said. "I've never seen Noah so happy. I was so afraid that no matter what I did, he might never be happy again."

"There will still be those days," Helen said. "Right now he's too busy to dwell, but that longing for his mother will come and go. You're right to enjoy these days. And your color is so good, too. You've been spending lots of time outdoors, haven't you?"

Hannah told her everything they'd been doing from swimming to piggyback hiking, ice-cream sundaes at Rob Shandon's pub.

"Rob is married to my niece," Helen said. "That makes him like a son-in-law."

"My God, this whole town is connected!"

"Talk about a family tree . . ." Helen said.

"And Noah is taking pictures now. Owen gave him an old camera and showed him how to focus and shoot. Then they look at his pictures on the computer and he's thrilled."

"Isn't Owen the loveliest man?" Helen asked. "The second I met him, I knew he was special. I love talking to him about his travels, about his accidental success. Well," she laughed. "Accidental in that he didn't plan it or expect it but when you look at those books of his, read his descriptive prose, it's unsurprising. It was bound to happen. He has the heart of an angel."

"I know! I admit, I'm thoroughly captivated! He's made such a difference in Noah's life. And mine! He seems like such a pure soul. But, Helen, I know you've been in my shoes — will you please give me your three or four strongest tips for learning to be a sudden mother? My friend Erin, though a single, working mother, was the most wonderful mother I've ever known. There's no way I can ever measure up!"

"Oh, you'll do fine. I had to build a network, not just so I could survive, but so Leigh had connections, too. Neighbors, mostly. I had to get cozy with her teachers, making sure they all knew it was just the two of us."

"I have two other best friends who aren't far away. They were also close to Erin and Noah. They promise to help and they have kids who are great with Noah. And I'll get him going on a new physical therapy program. Although, if Owen has his way, Noah will be walking on his own before we leave."

"I have something important to tell you, something I struggled with. You must always remember Noah's mother's death wasn't your fault. He'll need sympathy and re-assurance but don't let a cloud of guilt cause you to make bad decisions. Don't overindulge or let him get away with being naughty just because you feel bad for him. That won't help him. And my best advice — tell him you love him often but also tell him how much you want him. You miss his mom, too, but what a gift she gave you."

"Yes," Hannah said. "The first week I lived with this gift, that first terror-stricken week, all I could think about was how impossible it would be. By the end of that first week, after cuddling him at night a few times, after watching him soldier on despite how much it hurt, I knew I couldn't live without him. How does a person fall in love with a child that fast? A child not even my own?"

"Doesn't take long for that child to be-come yours, does it? Takes about twenty-four hours and you need that child as much as he needs you."

"I didn't realize . . ."

"Sadly, that's not always the case. Some

people don't bond with their children, even the children that came out of their own bodies. I count myself so lucky in that regard. It was very hard at times but I was so lucky to fall in love with the child I would raise."

Hannah remembered. She always felt her mother didn't love her. There was a coolness about her when she dealt with Hannah. She always felt it was because she was adopted and didn't look like her sisters. Hannah grew up being the least loved in the household, the only one with a different last name. She was resented and she knew it; she'd always known it. She had felt it long before she could put a definition to it.

It was *not* going to be like that for Noah. She would be his champion. No matter what it took.

"How did you manage a full-time job?"

"So much juggling. I was close with my neighbor who was a stay-at-home mom. On those occasions Leigh had to stay home with a cold or flu, my neighbor would look after her. Sometimes Leigh came to my classroom in the late afternoon. Oh, hell, she went everywhere with me. When she was a little older, she could go to a friend's house after school. There was a lot of trial and error the first couple of years while we were figuring things out. Keep an open mind, Hannah. New ideas will present themselves."

"I bet you were wonderful fun to grow up with," Hannah said.

"On some days," Helen said. "Are you doing all right, girl? You look like you're happy."

"I dread going back to the real world. But that's where my network is. This has been like a fantasy."

"Let's walk over to the store and let Sully feed us." Helen hooked her arm through Hannah's. "A lot of us live here full-time, you know. And it might seem like a fantasy but I guarantee you it's real life. It's also real nice. I even made it through winter and I hate winter."

"What's winter like here?"

"Not too bad," she said. "Don't tell Sully I said that. It will take all the starch out of my complaining."

"He dotes on you," Hannah said.

"Oh, yes. And all winter he dotes more, bringing in firewood and making soups. He only knows four soups, by the way. And they're a lot alike. This next winter we're going to find some new recipes so I don't go bat shit crazy."

When they got to the store's porch, Sully

and Noah were sitting at a table playing checkers. And it looked like Noah was winning.

Owen was all too aware that he was counting the days. Counting down, actually. At first he was thinking they had ten days left and that seemed like plenty. Then it was seven. Then it was five.

From the first moment he saw Hannah, he was smitten and the more time he spent with her, the more he was intrigued. Her skin bronzed up at once, glowing in the warm Colorado sunshine. She had some freckles on her cheeks that made her look fresh-faced. She wore no makeup and pulled her hair back in a simple ponytail, and when she let it loose, it fell below her shoulders. She was beautiful, long-legged and athletic. Her smile was contagious, her laugh loud and unrestrained.

Every day they swam, hiked, took pictures, looked at the pictures they'd taken. Hannah and Noah read together every afternoon, often in the hammock. They all went to the market together and got ice cream. They had breakfast, lunch and dinner together. Then he would sit on the porch with Hannah after Noah went to bed. He wasn't sure what part of each day and night he loved the most.

Sheila called him late one night just as he was getting ready to turn in. "How was Taiwan, Owen?"

"Oh, Sheila, I guess I should have called you. I never thought . . . My trip was canceled. Severe flooding. At first they wanted to delay it five days, but I couldn't see making the effort then."

"I'm sorry to hear that," she said. "Did it cost you a fortune?"

"Nah, I've learned to always insure the trips. The places I like to go are sometimes isolated and inhospitable."

"What's your next trip, then?" she asked.

"This is the best. Hang Son Doong, the largest underground cave in the world. Vietnam. I'm going on an expedition. I'll be gone two weeks, about one week in the cave. Look it up sometime — it's amazing."

"Didn't you have someone renting the house?"

"I didn't cancel them," he said. "I've been staying in the barn. And I'm glad I didn't cancel — they needed this place. It's a young woman and her boy. They're in a challenging place—his mother was her best friend and she passed away suddenly. They've known each other, the boy and Hannah, but he's only five and on top of that he has a mild case of CP affecting both legs. Smart as a whip, this kid. Romeo has been helping him adjust to what will be a new life."

"And are you helping them adjust, Owen?" she asked.

"He's a brilliant, hilarious kid," Owen said. "Kind of reminds me of someone. You know?"

"We'll always miss him," she said. "That's something we'll live with forever."

He laughed, though not with humor. "You do it so much more gracefully than I do. I buried myself inside myself."

"I don't know that I'd consider my coping graceful. I became a roaring dragon. As for you, it sounds like at the moment you're not buried," she pointed out. "Rather, you seem to be surfacing a bit."

"Noah probably brings that out," he said. "He's so alive. So funny and engaging. Despite his vulnerability, his neediness, he might be the strongest one of us on the property."

"I'd say we've come a long way, both of us. And what's she like, Owen?" Sheila asked.

"When we first met, she'd only had Noah for a few weeks and she was still on shaky ground, trying to figure out how to be a mother. She's a single woman and though she'd promised her friend, this was the last thing she expected. This little retreat has been good for them. I can see the difference in her confidence already."

"How much longer will they stay?"

"Five more days," he said. He wondered if his voice lowered in some despair. "She lives in Minneapolis."

Sheila was quiet for a moment. "Maybe they'll decide to stay a little longer. Since it's working out to be good for both of them."

"I don't know," he said. "She keeps talking about all the details she has to get in order so she and Noah can get back to school and work and, you know, real life."

Sheila laughed. "Sometimes real life is way overrated."

And sometimes real life is what and where you make it, he thought. "How are Lucas and your girls?"

"Lucas works too hard on the foundation, but he's getting so much accomplished. And the girls are busy and happy. We should book some time at your cabin and come for a visit. Soon."

"Sheila," he said with a laugh. "What kind of woman visits her ex-husband? With her new husband?"

"It takes a special ex-husband," she said. "Listen, this woman and her boy —"

"Hannah," he said. "Hannah and Noah."

"Maybe you shouldn't let them get away. Life's short."

"I know. Listen, I was just getting into bed but I'm glad we got to talk."

"Ah. That's Owen telling Sheila to mind her own business."

"Not at all. Say hello to Lucas for me. Tell him to slow down — the work will never go away."

"Speaking of work, are you getting any good pictures lately?"

"Fantastic pictures," he said. "I'll email you some. No, wait—I'll email you some after the cave."

"Sounds great, Owen. Take care of yourself."

"Absolutely."

He had been getting some great pictures. Noah swimming beside Romeo. Hannah in the hammock with a book, one leg out to push her into a slight sway. Hannah with some hair blowing across her face. Hannah and Noah with ice-cream cones, laughing, ice cream on their noses. A selfie with Hannah and Noah. Noah pitching the ball to Romeo. Noah sleeping against Romeo's belly.

He could tell Hannah didn't know how beautiful she was. Her brown hair was so thick and soft it begged for a man's touch. Her eyes were dark with small flecks of gold. She wasn't very tall next to him; he towered over her. She was always concerned about other people — him, Noah, her friends back home, literally everyone she was in contact with. She was thoughtful and kind. And her humor snapped like a whip. She was so tender with Noah. He knew in one day Noah was in good hands with her.

Maybe you shouldn't let them get away.

*I love the man that can smile in trouble,
that can
gather strength from distress,
and grow brave by reflection.*
— THOMAS PAINE

5

Hannah was doing laundry when Owen found her. "Hannah, Helen Culver just called. She asked me to invite you to meet her for lunch at the pub. She would like you to meet her niece, Leigh."

"The niece she raised?" Hannah asked.

"There's only one," Owen said. "I think you and Leigh are about the same age. Why don't you go? Noah and I can stay out of trouble without your supervision."

"Don't you have work to do? I hate to impose. Helen probably wouldn't mind if I brought him along."

"I will always have work to do," he said. "And I will always have great excuses to avoid it. I bet Noah would rather have PB&J with me than go to the pub with a bunch of women. But would you stop at the market? I have a short list."

"Are you sure?"

"Absolutely. We'll have some chicken and

grilled veggies tonight. And if you think Noah would rather have something else, get it. Okay? Helen said to meet her at noon."

"Should I call her back and accept?"

He grinned. "I already accepted."

Her expression was momentarily shocked. She looked at her watch. "I have to shower! Where's Noah?"

"He's waiting for me on the porch," Owen said. "I told Romeo not to let him off the porch till I get back."

"Oh, you and that silly dog! Get back out there and make sure Noah's safe," she said, rushing off to the master bath.

"I won't tell him you said that," Owen said.

"Just be sure *you* watch Noah and aren't just giving orders to Romeo!"

"Yes, ma'am," he said.

Hannah hurried to shower, change and spruce up a little, finding herself really looking forward to this lunch. It would be great to see the adult version of the little girl Helen had inherited. A doctor, no less. What if Noah wanted to be a doctor? How in the world would she manage that? Her salary was good right now but if she had to change jobs to travel less, that could mean earning less. There was a trust to help — Erin's estate and insurance money. The more she used now, the less there would be for college. Hannah realized once again she was going to have to plan carefully.

When she got to the pub, she found that Helen and her niece were already there, seated in a roomy booth.

"I'm sorry if I'm a bit late," she said. "I was in the middle of laundry and —"

"You're not late," Helen said. "Sit here beside me. This is my niece, Leigh, and she is holding my great-niece, Lily Culver Shandon."

"Happy to meet you, Hannah. How do you like our little town?" Leigh asked.

"The whole area is wonderful. It's been a perfect escape for me and Noah."

"I told Leigh all about your situation. I hope you don't mind," Helen said. "It so closely resembles our own. Leigh's mother was my sister, but she was ten years younger so we weren't exactly best friends. But like you, I suddenly found myself a single mother."

"And I nearly found myself in the same position," Leigh said.

"How's that?" Hannah asked.

"Well, I had barely started seeing Rob when I found myself pregnant." She took a sip of her water. "It was a little ahead of the marriage. I was looking at being a single mom but fortunately he wore me down and I did marry the most wonderful man in the world. A man with two teenage boys and a business. And I'm the primary care physician at the local urgent care. My hours are not short and I'm afraid his are often worse. Keeping an eye on a business that's open seven days a week is demanding."

"How do you manage with a baby? Does Helen help out a lot?"

"No," they both said in unison. Then they laughed.

"I help out a little bit, but I have a job," Helen said. "I told Leigh to start interviewing babysitters."

"Right now, while Lily is still so young, we're shuffling her back and forth. She's very portable. Rob is home in the mornings, she comes to the clinic with me some afternoons, and her brother Sean, a junior in high school, helps out when he can. Sean and his older brother, Finn, will not admit it but they're putty in her little hands. When she's moving around faster, we're going to have to make adjustments."

"The hardest part is trying to remember to enjoy these days when you're so busy just getting through them," Helen said.

"Who is your support, Hannah?" Leigh asked.

"Right now, it's Owen. He's wonderful with Noah and I'm sure he's enjoying every second. Back in Minneapolis I have a couple of girlfriends who were also close to Noah's mom and they've promised to help me as much as possible. But they're working mothers. I'm going to have to reach a little further. I'm on family leave right now. I have a little more time to think. And if I need to, I can extend my leave, without pay."

"Then you should stay here awhile longer," Leigh said.

"I wish I could," she said. "But I've got a house in Minneapolis and with that house comes a mortgage. Noah has to get established with new doctors — he and his mom lived in Madison. I have to keep up with his therapy, although," she added with a laugh, "I think Owen has taken on that challenge. He bought himself and Noah wet suits so they can swim in that cold lake every day. Noah is five and he told Sully the wet suit was so he wouldn't freeze his nuts off."

"Oh, Lord, that's going to be Lily," Leigh said, leaning her head into her hand. "I have the worst mouth."

"And she got it from me," Helen admitted. "We're doomed."

Rob Shandon was beside their booth.

"What can I bring you beautiful women today?"

"You know what to bring me," Leigh said. "And I'll have the diaper bag when you get a minute."

"I'll have the chicken Caesar," Helen said.

"I guess I'll have that, too," Hannah said.

"Try the chicken Caesar wrap," Rob suggested. "It's a big seller."

"Whatever you recommend," Hannah said.

"I hate to brag," Leigh said, "but I was smart enough to marry a man who cooks. For the past ten years he's been going home at dinnertime to eat with the boys, to make sure they get nutritious meals. Now he's taking care of me."

Owen cooks, Hannah thought.

"What if you're called to work?" Hannah asked.

"That doesn't happen too often, but I have Sean as a backup when he's around, and Rob has a good assistant management crew. Most of the time he can sneak away from the pub if I need him. And there's always Helen in a pinch, but she has been firm — I'm not allowed to take advantage of her."

Helen shrugged. "I'm afraid I'm not that flexible," she said. "Ask Sully. I like a schedule. I'm a slave to routine. It's what helped me survive when Leigh was young and I was working two jobs. Old dogs, you know."

They talked and laughed all through lunch. Hannah learned sudden single motherhood wasn't all they had in common. Leigh and Helen were also transplants from the Midwest area, having made their home in Chicago. Leigh wanted a slower pace after years of being on call and fighting traffic to put in long hours. She had accepted the contract in Timberlake as an experiment but it turned out to be such an improvement over her city lifestyle. "Don't let the size of the town mislead you — everything you'll ever need is at least nearby. The views are pretty, the air is clean, the people are helpful. It's a healthy place. Now that I have Lily, I'm so happy to be raising her in a place like this."

It was one of the best girlfriend lunches she'd had in a long time. She was astonished by the success of these two women—Helen, a bestselling author, and Leigh, a physician. Both of them had found true love in the year they'd been here. As hard as they worked, they had satisfying personal lives.

"And so will you," Helen said.

"I don't know about that," Hannah said.

"True love seems doubtful, except for my true love with Noah. I'm pretty reluctant to try a man again after calling off two weddings! And now I have a child to think about."

"I think you should stay a little longer," Leigh said. "Just until you feel like you have your sea legs in this new life you're taking on."

"That would be great, but every night when I close my eyes I dream about that list of things I have to settle before Noah and I can get on with our lives — registering for school, returning to physical therapy, establishing with a good doctor, finding the right sitter, getting back to work . . ."

"When Rob was married to his first wife, he had a big job in a big city. He was an assistant manager in a five-star restaurant. After her death, his sons were just five and seven years old and he decided the best thing he could do to make his life manageable was find a small, safe, friendly town where he could open a restaurant. A place that was close to home and school so he could keep an eye on his boys. Now here we are with a little girl and he's doing it again, very comfortable with the baby in her swing or napping in his office or in her carrier on his back. I think business has picked up since Lily came along. Everyone wants to see the baby. And it's the same at the clinic. My nurses love helping me care for her — she's become a fixture around there. This wouldn't have been possible in a big Chicago hospital. I can't imagine how the senior staff in the city emergency room would have reacted if I said I had to go home because the baby has a fever. But here? Fifteen people would offer to back me up. My patients would happily wait while I checked on the baby."

It was definitely food for thought.

Later that night, after dinner, when Hannah was telling Owen about her lunch, he said, "Why don't you think about staying awhile longer? It kind of sounds like you're not sure how this is all going to work out. I don't mean to project, but if you have some anxiety about it, take your time. Here, every day is a good day for Noah and it's one more day you have to put the pieces of the puzzle together in your head. You'll still have the whole summer."

"Owen, I need to face this. I have to get back to earning some money rather than just spending it. I love your house but . . ."

"Hannah, I think you know having you here has been good for me, too. I wouldn't charge you to stay in the house. In fact, if you hadn't already paid the rental in advance, I'd tear up the bill."

"Why, Owen? Why is this good for you?"

"It must be the timing, that's all I can think of. It's been a little over ten years since my divorce. I can honestly say I haven't been too lonely. My relationships with women were few and brief. I haven't spent this much time with a woman and child in all that time. My wife remarried. A very nice fellow. I like him. They have a couple of little girls." He laughed with some embarrassment. "I talked to her a couple of days ago and she suggested bringing the family out here for a visit and I asked her what kind of woman visits her ex-husband." He shook his head. "But from the day you and Noah got here, it's felt so ridiculously normal. I understand if you need to go. Maybe we'll stay in touch. Maybe you'll come back. I think it's less odd if you and Noah visit than if my ex-wife and her new family visits, don't you?"

She laughed a little. "I suppose."

"I'm used to feeling odd," he said. "I'm known around here as that skinny guy with the camera. For some reason, I don't feel that odd with you."

"But you're not odd. You're the most real

person I've met in too long. And I don't think you're skinny at all."

"I could get things off the top shelf for my mother when I was twelve. I can get things off the top shelf for you. I can swim with Noah. He's thriving here."

"I think it's my responsibility to help him thrive in his forever home, in the place we're going to live from now on. I have a plan. I should stick to the plan, no matter how uncertain I might feel."

"This is usually an uncomplicated place," he said. "You have a couple of days before your plan says it's time to go. Think about it, okay? Think about giving yourself this gift of time. It's working for all of us."

"Please tell me you won't hold it against me if I feel I have to go," she said.

"Of course not," he said. "We've become good friends. I only want you to be happy, to be doing exactly what's best for you."

She smiled at him. "Why do I have the strangest feeling those were your words when you decided to divorce? Were you polite and supportive even then?"

His shoulders shook with a silent chuckle. "Found me out," he said. "It was very much like that. Poor Sheila, she has so much energy, has so much to say, so much to give. She's a total people person. She said that

134

sometimes I was quiet for days. I never thought it was that bad but I didn't crave large groups of people. It's true I began seeing more of my world through a lens. I'm afraid I enjoy quiet dinners, sunsets, long walks, campfires, people who don't have five hundred friends but only a few good ones and count me as one of them. I walked around the Colorado countryside for months and then stumbled on this place, where I could be as quiet, slow and easy as I wanted to be."

"But you travel to so many exotic places," she said.

"I know. I have an insatiable curiosity about things I haven't seen and I do have to make a living. Not always in exotic places, though. I've traveled to many ordinary towns to witness a soldier coming home from deployment or being released from a hospital on his new legs. I shot some amazing soup kitchens and some real raw homelessness. But I love places few people get to go. I think that, like you, there's a puzzle in my head and I'm putting the pieces in place."

"I don't know how I can ever thank you for your kindness and generosity to me and Noah," she said. "It's been such a privilege to see some of your work."

"Now you're just flattering me," he said.

"Ha! Not at all. I envy you that talent and drive. I have no idea what to do with my life! My job is a good job. The company is a good company. It pays well but it's only rewarding to me in the area of income. Everything else about it has worn me down."

"Hannah, that happens to most people, I think. No matter what field. I was a different kind of photographer before my divorce. I shot weddings, ball games, school photos, babies and Christmas card photos. Then I had this uncomfortable freedom and I started to change."

"Did I tell you when I was here last? Did I tell you about our team building exercise?"

"Well, that you were here for a company retreat. Right? I was away."

She told him about the trust exercises, about the sexy moderator, about her male colleagues getting stoned, about going home to find her fiancé boinking her administrative assistant.

And he laughed. "Oh my God, I apologize. That wasn't really funny. Was it?"

"It's getting a little funnier as time passes. By the time Noah is older, I might tell the story at his wedding . . ."

"I hope I'm there," Owen said. "That

136

sounds like something in a sitcom."

"I picked the lock on your closet door to get my phone and laptop," she said. "The moderator took our devices away so we'd have to communicate the old-fashioned way. I should've picked the lock on the wine cellar . . ."

"Ah, but then you wouldn't have caught the fiancé and the admin."

They looked at each other and burst out laughing. They enjoyed another glass of wine. When they said good-night, Owen kissed her on the forehead. "This is a slow, safe place. If you think it would be good for you and Noah, you can stay longer."

"You're such a kind man."

"Sometimes I'm a little bit selfish."

"Kate," Hannah said into the phone. "Can your life change in two weeks? Completely? Can everything you once wanted become things you'd like to be free of and things you thought you'd never want mean everything?"

"Hannah, Hannah. That can happen in two minutes, haven't we learned that much? Are you okay?"

"This place is like heaven and I dread going back to Minneapolis," she said. "I'm afraid I'll be so lonely. I'm afraid Noah will somehow slip through my fingers, that I won't be able to do my job and keep tabs on him. What if I can't find a good baby-sitter? What if I find out I got a bad —"

"You don't have to rush back to work," Kate said. "You can take all the time you need to make adjustments. Sharon and I will help you as much as we can. We're pretty well connected in the kids' arena. Experienced, too. We can help you find the right support system. But you don't have to rush back if you don't want to. It's only been two weeks."

"Owen offered me another two weeks, if I want it. He said that our being here is work-ing for him, too."

"Why don't you take it?" Kate asked. "It's not that long. You'll still have the whole summer to settle in. Does Noah need any medical attention?"

"He seems to be fine. Improving, in fact. And I've gotten friendly with the town doc-tor — if I need anything, I'm sure she can direct me."

"So, you and Noah are getting along?"

"Oh, yes, absolutely. I adore him and I think he's growing to love me."

"Then trust yourself. Take a little more time, then come home. We'll have all sum-mer to adjust and we're here to help. It's going to be all right."

"You're right," she said. "I want to stay. Not just for Noah—I need this, too."

"And you're more than a little curious about the man," Kate said. "Might as well see what you can learn about him."

Hannah chuckled with a tiny spasm of embarrassment. "Yes, that, too."

The next morning Hannah told Noah first. "I've decided we can take another two weeks, since Owen offered. But then we absolutely have to get back to Minneapolis. We have lots to do!"

"Yay!" he said. "What did Owen say?"

"I haven't told him yet. Do you want to tell him?"

"I'll tell him!" Noah said.

Noah got dressed and into his braces the fastest he ever had, and with the help of crutches he was practically running across the yard. He was careening like a drunken sailor and so cute. Hannah readied herself to run and pick him up, but he made it all the way without falling. From her place on the porch she could hear Noah yell, "We're staying longer!" And she saw Owen pick Noah up and toss him into the air. One of Noah's crutches hit Owen in the head. He winced and laughed.

For just a moment, she worried that by

taking two more weeks she had worsened the problem, making leaving even harder.

Owen carried the boy across the yard, his crutches dangling from his arms. Romeo was prancing along behind, taking a detour for his morning constitutional. Owen's smile was wider than she'd ever seen it.

"This was good news to wake up to," he said.

"I hope this doesn't make it worse, like if Noah and Romeo bond even more . . ."

"Don't be silly," Owen said. "They couldn't possibly bond any more."

"You do understand that's all I have. Two more weeks. After that, I'm almost into my unpaid family leave."

"I get it. And you'll be leaving before summer really hits," he said. "You'll still have plenty of time to establish your routine."

"That's right," she said. "So, now what?"

"We have many things to do — swimming, fishing, visiting neighbors, taking pictures and taking walks. Maybe we should take a road trip or two and visit some of the small towns around here, check out their pubs, diners, galleries, bookstores — everything. Don't worry, I think we'll be busy and have great fun, so let's not burn daylight."

Owen was back to counting days. At first,

with the gift of two more weeks, it seemed he would have forever with Hannah and Noah. The May wildflowers were popping up along mountain roads and around ranches and houses. They planned a full day every morning. They chose where they'd have their meals, some days staying home all day. No matter what they did during the day, each one ended on the porch, where Hannah and Owen talked and talked.

Their routine was full, exhausting for Noah. The little guy had an hour or two nap most days. There had never been so much life in Owen's home before.

Then he was down to a week left. Then a couple of days.

"You know, you can stay longer if it will help things," he said to Hannah.

"Thank you, that's very sweet. But staying on any longer is like running away from a reality Noah and I really should face. Are we invited back for a visit?"

"Many visits," he said. "You are always welcome."

She was feeling so comfortable and content that it all seemed too good to be true. Then there was a strange occurrence—she saw a missed call on her phone. Wyatt. There was no message. No text. She decided it must have been a pocket dial. But it

brought back that uncomfortable feeling —
*maybe I'm no good at knowing a good man
when I find one.*

A couple of hours with Owen made her
stop worrying about that. Or stop caring,
she wasn't sure.

She went to bed, night after night, telling
herself it was time to go. And then it was.
She told Noah they had one more day.

The next morning, Hannah woke up to the
sound of drizzle. It would be good for the
flowers and vegetables in Sully's garden, but
it was a shame that on their last day with
Owen, they'd be driven inside. On top of
that, someone woke up on the wrong side
of the bed.

"I said I'm not hungry! I don't want
stupid cereal!" Noah said angrily.

Hannah was stunned. The perfect child
had gone sour. "Would you like eggs? Toast?
Pancakes? I think we have some —"

"I'm not *hungry*," he yelled, hitting the
table with his fist and tipping the cereal
bowl so that milk and Cheerios ran all over
the table and dripped on the floor.

"I guess what you want is a time-out. Go
to your room. I'll be in to talk to you in a
minute. After I clean up."

"I. Want. *Romeo!*"

142

"I don't think they're up yet. If I have to drag you to your room, I will. Let's move it."

"I don't want to," he said. Then he burst into tears.

Hannah left the spilled milk and crouched beside Noah's chair. She felt his head. "Are you feeling sick?" she asked. "Do your legs hurt? Are you still tired?"

"I'm nothing," he said, grinding his little fists into his eyes.

"Why are you in a temper?" she asked. "I've never known you to be so awful and mean."

"*You're* mean!" he said.

"Okay," she said, picking him up. "You need a little time alone and I need to clean up the mess you made. I don't want to see you until you're ready to apologize. And I know you know what that means."

He started to struggle and kick. He had his heavy tennis shoes on and got her a good one in the shin.

"Boy, you might be in here all day," she said, depositing him on his bed and closing the door on the way out. She vigorously rubbed her shin, then limped to the kitchen.

A couple of minutes later there was a knock on the door and she opened it to Owen and Romeo. Romeo had a towel draped over his back, sopping up the drizzle. "Was that Noah screaming?" he asked.

"Yes, Mr. Cranky Pants came to breakfast this morning."

"Is he like that often?"

"No! I have no idea what's wrong. I hope he's not coming down with something. We've been together 24/7 for over two months and I've never seen behavior like that before. Not even with losing his mother."

"Maybe it was bubbling up," Owen said. "If it was, it's good to get it out."

Romeo sat beside Owen, quiet and stoic. In fact, it looked to Hannah as if the dog frowned slightly. "Want some Cheerios, Romeo?" she asked, standing aside with a rag in her hand. The dog very happily cleaned up the rest of the mess on the floor.

Hannah poured Owen a cup of coffee and they sat at the table.

"Why does your coffee taste so much better than my coffee?" he asked.

"Because you didn't make it. You want me to mess you up some eggs?"

"I'll wait awhile, maybe eat with Noah. When he recovers. What are your plans for the day?"

"I was hoping Noah would play outside and I could gather up our stuff. We're going to get our bath and shower tonight, and in the morning we'll just dress, have a little breakfast and hit the road early."

"I can entertain him in the barn with pictures," Owen said. "Hopefully it'll clear up later."

"I want to go over to Sully's and say goodbye," she said.

"You'll come back here for a visit, won't you?"

"Of course! Yes! I promise!"

"I'll look forward to it every day."

"I don't know when, Owen. I have to figure out some things at home first, you know. I have to find my comfort zone. *Our* comfort zone. Then I can try to plan a visit with you. That will give Noah something to look forward to."

"And me," he said. "I'll be sure to give you the dates I'm going to be away so you . . . Come when I'm here, okay? I can help with Noah and Romeo won't be with my sister, and you know Noah wants Romeo here. You take his wet suit in case you want to take a dip in one of those icy Minnesota lakes . . ."

"I know I seem crazy, but I'm not."

They stopped talking when Romeo got up, dropping his towel on the floor. The dog walked across the great room to where

Noah stood, holding his blanket.

"Sorry," he said very quietly.

"Feeling a little better?" Hannah asked. When he nodded, she said, "Come here, honey."

He shuffled over to her and let her draw him up onto her lap. Romeo was right there, his big head on Noah's lap. She kissed his temple. "Owen waited to have breakfast with you. What would you like?"

"What's Owen having?"

"I'm having eggs. Messed-up eggs."

"I could do that," Noah said.

"Good," Hannah said. "You sit right here. I'll make you boys some breakfast."

While she was in the kitchen, she listened to them talking.

"Let's have some fun today, since you have to leave tomorrow."

"What kind of fun?"

"Well, while it's rainy, we'll go to the barn and tinker with some pictures. You took a lot of pictures and I can put them on a flash drive for you to take home. I showed you some flash drives. You can plug it into Hannah's computer or tablet and look at your pictures."

"Can I have some of yours, too?"

"Of course. You can show me which ones you like. Then maybe we should have lunch at Sully's place."

"Can Romeo go?"

"If it's not raining. If it's still drizzling and the ground is all sloppy, Romeo has to stay home. He's a very bad influence on Beau."

"And Sully doesn't feel like washing him."

"And I don't feel like taking a muddy Great Dane home in the truck. Or Hannah's car."

"Thank you for that," Hannah said. She brought over two plates. "Here you go. If you want something more, just say so."

"Thank you," Noah said.

"That was very polite of you," Owen said. "I'm glad your manners are back."

Noah shrugged and sank his fork into some eggs. "I had a temper before."

"I heard," Owen said. "It was awful. Don't give Romeo eggs or he'll poop all over. Eggs give him the trots."

Noah laughed.

"He cleaned up your cereal mess and I'm bracing myself," Owen said.

"Yet another reason Romeo shouldn't go for a ride in my car," Hannah said.

"After we get back from Sully's, when all your stuff is gathered, I'll help you load up your car," Owen said. Noah instantly dropped his gaze and started stirring his eggs. "Buck up, kid. Hannah said you guys will be coming back for a visit this summer. Don't spoil it by being angry."

"We are?" he asked Hannah.

"Sure. We'll figure out a good time. But we have things to organize at home first. Then we'll come for a visit. Will that help you enjoy today?"

"Yes," he said. "Except, you know, that's not really where I live."

Hannah lifted his chin. "I'm sorry about that, Noah. But it's the way things are now and we're going to make it good. We're going to make new friends just like you made friends with Owen and Romeo. And we'll visit Owen and Romeo as soon as we can. We have a big job to do and we can't be on vacation forever. Will you help me? Just help me by trying to get along?"

Noah locked eyes with Owen and at Owen's very slight nod, Noah said, "I can do that."

"That's my guy. Now, I'm going to do the dishes and clean up the house while you and Owen and Romeo pick out some pictures."

"'Kay," he said meekly.

Once they left, Hannah, alone in the kitchen, cried into the sink. Because she didn't want to leave, either. She wanted to stop the clock, burn the calendar and just make this the rest of her life.

Hannah and Owen were so forcibly cheerful, she was certain Noah noticed it wasn't real. They went to Sully's and had lunch on the porch. The sun came out and Romeo loped around the campgrounds with Beau; Sully and Noah threw the ball for them for a little while. Hannah was able to thank Helen for all her help and advice.

Back at Owen's, Noah and Owen did a little fishing while Hannah gathered up all their things and packed everything except what they would wear to bed and then put on in the morning. Owen helped her load up her car and she proved to be very controlling about how things were arranged, making them both laugh.

Owen cooked dinner. He made Noah's favorite meal of hot dogs and mac and cheese, except his mac and cheese was rich and thick and made from scratch. Hannah had the passing thought that if she were to stay longer, Owen would make her fat. Nothing stuck to him; he ate all the most fattening things and was still thin.

They played a rousing game of Candy Land after dinner. The sun just didn't want to go down, even with the help of the Rockies to the west. Finally, Hannah told Noah it was time for his bath and bed. She even allowed that Romeo could help him go to sleep.

It took about a half hour for bath, book, settling in. When she got back to the porch, Owen had lit a couple of candles, opened a bottle of wine and had some soft music coming out of the walls. She had no idea how he'd done it. This house he'd built, it had everything. It was a magic house.

"Would you like me to clean out the refrigerator?" she asked him. "There's not much and nothing has gone bad."

"Leave it all and sit down."

She sat and accepted a glass of wine. "I'll strip the beds and toss the sheets in the washer before we leave in the morning."

"Please don't," he said. "Please leave me things to do. I think I'm going to want to be busy tomorrow. And can you check in sometimes? Let me know your progress and how the drive is going."

"Sure, but please don't worry."

"It was a very good vacation," he said. "I hope you feel refreshed. The weeks leading up to you coming here were so hard for you."

"It's been a wonderful escape." She sipped her wine. "My fiancé's name was Wyatt. He betrayed me. I had to cancel a wedding. I lost hundreds of dollars in deposits. And I haven't given him two thoughts in four weeks."

A huff of laughter escaped Owen. "That really was a close call."

"I'm going to think about you a lot," she said.

"Good. Because I want you to come back. Or summon me to Minneapolis. We spent every day together and yet there are so many things left to talk about. I'd like you to meet my mother. My mother and sister — they're probably the best parts of my life. I'd even like you to meet my ex-wife. She's a remarkable woman."

"I'd like to work as your assistant and go on some of your trips with you."

His eyes lit up. "It just so happens, there's an opening! When can you start?"

She smiled but shook her head. "You know I have to go. I have to get Noah settled. We have to find a routine. A routine will help him a lot, I think."

"You're going to be a wonderful mother," he said. "You're already a wonderful mother."

"Everything has changed now. I was on the fast track to become regional director of sales. If I performed well in that capacity, I stood a chance of eventually being vice president of sales. Now none of that seems important. The only thing that matters is having enough time for Noah. Enough time and money to do right by him. I'd quit working altogether, but that's just impractical — we need medical benefits and income. I think I'm going to look around for a job with more flexible hours and far less travel. Maybe there's something in my company . . ."

"A transfer to a different department?" he asked.

"I don't even know what to look for," she said.

"Maybe you should see a counselor," he said.

"I don't think I need counseling," she said, bristling a little bit.

"Not a therapist," he said, laughing. "A career advisor. Your circumstances might be special but lots of people reach a point when their work is less than satisfying and they want to make a change, but they just don't know where to turn."

"Huh," she said. "I never thought of that . . ."

"You could take your time. There's no deadline."

"You make everything sound so easy."

"Hannah, it won't be easy. But it doesn't

have to be an emergency. You and Noah can move forward at your own pace. You'll find your groove."

They talked through two glasses of wine each, like every other night. Then he took her empty glass, set it aside and pulled her to her feet. He kissed her brow, a tender smooch that didn't quite live up to the feelings she had. "I want you to get a good night's sleep but I don't want you to wake up with a hangover—you have so far to go tomorrow." He wrapped his arms around her and pulled her close. "I'm going to miss you. And Noah. I think poor Romeo might sink into depression."

"You'll have to give him extra attention."

"What time are you getting up?" he asked.

"About six," she said. "That should be early enough. We'll dress, have a quick breakfast, hit the road."

"I'll be up," he said. He lifted her chin and pressed his lips against hers in a sweet, firm kiss. Then he rubbed a knuckle along her cheek. "This isn't really goodbye. We'll talk all the time. Probably every day. We'll see each other again soon."

"Sure," she said. "Sleep well. See you in the morning."

The family is the test of freedom;
because the family is the only
thing that the free man makes
for himself and by himself.
— GILBERT K. CHESTERTON

6

Hannah feared it was goodbye. Owen lived a somewhat adventurous, reluctantly famous life and in between his travels, he hid out at his cabin and put together his photos and collections. What did she really know about him? She loved his temperament and his humor, loved the way he related to Noah and even Romeo, but she had no way of knowing if he had that occasional dark side. His ex-wife, who he described as a fun- loving extrovert, said he could be quiet for long periods. She hadn't noticed that in the time they'd been together. Would that be okay after a while? Or would it become tiresome and lonely?

Still, she felt the threat of tears while she was in the shower. She had to be so careful. It wouldn't take much to get Noah going — he was already grieving the end of his vacation, already missing Owen and Romeo. The poor little guy had done so much grieving lately.

But the press of Owen's lips had left an impression. The safety she felt in the circle of his arms was so promising. Being near that calm, strong confidence was inspiring. He was not like any other man she'd ever known. It was true — she had hardly thought about Wyatt. If she hadn't gotten that errant phone call, the one she hadn't even answered, she might not have thought about him at all. Not even in the dark of night. *Close call.*

There was one thing that left her unsure. It was clear that he adored Noah but how did Owen feel about *her?* In four weeks of constant companionship Owen had hugged her a couple of times. Very polite and platonic hugs. He'd kissed her brow a few times. He'd kissed her lips only that once, and it hadn't been a passionate kiss filled with longing. With the exception of his kindness, his generosity and warmth, she didn't get a strong sense of desire from him. He'd said since his divorce, relationships had been rare and brief.

She dried her hair so it wouldn't be all wonky in the morning and slid into bed. She thought about keeping Owen in the back of her mind, handy. Waiting. They would get to know each other better on phone calls. She would visit him again. If she didn't learn what she needed to know after another visit, she might plan to visit him the following summer. After all, she'd reconciled herself to the fact that she was going to be a single parent. She'd called off two weddings, proof she wasn't a great judge of men.

Morning came too soon and she was tired. She'd slept but not well. She was relieved to see the clock read nearly six; she wouldn't have to fight it any longer. She got up, dressed, put on the coffee, stowed away her pajamas and yesterday's clothes and her toiletries. She put her suitcase by the door.

She roused Noah and he groaned miserably. "Get up and put on your happy face. I'm going to want you to take pictures of our road trip that you can send to Owen. He'll be coming over for breakfast so let's get moving."

"Do I have to?"

"Well, I can carry you to the car in your pajamas and you can get dressed later, but don't you want to see Owen and Romeo before we leave?"

"Uh-huh," he muttered.

She helped him get dressed and get his braces on. While he brushed his teeth, she stripped both beds and put the sheets in the washer, but she didn't start it. She made a neat pile of blankets, comforters and pillows, and her nose told her the coffee was ready. She gave Noah a bowl of Cheerios, poured two cups of coffee and opened the door — that was their signal.

Romeo came bounding inside. "Here, boy, here," Noah called and the Great Dane ran to him and licked his face.

She carried the coffee to the porch and there he sat in his favorite chair. "How long have you been waiting?" she asked, handing him a coffee.

"Just a little while," he said.

"Aw, you're looking a little bit tired," she said. "It's going to be all right, you'll see. I have it all worked out in my head. We'll talk on the phone. We'll FaceTime and text and get to know each other even better. We'll have another visit before the end of summer. Maybe you'll come to Minneapolis even though, for a man like you, that can't seem very interesting. But this has been wonderful, Owen. You're wonderful. Thank you. I think it was the best month of my life."

"Mine, too."

"Can Noah borrow that camera you showed him how to use? He can take pictures from the car and we can email them to you. I'll send the camera back —"

"You don't have to send it back. He can have it. Tell him to take pictures of you, too. And I'll take pictures of Romeo."

"Why do you call him Romeo anyway?"

He smiled. "He was just a pup when I found him but that didn't keep him from flirting with every animal in sight. I even caught him trying to have his way with a fawn. Thank God that didn't work out for him. Can you imagine the ugly beast we'd have gotten?"

"You're making that up."

"I wish I were. Do you need help gathering things together?"

"Nope. We're ready. The snack pack, little cooler and Noah's backpack with his tablet and toys go in the back seat. My little overnight bag can go in the front seat with my purse."

"Have you eaten?"

She made a face. "I don't think I can, Owen. I might have a little travel tummy. But let me mess you up some eggs if you want."

"Nah," he said. "I'll do that later."

A small voice came from inside the cabin. "Take care of Owen and Beau and don't be a bad influence. Be very good. Owen can

160

show you my face on the phone when I call. I love you more than anything."

Hannah put her hand over mouth. Her eyes watered and she fought tears. "We need to go. We need to not drag this out. Please understand."

"I understand," he said.

"Let me rinse the cereal bowl . . ."

"Hannah, I'll get that. Just come here." He wrapped his long arms around her and said, "Let's be grateful for how this worked out and not make it negative. It was incredible. I can't wait for the next time."

A hiccup of emotion escaped her and she got on her toes to kiss his cheek. "How does it feel to be the second best man in my entire life?"

He grinned. "Very good, that's how it feels." He walked into the kitchen, grabbed Noah and lifted him. "Come on, cowboy, let's get you situated. Hannah will get all your back seat stuff. Do you have to go to the bathroom?"

"I went."

Owen settled Noah into his seat and kissed him on the cheeks. "Thank you for visiting me. Please visit me again soon. I'll miss you so I'll call you."

"'Kay."

Owen took the things Hannah carried and

put them within Noah's reach. She came back a second later with her small bag and her purse. She hugged him again and slid into the car. "Have a wonderful time in your travels, Owen."

"Thank you. Be very safe and careful."

"Of course. You, too."

He closed the door and she pulled out of her space by the house and drove down the road. She gave the horn a little toot and heard Romeo bark. And she thought, *Thank God we don't have to face goodbye anymore.* She checked the rearview mirror and saw that Noah had tear streaks down his cheeks. "You okay, buddy?" she asked.

He nodded. "I wish I didn't have to go away from everyone I like."

She felt the dampness of her own cheeks and decided it was best just to say nothing. They were entitled to a little cry. She drove toward Leadville.

Owen had another cup of coffee on the porch. Romeo kept putting his big head in Owen's lap. "We're bachelors again, Romeo," he said, scratching Romeo's ears. "We'll be fine."

After all, he'd been fine for years. He had no one to answer to, he'd developed some wonderful pictures and collections and it was time he focused on that again.

He'd also liked their company. He'd been so surprised. You'd think in ten years he'd have met someone that made him feel connected again, but no. It wasn't until Hannah and Noah. Either they were special or he was just ready and they were in his crosshairs.

He hadn't wanted them to leave. Of course he couldn't make them stay. He'd offered. He'd said, *Stay longer. Take your time. You have family leave. You can sit and think.* Had he said, *Please don't go?* Probably not. Owen was always hesitant to push his affection or, worse, his needs on another person. Had he told her she was beautiful? He supposed not since he was a little shy. Shy and sometimes uncertain. And he hadn't told her he'd been a father. Telling anyone about that part of his life always sent him into a panic. He could see the horrified look in the eyes of the person he told. Because it was horrifying! Not only could other people not imagine how anyone could survive that, Owen had trouble imagining that himself.

He should have told Hannah there was a reason why he picked up on Noah's vulnerability. Their losses fit together like puzzle pieces. Not just Noah — Hannah, as well.

She'd lost so much and yet managed that with such grace and strength. She was clearly struggling to figure out what her life with Noah should look like, feel like.

Ach, he was a lamebrain! Would he ever learn to tell people how he felt? Sheila used to tell him, *Just say how you feel! That's all you have to do!*

He rinsed the dishes, wiped the table where Noah had slopped, looked in the refrigerator to see so much good food was left that he was certain he wouldn't be able to eat. He went to the bedroom. She'd stripped the bed even though he told her not to bother. He picked up a pillow and held it to his nose. Oh God. How long could he preserve the scent of her?

He went back outside and sat on the porch.

What if I tell her how I feel and she falls for it, gives me a chance, and in due time she discovers I'm a dark, quiet, solitary person and she can't live like that? What if it's only a year and she can't take me and my preoccupation and silence?

"I don't know, Owen," he said aloud, answering his own question. "Do you still get the year with her?" Because right now a year seemed like enough time to learn to be more open, more loving and emotionally available.

I'm such an idiot, he thought. He pulled out his cell phone and called her.

"Owen, I'm fine," she said. "Are you okay?"

"No," he said. "Where are you?"

"I'm almost to Leadville."

"There's a rest stop and park right before you get to town. Pull over. I'm coming."

"Why? Why are you coming?"

"I have to tell you something! Will you wait for me? It's very important."

"Well . . . sure . . . but are you all right?"

"I'm fine. I'm only fifteen minutes behind you." He disconnected.

He shuffled Romeo into the house but he had to stop and put down water for him. "Behave. I'll be gone an hour."

He jumped into his truck and began to drive. When he saw the speed he was going, he eased off the gas. Dying would be inconvenient. He practiced what he would say when he caught up with her and everything sounded so stupid, he had to stop. She was going to think he'd lost his mind and if she ever had a reason to run back to Minneapolis, his lunacy would be it.

Then he began to rehearse how he would behave when she explained she just couldn't stay with him — she had things to do, things to put in place so she could be a single, working mother. He would say, "Okay, but I had to try."

By the time he got to the rest stop, he was totally jumbled. He pulled up right behind her car and honked his horn. He put the truck in Park, jumped out, ran to her car door just as she was getting out. She had a mystified look on her face as she stepped out of her car.

Owen cradled her face in his hands, threading his fingers into her hair, and covered her mouth in a powerful kiss. Her lips parted, inviting him in, and he devoured her, so hungry. He couldn't let her go completely. Against her lips he said, "I want a chance to fall in love with you. I need you. You're the best thing that's ever happened to me. Noah is the best thing, too. I want you to stay. Please stay. Stay the summer. Let's see what we know after summer and if you don't think we're a good idea, okay, I give up. But I think if we give it the summer, we'll fall in love. I'm probably already in love. I must be. I've never felt so awful before." "Awful?" she asked in a whisper.

"You leaving gutted me. Please stay."

"But Noah . . ."

He kissed her again. Long and deep. She wrapped her arms around him. "We have everything he needs. We have doctors and dentists and neurologists . . . Okay, maybe not, but they're close enough. Physical therapists. Schools, babysitters, one Great Dane. You don't have to worry about money. I don't mean to say I don't want you to work . . . Shit, I've never been good at this."

"Good at what, Owen?" she asked. But she was smiling.

"Begging."

She held him close. "Yes, this is what was missing." Then she got up on her tiptoes and kissed him. Long and lovingly. He lifted her off her feet.

"Will you give it the summer? To see if you can stand me? To see if we three belong together? Because I know, firsthand, how suddenly happiness can be snatched away, and since you've been here, I've been so happy. If you're happy, too . . ."

"I've been happy," she said, her lips still against his. "So happy . . ."

"The summer, then," he said. "For starters. Let's at least give it the summer."

"I think that's perfectly reasonable. Yes, I want to find out."

"Oh God," he said, clutching her tightly to him. "Oh God."

And then a small voice said, "Hey! Whatcha doing out there?"

Owen wanted to be the one to tell Noah. He opened the car door and said, "Noah, you and Hannah are going to come back to my house. Hopefully for the whole summer."

"How long is that?" he asked.

"Long," Owen said. "Months. Till it stops being summer. Can you live with that?"

Noah's face lit up in a huge grin, a light shining from inside the little guy. "I could do that," he said. "Does Romeo know?"

"You can tell him."

Noah was full of questions on the way back to Owen's house. "Why do we get to go back? How long is summer? Is it almost a year? Can I fish today? Can I swim? Do I have to have quiet time again? Should I tell Sully? We could call him or we could go over there. We're taking all this stuff back in the house, right? We don't have to leave it in the car for summer, right?"

Hannah was laughing, but she was also driving. "Summer is a long time. Yes, we're going to take all our things in and put everything away in the drawers and closets. Play a game while I drive!"

Owen carted all their belongings back into

the house and while the boys hung out, fished, threw the ball for Romeo and read in the hammock for a while, Hannah was busy putting things away and calling her girlfriends.

"I'm staying for summer," she said. "I'm staying to see if I love him. I'm giving it a chance to see if I love him like I think I do."

"I had a feeling," Kate said.

"I'm not crazy. You'll meet him and you'll know. I don't fall in love fast or easy. I may have picked a couple of bad apples but not because I was impetuous — because they were wrong. Owen is . . ." *Right,* she thought. "I have to know. We're happy here."

"Are you sure this is a good idea?" Kate asked.

"Yes," Hannah said. "I'm not sure of the outcome yet but it's what I want. I wanted so much for him to say, 'Let's see if we're right together.' When you meet him, you'll understand. He's amazing."

"Will this be okay for Noah?" Sharon asked.

"I think it will be the best thing for Noah, but you shouldn't worry about that. I will always put Noah first and if it ever becomes a negative for Noah, I can have that car loaded in thirty minutes. But Noah loves Owen even more than I do."

"You said *love*," Sharon said.

"I'm not getting ahead of myself," Hannah said. "I'm not sure it's true love but it feels like it. That's why we're giving it the summer. Before the leaves change color, we'll know if we should be together."

"Hannah, you should wait. Don't move in together so fast. Take your time."

Hannah laughed. "I waited a year with my first fiancé. I waited two years with my second. Both were excruciatingly bad choices. Neither felt like this feels. How long should I wait? Owen makes me feel better about myself than both of those fiancés put together. And Noah is too young and sweet to have to leave behind another person he loves. We're going to stay with Owen for the summer and if we belong together, it will be longer. I have shortcomings of all kinds but you must believe me — I will protect Noah. I love him to the moon and back."

"We're going to have to come and visit," Sharon said.

"By all means," Hannah said. "But when you fall in love with this place and the man, don't think you get the whole summer!"

It was a slow and languid day because everyone was tired. Apparently the stress of knowing they had to leave and all the getting ready wore everyone out. The sun was trying to sneak behind the Rockies when Noah was snuggling on Hannah's lap, yawning.

"I think you need a quick bath and bed," she said.

"Can Romeo come?"

"Owen?"

"If he wants to. And if I know Romeo, he wants to."

By the time she got back to the porch, he had opened a nice bottle of wine. Instead of sitting on her favorite chair, she slid onto his lap and put her arms around his neck. "I hope you don't regret this," she said.

"I almost didn't catch you in time," he said. "I almost let you get away."

"My girlfriends are worried about my judgment. They'll come for a visit, check you out, decide whether I've lost my mind."

"How soon will they be here?" he asked, nuzzling her neck. "I get a couple more days to seduce you, don't I?"

She laughed. She also shivered at the sensation of his lips on her neck. "You don't need all that much time, Owen. But when did you discover you felt this way? I had no idea."

"It was pretty quick. Not immediately, but within a day I was asking myself, what is this feeling? I couldn't risk scaring you away so I made myself slow down. You guys had been through a lot and the only thing I wanted was for you to feel safe and happy here. And with me — here with me."

"Owen, maybe you should have told me how you felt. When you were offering me a chance to stay longer . . ."

"It's been such a long time since I was in love, Hannah. You're going to have to be patient with me. I'm a solitary old dog. But what I want is to be part of a family like yours. What I really want is to not let go of you for twenty-four hours. At least."

"Are you offering to tuck me in tonight?"

"I could do that," he said, aping Noah's best-known phrase.

"You'll have to have pajamas," she told him. "Noah sometimes wakes up in the night. Do you own any?"

"There's a trunk in the master closet, filled with my more personal items that I don't bother to pack or move into the barn. There are some T-shirts and boxers in there. Will that do?"

"That would be nice," she said, giving him a kiss.

"Do you have pajamas?" he asked, pulling her closer.

"Of course."

"I don't think you're going to need them

for a while," he said. Then he kissed her with every fiber of emotion running through his veins. His hands wandered under her shirt, stroking her back, sliding under her bra to fondle her breasts and tease her nipples. His tongue made a playful tour of the inside of her mouth and both of them were breathing hard. He lifted his hips slightly. "Do you think he's asleep?"

"He was almost asleep when I tucked him in, but I'll check." She laughed softly. "I'm not going to get a glass of wine, am I?"

"I'll bring it. We'll have wine. And other things." He lifted her up so he could stand, placing her on her feet. "Come with me, sweetheart. Tiptoe. No need to wake anyone."

The front door was locked, the lights turned off, Noah and Romeo looked in on, the covers on the large, extra-long bed pulled back. The bedroom door had to be closed. A bottle of wine and two glasses sat on the bedside table. "Have you missed your bed?" she asked him.

"It wasn't the bed I've been wanting," he said. He pulled her shirt over her head and kissed his way from her neck to her shoulder and down her arm to her wrist. He pulled his own shirt off and pressed her close against him, letting her soft breasts tease him. He pulled her down on the bed and lay facing her, leisurely kissing her and running his fingers through her hair, tucking a lock behind her ear. "I was afraid this might never happen. You were so insistent that you had to get back to Minneapolis."

"I have a cute little house there," she said. "It comes with a cute little mortgage. I was so proud when I was able to buy it. My life has changed ten times since then."

"I hope from now on your only changes are welcome." He slid her shorts down and flipped them away. "Starting here," he added, sliding a hand over her belly and down. His long fingers glided toward her most private places and she opened her legs for him.

She unsnapped his shorts and slid a hand inside. "Starting here," she added with a soft, wicked little laugh. Her hand slid over his erection and he moaned. "Owen," she whispered. "Get rid of these shorts and let's get under the sheet."

He rolled with her right, then left. He pulled her under him and settled himself between her legs, gently prodding her. "How's your birth control?" he asked.

"I guess that means you don't have a condom . . ."

"I have some mighty dated ones in that

trunk in the closet. If I wasn't prepared it's because I didn't expect to be this lucky. How is this so far?"

"Almost perfect," she said. "I'm on the pill and it's served me well." She pulled his face down to hers and kissed him while her hands roved all over his back and butt. He was so beautifully put together, his muscles long and lean, his male butt solid and round.

He pampered one nipple, then the other, then licked his way down her stomach again, this time not stopping until he reached the center of her body. He spread her legs and briefly buried himself in her soft flesh, his tongue torturing her. Her fingers were in his hair, gently massaging his scalp. Thankfully he didn't waste a lot of time because she was struggling. He came back to her lips and whispered against them.

"Anything you want," he said. "Anything."

"I want you inside me."

"Thank God," he said, immediately sliding into her. He pinched his eyes closed and was still a moment, then began to move. She moved with him, clutching him tightly to her. She whimpered slightly, reaching for that moment. Her legs came around his waist and he grabbed her butt, pounding into her with hard strokes, pressing into her, reaching deeply.

She had a powerful, blinding climax in his arms. He opened his eyes, looking down at her. She closed her eyes and bit her lower lip, riding it out. "Honey," he whispered. "Hannah." Then, unable to wait her out, he pumped a few short times and exploded with her.

When he stopped panting, he covered her lips with short kisses, leaning on his elbows to keep his weight off her.

"I hope that was okay," he said in a rough whisper. "Because I think after that one time, I'm addicted."

She laughed softly. "It was very good," she said. "Can you do that again?"

"In a little while," he promised. "Right now I want to feel your whole body against mine. You're so soft. So sweet." He turned her a bit so he could spoon her. He nuzzled her neck. "I'm so happy my trip was canceled."

She chuckled. "Me, too. What do you suppose people will say when they notice I'm still here?"

"I don't know what they'll say about you but I think they'll decide I'm less strange."

"I'm not sure anyone thinks of you as strange," she said, holding on to the arms that held her.

"They must. I even find myself strange. But right this moment? I find myself to be the luckiest man alive."

"We should put on our pajamas and open the door to listen for Noah . . ."

"In just a little while," he murmured. He turned her toward him and pulled one of her legs over his hip. "We can take a little more time."

"Oh, Owen. I do love the way you touch me."

"Good. I'm going to touch you every chance I get. Hannah, Hannah, you make my heart feel so full . . ."

"So far . . . this is an excellent idea. I think photography isn't your only gift."

A couple of hours later, still cuddling but pajama clad, Hannah opened her eyes to see Noah at the side of the bed.

"Hannah?"

"Noah, did you have a bad dream?"

"No, but I was done sleeping." He yawned. "For now."

"You can come in the bed but let's take your braces off."

"'Kay," he said. "Hannah, is that Owen right there? What is he doing there?"

"Well, this is his bed I've been using so I imagine he'd like it back. And I don't mind sharing," she said, sliding off the braces.

"Come here on my side. No, Romeo. You have to lie on the floor. There you go. Snuggle up, Noah. Close your eyes, please. I'm not done sleeping yet."

"'Kay. You sure do fit a lot of people in this bed."

"It's better when it's not too many," she said. "Shhh."

Helen said she was relieved and not at all surprised that Hannah and Noah stayed. "I figured you for a smart woman," she said.

Leigh Shandon said, "I'm growing a nice little group of women friends. Maybe I'll start a book club."

At the thought of books, Hannah remembered that great shelf in Owen's library of children's classics, each one too long to finish on a short vacation. *Treasure Island, Swiss Family Robinson, Alice in Wonderland, Watership Down, Where the Red Fern Grows, Peter Pan,* all the Harry Potter books. Since they were only going to be here for a couple of weeks, she'd been reluctant to get into too many of the classics, though she fell in love with them. Beautiful paper, illustrated, leather-bound. Because she thought time was short, she'd done most of the reading. They were reading *Treasure Island.* "Help me read a little bit, Noah," she said.

178

"I can do that," he said.

Noah was able to read whole sentences even from this complicated book. He had done this before when he'd been reading his own books, but she assumed his books were so familiar to him that he did it a lot of it from memory. "Noah, you're a very good reader!"

"Sometimes," he said. "Not the real hard words."

"Who taught you to read?"

"The teacher. And Linda. And Mom."

"Wow! You're amazing!"

He just shrugged. "I'm not that active."

"You're sure active here!" she said.

"I think it's 'cause there's no other kids," he said. "When there are kids, I'm the slowest one."

That stopped her for a second. But then she said, "That's going to change, too. And when you catch up to the other kids, you're going to be able to read!"

"A little bit," he said.

"Read me what you can of this page," she said.

He barely stumbled. He sounded out phonetically the words he didn't recognize. Sometimes they had to talk about the meaning. Owen came from his barn to sit on the porch and listen for a while. He smiled and nodded at Noah. After about ten minutes, Owen went back to the barn and Noah read with Hannah.

The temperature dropped, it rained a little and Owen made beef stew with biscuits for dinner, ice cream for dessert. Instead of sitting on the porch, they found a movie and lit the fire. When Noah was in bed, Hannah snuggled up against Owen in the great room.

"Did you hear how brilliant Noah is?" she asked him. "I don't know anything but I bet he's reading at a fourth- or fifth-grade level. He'll turn six before the end of the year, but c'mon, he's only five! You are so smart to have some kids' books. I guess that's for the families that rent your house . . ."

He was quiet for a moment. "I didn't buy them for future rental guests. I bought them for my son," he said. She slowly turned her head and looked up at him. "I have some things to tell you," he said. "Some things that are going to be hard to hear."

*New beginnings are often
disguised as painful endings.*
— LAO TZU

7

"His name was Brayden and he was the victim of a violent crime when he was seven years old. He was kidnapped from the sidewalk in front of our house. Well, two doors down. I was in the open garage. I never heard a car. He never yelled. His body was recovered eighteen months later. That's when I left California. And I haven't been back."

"Owen," she whispered after a long moment of silence.

"I know. It's horrendous, I know."

"It must be so hard to talk about it," she said, giving his cheek a gentle stroke.

"I can talk about it. What's hard is watching someone hear about it. Especially someone I care for. I usually talk about it with people who already know — my mother, my sister, even my brother-in-law. I know it's shocking . . ."

"It's heartbreaking," she said. "I don't

know how you survived it. Do people around here know?"

"No one has mentioned it. Nor has anyone asked me. This is a long way from LA but the case of Brayden Abrams missing, found murdered, then his killer's arrest — all of that was at least regionally famous. And my ex-wife is still nationally known as an activist in child advocacy. She is still called Sheila Abrams even though she's remarried. Not for me but for him. For Brayden. The short answer is — I don't know who knows. I haven't told anyone around here. For the reasons I explained. It changes the landscape of the friendship. Things become so awkward. Not for me — I live with that awkwardness every day."

"Is that why you took to Noah?" she asked.

"No. I can honestly say no. I like children in general. I used to take pictures of kids — portraits, family pictures, school pictures, all that. From babies to graduating seniors. I've always gotten along better with kids and dogs than adult humans. Sheila said it was because I'm immature and hard to train. I hope she was kidding, but it's possible . . . Ah, well, I think you know — Noah is special. Your friend must have been the most wonderful parent. And you're wonderful, too."

"I guess that's why your marriage didn't survive," she said. "Whose could?"

"That's a little more complicated," he said. "We approached our loss in different ways, opposite ways. We were both devastated and, until he was found, terrified. I withdrew into myself. I hounded the police, studied other kidnappings and searched. I looked everywhere — on playgrounds, malls, diners, alleys, in dumpsters. I didn't work, I roamed. Sheila went public, spiking awareness, bringing attention to the danger, the problem, the vulnerability of innocent children and she was brilliant at it. To be fair, she'd always been brilliant in front of an audience and I've always hidden behind the camera, an observer. Sheila is a lawyer and she's incredible. And I've always been . . . I've always been like I am — someone who watches.

"She wanted me to join her in her crusade to bring awareness to the problem so that something positive could come of it, even if it saved only one child. But that wasn't my path. Grief is a poison and every human being has a unique approach to purging that poison. I wanted to feel that same fire Sheila felt but all I felt was despair. Sheila is now one of the most well- known advocates for lost and stolen children in the country. She's a highly paid speaker, a media personality, a lobbyist. She's testified in front of Congress and written laws. I can't describe how much I admire her."

"You still love her," Hannah said.

"I will always love Sheila," he said. "But I'm not in love with her. I'm in love with you."

She held her breath for a moment. "You can't be sure of that."

"I didn't say that so you'd say you love me, too. It took me a long time to even be open to the idea of loving someone. Sheila was stronger and better at moving on — she married an attorney who is much more like her. He's a former cop, a smart and socially conscious man. They worked to- gether, fell in love, married, had a couple of kids. One of them will eventually run for of- fice, I'd bet my kidney on it. But when I met you and Noah, I knew in a day I had found a woman to love. I wanted to love and protect you both."

"But would you love me if I didn't have Noah?" she asked. "Because you lost a child and Noah is so vulner —"

"So smart and vulnerable and funny and sweet, and that's the scariest part for me.

Can you imagine what would become of me if we lost him? It's almost enough of a reason to deny myself a relationship with you! But I can't. I knew in twenty-four hours that if I could somehow manage to be the man you wanted, I was in. But I also knew you'd have to be willing to live with this ghost of mine. I believe it's called *baggage* and it's hefty. I'm damaged —"

"No, you're not," she said. "No more than any of us. In fact, I think it's what makes you special. I'm so sorry for what you went through but I don't think of you as wounded. You're gentle and kind and stronger than anyone I know. You're good for Noah but you're also good for me. Still, I think giving it at least the summer is a good idea — who knows what we might discover about each other once we dig beneath the surface? We deserve a chance to see if we can be good for each other."

"I know you'll be good for me," he said. "The question is, will this broken man weigh you down? Because I'm tired of feeling crippled and sore. I want to be good for someone. I want to be good for you."

"You have been so far," she said.

"Promise me," he said, lifting her chin with a bent finger. "Don't accept me out of pity or because you think you can fix me. I was quiet and a little moody before I lost Brayden. That didn't bother Sheila. She said she was happy to do all the talking."

Hannah smiled. "I can't wait to meet this woman. Is there anything else you want to tell me?"

"Not that I can think of, thank God. I'm sure that was a big enough load."

"Good. Then let's go to bed and hold on to each other. I need some rest. I have to go into town tomorrow and get some referrals from Leigh Shandon. Even though I've kept up with Noah's exercises the past few weeks, it's important not to ignore his therapy protocol. We have to get back in the program."

"Good. Even though we've been having fun, I haven't forgotten he needs routine therapy. And listen, if you'd rather have some space tonight, to think over all the stuff I just dumped on you . . ."

"Don't push it, Owen. Come to bed. Love me. I could use a little reassurance."

He grinned at her. "Amazing. I didn't scare you off."

It happened to her again — a missed call from Wyatt. Well, when you were having summer at the lake with your best guys, you didn't look at your phone much. The only other calls she'd gotten were from Kate, Sharon and a couple of other friends who just wanted to check on her and see how she was doing. There were also a couple of numbers she didn't recognize, which she chalked up to telemarketers. No messages, no texts. She'd looked at her email about once a week. She didn't miss it at all.

Wyatt must have lost control of his phone. Another pocket dial. If he wanted to reach her for some reason, he could text or leave a message but he hadn't. And she found she had no desire to text him, hear from him. She definitely had no desire to see him.

She'd been prepared to marry him and now, because of Owen, she realized she hadn't had the depth of love and trust a lifetime commitment required. She had let it be enough that she usually felt happy when they were together. Usually.

Then Owen came along. Owen made her feel brand-new. Fresh, happy and utterly safe. She felt as though anything was possible.

With each passing day, it was easier for her to ignore Wyatt's accidental call and not give him a thought. She was exactly where she wanted to be.

Hannah took Noah into Timberlake to visit

the doctor, giving Owen some time to work. Leigh was very encouraging by echoing what his neurologist had told her before they left Madison — his case was very mild and with the right therapy, possibly medication, possibly Achilles tendon surgery after puberty, he would probably walk without leg braces. He might have a lifelong hitch in his step . . . or not. But he was so fortunate that was all he was dealing with. A large percentage of those afflicted with CP had seizures, had full-body involvement, had other affected areas of the body from speech to mobility and would never leave a wheelchair. Leigh called Maggie Sullivan, Sully's daughter, who was a neurosurgeon, to get her recommendations on doctors and therapists, and Maggie also suggested a counselor she knew — someone to help Noah with grief counseling and adaptation to relocating and dealing with a disability. "I'm prone to do too much as opposed to too little. We'll drop out some of the players as we go along," Leigh said.

"I agree," Hannah said. "Let's cover all the bases. Especially now, when it's summer and school is out."

Hannah thought that Romeo was probably the best counselor of all. What luck that was.

For the first few weeks Hannah was on leave, there had been a never-ending stream of emails asking her questions about accounts and business associates, but that had dwindled considerably since. She kept in touch with her boss, though just a bit and only because she wasn't ready to burn that bridge. She sent pictures of Noah, Romeo and even Owen to her girlfriends back home, corresponded with her lawyer and Erin's former boss, who had helped Erin with her will.

And when she had a little time alone with her laptop, she looked up Owen. Of course he was very well-known in both photography and book circles and there were a couple of brief references to the fact that he'd had one son who died at the age of seven.

But it was Sheila Abrams whose internet references were too many to read. Her advocacy work was global. Sheila Abrams was stunning and widely respected. She spoke not only at rallies and advocacy gatherings but also graduations and conventions. Hannah watched interviews she did on *Oprah* and on *Ellen* — she was so well-spoken, powerful and so brave.

There were pictures of Brayden as well and even a little bit about his killer, who traded information about other victims to take the death sentence off the table, not that it did him any good. He confessed to killing four children, was sentenced to 142 years in prison without parole and was killed in prison before he could file his first appeal. There were two pictures — a mug shot at his arrest in which he looked like pure evil and a picture taken just outside the courtroom in which he looked like a perfectly safe guy from church.

It was strange, she could see Owen and Sheila together—yin and yang — the quiet and stoic observer and the lion queen. The thing that made Hannah happiest was knowing how much Owen respected the choice Sheila had made. It was perfectly understandable. Some people were born to lead with a strong voice. Owen was born to capture the world and its people in all its beauty and unpleasantness, subtle and bold. Their hurt was probably equal but, as he had said, they took different paths.

They worked and played through the first couple of weeks in June, seeing the doctors and therapist, making progress. The combination of playing with that rambunctious dog and swimming almost every day was telling on Noah — he was nearly running!

The days would start out energetically and end with Noah exhausted, sweaty and smelling gamey. Owen put a rubber mat on the shower floor and installed a grab bar on the wall so Noah could shower. "Like a guy," Noah said, ecstatic. "Now Hannah doesn't have to wash me!"

"I will still check behind your ears."

Of course, the first solo shower he fell and Hannah ran for the bathroom door. Owen grabbed her arm, stopping her. "You okay in there, Noah?" Owen yelled.

"Okay!" he yelled.

"Need help?" Owen asked.

"I got it!" Noah yelled.

"What if he hurt himself? What if he's bruised?" she asked.

"Ask him if he checked to see if he has a bruise or is sore anywhere," Owen said. "Hannah, he falls a lot. It's one of the complications. But he's getting stronger by the day."

"I know, but I like to check," she said.

"Check behind his ears for dirt and check his teeth to see if he's brushing. And let him be independent."

She looked up into Owen's warm and smiling eyes. "He has a loose tooth, you know," she said.

"Hey, that's great! What does the tooth

fairy pay these days?"

"I have no idea! Call Sheila! Ask her!"

He laughed and pulled her into his arms. "I haven't exactly told her you stayed."

"Are you keeping me a secret?" she asked.

"Actually, I can't wait to tell her. But there's something we have to talk about. Noah says he doesn't have a father. That his mother got him at the store."

"Oh, crap," she said. "This might be above my pay grade."

"Hannah, even though it's hard, you have to tell him the truth. We can talk about it and I'll help if I can. But he needs to know —"

"That is the truth," she said. "She got him at the store. Sort of."

He just looked at her for a long moment, holding his lips in a straight line. Then he slowly shook his head. "Tonight's fireside chat is going to be so revealing."

The bathroom door opened. Noah was hanging on to the door handle for balance and assistance, the towel wrapped around him, a big grin on his face.

"Look at you, standing all on your own," Hannah said.

"I'm just about done doing that, too," he said.

"I've got this," Hannah said, scooping him

up. "You can sit down on the bed to get into your pajamas. I can help if you want me to."

"I can do this," he said. "But I'll take a ride. Romeo and Owen just about wrecked me today!"

"Are you too tired to read for a while?" she asked.

He yawned. "Maybe. But I have a little listening left."

She snuggled him close and carried him the rest of the way.

When she got to the porch, Owen had lit a couple of fat candles and was comfortable in his favorite chair.

"Would you like something to drink?" he asked.

"I think tonight deserves something a little strong," she said. "How about a Crown, if you have it."

"Water?" he asked, lifting an eyebrow.

"Not too much. Mostly ice."

"Look out, Owen," he said. "She's drinking hard tonight."

Who can blame me, she thought. When he brought back the drinks, she lifted hers in a little toast and said, "Here's to motherhood — on-the-job training."

"You're doing fine, you know."

"I have to clear up that little misunderstanding about where Noah came from. I know what happened — Erin told me about it. She had a pamphlet about explaining eggs and sperm to young children. I think Sharon or Kate gave it to her. It wasn't that long ago, a year or so, when he wanted to know where his father was. Erin told him he didn't technically have one, at least not in the usual way. Usually married ladies make their babies with their husbands but Erin didn't have a husband and she still wanted to be a mother more than anything. She explained that not all married people are lucky enough to have babies — not all women have the eggs and not all men have the sperm and it takes those two things, every time, in almost all animals on earth. But for human men and women sometimes when someone has more than they need, they donate for people who don't have enough. So even though she didn't have a husband, there was a place she could go and get that donated sperm. She told him she went to a sperm bank to find a father for her baby and she must have picked the best one available because he was perfect. She explained it as a little like adoption except this way she got to be pregnant and feel him grow inside her, which was so special. She tried to explain that it was private business and if anyone wanted to know where his father was he should just explain that that's private family business. Somehow the 'bank' turned into a store in his mind and he forgot it was private. And isn't it a wonder no cabbages were thrown in, as well."

"Well, that's just remarkable," Owen said. "What an amazing mind he has."

"I know. He's teaching me things every day. I think he's done letting me see him in his underwear now."

"Kind of sounds like it," Owen said.

"I have a huge, huge favor to ask you."

"No, I'm not going to explain the sperm bank to Noah . . ."

"Not that," she said. "Even though I didn't get a clear job description, I know what I have to do. No, my girlfriends, Sharon and Kate, they want to see us and get a look at you. Can you stand a lot of company? I could ask them to wait until you go to Vietnam but Sharon doesn't have much time to screw around. She's due to have a baby in about six weeks. And they do want to get to know you."

"Bring them on," he said. "How many of them?"

"Kate, Phil and only two of their kids — Phil's three kids from his first marriage will be with their mom. Sharon, John, their three-year-old and Sharon's big belly. So, not counting the belly, seven."

He smiled reassuringly. "If I pass this test, can I keep you awhile?"

"You might be stuck with me either way."

"I can do that," he said.

Hannah was conscious that for the first time she was not at all nervous at the prospect of introducing her best friends to her boy-friend. Not only was she completely confident in Owen, she also didn't care what they thought — she adored him.

The third weekend in June would bring the friends for a long weekend — from Thursday to Tuesday. Owen asked her to go shopping with him to stock up. He wanted to fill up the kitchen with food, drink, plenty of ice cream and needed her input. The kids were three, four and seven. Add in Noah, who was five. When she tried to help pay, he wouldn't have it. "Come on, let me play the host. Unless my sister or ex-wife visits, I'm mostly alone or on the road."

"You must make sure Sheila and her kids come soon," Hannah said. "I can't wait for that."

"I have a feeling the two of you will roast me."

"But not badly."

He also wanted to make sure there were plenty of fishing poles, life vests, floaty toys and games. He dragged out corn-hole boards and beanbags for pitching games, the small firepit with a screen cover for safety and to keep sparks at a minimum, some fireworks and sparklers.

"Are you going to buy a boat?" she asked him.

"I wish I had a boat," he said. "The truth is I have no interest in a boat, but just now I wish I had one."

He complained that he'd gone through a lot of wine since meeting Hannah and he usually ordered his wine from various vintners but this time he had to make do with a case from the liquor store, along with beer and sodas.

There were plenty of towels, since he was set up as a rental home. Mrs. Bourne with her daughter and daughter-in-law came to give the place a freshening and Hannah couldn't help herself. She pitched in, cleaning with them. Mrs. Bourne chattered the whole time.

"So you've been here over a month, is it? And staying on, are you? With that cute little boy of yours? You and Mr. Owen must be working out just excellent then, if you're still here. I've been looking for a woman for that kind man and I have to say, he did right well with you! And little Noah will go to school in Timberlake? And maybe take some trips with Mr. Owen, I suppose. And I guess I'll be cleaning up for a wedding one of these years! No pressure — you should be sure — but I don't know how much better you can do but Mr. Owen!"

Hannah found if she said nothing at all, Mrs. Bourne didn't notice. At one point her daughter, Rebecca, said, "Mama, stop talking before her ears fall off!"

"Was I talking? Oh, never mind, Hannah don't care. Do you, Miss Hannah?"

Everyone arrived in the early afternoon on Thursday. They'd had an easy flight from Minneapolis to Denver and rented a van large enough for all of them and their luggage. Owen and Noah had been hanging out on the dock fishing to pass the time, and at the sound of a horn and Romeo's welcoming bark, Noah got himself up and made noisy running thumps down the dock. He was getting steadier and faster by the day. They might as well have been aunts, uncles and cousins, there was so much hugging going on.

Hannah glanced over at Owen and saw that he hung back a little. She smiled at him, for no one could look quite so alone in a crowd as Owen. His hands were sunk into his pockets and he had this little bit of errant hair that fell over his brow. He tended to always look like he could use a haircut. Today he was clean-shaven, probably in deference to guests, but usually he was just a little scruffy and Hannah loved it. She gestured him over.

John was first, grabbing Owen's hand. "How you doing, man? I'm John. This is Sharon and the bump, and this is Mandy," he said, picking up a three-year-old girl.

Then Phil stretched out a hand. "Hey, this is great of you, Owen, letting us invade like this. Kate, my wife, Jess and Alexa, our daughters aged four and seven. I guess the first thing to do is get the luggage in, then you tell us what to do and we'll do it. Chop wood? Hunt for food? Fish for dinner?"

Owen just laughed. "We get luggage in, then break out snacks. Hannah will show you which rooms she picked out for you. After that, the kids might want to swim or fish. I have plenty of life jackets and poles."

"Look at this place," John said. "It's a resort. You have ponies in the barn?"

"Unfortunately, Romeo is the only pony. That's my shop, where I work. If you're interested, I'll show you later." Romeo was in the middle of four kids, tasting each face.

"Don't worry, he's had his shots," Owen said.

"He's very nice but a little clumsy," Noah told them. "He knocked me off the dock and I almost drowned."

"You didn't almost drown," Hannah said. "Come on, you guys, let's get you moved in."

Chips and salsa, potato chips and dip, and a big bowl of fruit were put out for everyone to put a dent in their hunger so they could play. The kids chose swimming over fishing while the sun was out and Romeo was happy to join the kids, chasing his ball out into the water. Everyone wore their life vests even though Alexa was becoming a pretty good swimmer.

Noah showed them his stuff. With the buoyancy of the water and since this wasn't exercise time, he had flippers on his feet. He was doing some powerful kicking, chasing Romeo through the water. He might be slow on land but he was as fast as any fish in the water. Owen and the dads were in the lake, too, tossing kids around, throwing the ball for Romeo, laughing and taking revenge when they were splashed.

Owen put chicken and corn on the grill while Hannah managed deviled eggs. There were what Owen called high-density beans in the slow cooker — baked beans doctored with onion, peppers, bacon and mystery meat, which turned out to be leftover flank steak from the night before. With plenty of brown sugar and barbecue sauce, they were guaranteed to produce tons of calories and gas.

"Oh, man, we're all going to know each other very well by bedtime," John said.

"How about an after-dinner libation?" Owen asked. "Ladies?"

"I'll have a glass of any red you like," Hannah said.

"And I'll just take the whole bottle," Sharon said. "Oh, that's right — I get nothing until the bump arrives."

"Here's to Sharon and her many sacrifices," Kate said, raising a glass. And they all said, "Hear, hear!"

"You're too kind," she said, glowering at them.

The kids were bathed and settled in their beds, exhausted and asleep in no time. The adults enjoyed a soft summer night on the porch with the lapping of the lake and breeze through the pines as background music. Owen pulled out the firepit and lit a log and Romeo lumbered into the house to find Noah and curl up with him for the night. The adults stayed up talking, learning about each other. As many questions as the men had for Owen, he had as many for them, interested in their work as a teacher and airplane mechanic. Sharon was the first to head for bed. Owen was the last.

He curled his long body around Hannah and said, "Your friends are great. It's comforting. If for some reason I can't watch over you, I know they will. They're good people. They love you and they're committed to Noah."

"You're good people, too, Owen. You've made them feel very welcome."

As had become typical, Noah was awake first, raring to go. He had the other kids and their parents up with the sun. Their days were filled with swimming, fishing, food and fun. They all went to visit Sully and Helen and exclaim over their garden, the women went to town to poke around one day and then the whole crowd had burgers at the pub followed by ice-cream sundaes. They spent most of one afternoon looking through Owen's books and pictures, and from that point on someone always had one of his books in hand. Every evening found them on the porch with a fire.

"This is the life, Owen," Phil said.

"I know it's hard to believe but I actually

do work. In fact, sometimes it feels like I work hard. But I admit, it's fun."

"What's the best part?" John asked.

"There are so many best parts," he said. "The freedom to wander. Discovery. Every time I go after some shot, some scene, some experience, something I never expected pops up and usually sets me off in a whole new direction. The reunion collection started when I saw a clip on the news of a wrongfully convicted prisoner released from prison, his entire family waiting outside for him. I can't even remember the details but he served something like twenty years and then new DNA testing proved his innocence, and I wondered, was his family there because they never lost their belief in him or were there some in that big crowd who would ask forgiveness for not believing in him? I thought there are a million stories of reunions waiting for me. One sixty-second film clip and I put a lot of miles on. It grew like moss on the back of a tree. Soldiers reunited with their families, or how about their war dogs? But usually one photo per story. Never more than two. Photo stories."

"His writing is breathtaking," Hannah said. That caused Owen to turn sharply toward her.

"It is?" Owen asked.

"Yes," Hannah said. "So personal, so invested, so captivating. Heart-tearing drama and out-loud laughter. Since you claim to have hated every English class you ever had, you must be something of a natural."

He chuckled. "If you knew about the stomach cramps I get when I have to describe the moment, you wouldn't say that—natural."

"I love those books," Hannah said.

He told them about some of his trips, about the trip to Vietnam coming up and about some of his collections in progress. And then he did something that stunned Hannah. He told them about Brayden and how his death changed Owen's life and turned him into a completely different photographer.

"I'm sorry if I threw a damper on your vacation but you're here to check me out, to see if I'm a nutcase. You should know about me. I don't tell people often because I can talk about it but it's hard to look at the eyes of the people who hear about it. So, sorry for that. But it is a fact that after twelve years, after meeting Hannah and Noah, I feel myself changing again. This time it's a nice change."

There were a lot of muttered condolences

and reassurances. And Hannah looked at him and let him know with her smile that she was proud of him. He had done that for her and she knew it.

The night before everyone had to leave, Kate asked if she could tuck Noah in. She kissed him on the forehead and said, "I think you have yourself a good situation here, Mr. Noah. And a great pal with Romeo."

"I do," he said. "I think we should stay."

"I don't blame you, but you know that's up to Hannah and Owen, right? Because Hannah has to choose the best place for work, school, medical support and all those things. But I did bring you something. My favorite picture."

Kate pulled it out and gave it to him. It was a picture of the four best friends in a nice five-by-seven frame. "This was taken when you were just a year old. We were on a holiday. A girls' weekend, the four of us. You were still a baby and stayed overnight with Linda. There's your beautiful mom. And Hannah."

He held it and just looked at it. She had noticed he had a picture of his mom on the bedside table, but this was the group. "Do you miss her sometimes?" he asked.

"I miss her every day," Kate said.

"I miss her a lot," he said.

"That's why I brought you the picture," Kate said. "I don't have any proof but I bet she's near enough to hear your whispers. I bet she's watching over you. Over all of us."

He looked at the picture a moment longer. Then he hugged it to his chest and lay down in the bed.

"Sweet dreams, little man," she said.

She stood just outside the slightly open door for a long moment. Then she heard his sweet little boy voice whisper, "Night, Mommy. Night."

Hannah's cell phone chirped with an incoming call and it took her a moment to identify the sound — she no longer carried her phone around with her every minute of the day. It was in the bedroom on the bureau. Her best friends were with her so she wondered if it was another Wyatt misdial. Her friends had just started packing to head back home.

The caller was Judd Tamaris, Erin's former boss and lawyer. She closed the door to the master bedroom to listen and ask a few questions. Then she came back to the kitchen. Kate and Sharon were sitting at the table.

"Where are the kids?" she asked.

"Outside," Kate said. "Getting in the way while Phil, John and Owen load the luggage in the van. Hey, you look like you've seen a ghost."

"Something has happened. That was Judd Tamaris, the lawyer who handled Erin's will and the custody order. It seems Erin's mother has contested the guardianship. They were unsuccessful in serving me a subpoena because I'm not at home so they contacted Erin's attorney."

"Now what?" Kate asked.

"He knows we're in Colorado for the summer but I'd come back if he needs me to. He said he's been in touch with my lawyer and they're going to try to handle it without going to court. He wouldn't give up my address without a court order and told me to stay put. He'll call back tomorrow."

"On just what the hell grounds does she contest it?" Sharon asked.

"She's Noah's only family," Hannah said. "Oh God, she can't take him away from me, can she?"

"What does the lawyer say?"

"He says there's nothing irregular about Erin's wishes. He's well aware of the family situation. I don't know where Erin's half brother is but Erin said that he often went home to his mother and despite his issues, she'd take him in. This isn't good."

"Hannah, there's a trust, isn't there?" Kate asked.

She nodded. "Her insurance money, her vested retirement fund and eventually the proceeds from the sale of her house. It's a tidy sum, but stretched out over his lifetime, college and other expenses, it's not a fortune. Just the other day I was asking myself, what if he wants to go to medical school or law school? Of course I don't care about any of that. I don't plan to touch a cent until we know where we stand with school and our future. And I'm not the only person named in the will, as you know. Should anything happen to me, Sharon is next in line, then you. Probably that order because you already have five kids with your stepchildren."

"Since the Addisons had no relationship with Erin or Noah, I have to believe that's some of the incentive," Kate said. "Her stories of her home life were so sad. That brother of hers is the devil."

"What should I do?" Hannah asked.

"Stay calm," Kate said. "Get the facts. For God's sake, don't take any calls from the Addisons . . ."

"I don't know that they have my number.

Erin's been gone a few months. Have any of you heard from Victoria Addison?"

"Not me," Sharon said.

"Not me," Kate said. "It was Linda, the babysitter, who called Victoria. She showed no interest. It was Linda who told Victoria that Erin had chosen a guardian for Noah and Linda was keeping Noah until we three got to Madison."

"I didn't think she cared," Hannah said.

"I smell a rat," Kate said.

Great works are performed not by strength but by perseverance.
— SAMUEL JOHNSON

8

After a long talk with Owen and another conversation with Judd, Hannah made an appointment to see Cal Jones. She brought her leather folder with all the legal paperwork she'd acquired from Judd. Right after Erin was laid to rest, Judd had expedited the process of Hannah's legal guardianship through family court in Madison so there would be no interruption in Noah's care and he wouldn't suffer through any kind of fostering environment.

"Can you tell me how this guardianship came about?" Cal asked. "When did you and your friend decide you would be Noah's legal guardian?"

"We talked about it back in college when we were only girls. But then it was only girlfriend talk, fantasy talk — we promised that if we had children, we'd take care of each other's in such an emergency. We vowed to be better mothers than our mothers were. It was amazing how alike our upbringings were — we both had mothers who clearly preferred their younger children and often treated us like we didn't matter, didn't belong. They didn't beat us or anything, they were just emotionally unavailable to us. My half sisters got braces and tuition while I had to work my way through school. Erin's mother was constantly standing up for her son, Erin's half brother, even when he was at his worst. It's no wonder that Erin decided to have a child alone. When she asked me in earnest, of course I didn't hesitate. But who ever thinks something like this will come to pass? Erin was very specific in her will and even wrote a letter to the court to accompany her legal documents, explaining in detail why she wanted Noah taken care of by me and not her mother or half brother. I have copies of everything. I believe it's there, in that folder," she said, pointing to the letter. "She also specified alternative options if I predeceased her or if for some other reason I couldn't take him, like if I was sick. We have two other best friends listed as cosponsors and alternate guardians. We've been very close for seventeen years."

"And her family was abusive?"

She nodded. "Her father left them. Her

mother remarried and had a son. She separated from that husband years and years ago, and he died before Erin and I met in college. Roger, her stepbrother, has been in trouble since he could walk. He used to beat up on Erin. He's been in prison. Erin said her mother could have paid for a Harvard education on the amount of money she's spent funding his drug treatment and bail. Victoria didn't even come to Erin's funeral. And Victoria is contesting my guardianship, though she has yet to ask about Noah."

"She's not exactly contesting," Cal said. "I guess it could be interpreted that way — she's asserting grandparents' rights. She would like custody. She's asking for regular visitation at the least. She has an uphill battle on both — the court documents are filed in Madison, where Erin and Noah lived. Mrs. Addison filed her legal paperwork in Minneapolis and at the moment you and the child named are in Colorado. An interesting triad."

Hannah scooted forward in her chair. "Do I have to take him back to Minneapolis?"

Cal shook his head. "You're his legal guardian. You don't need permission to travel or vacation with him."

"Can I get some kind of restraining order?

At least preventing Roger from getting close?"

Again, Cal shook his head. "He might have a history of abuse but he hasn't abused or threatened you or Noah. You can't just sign out a restraining order because you don't like someone or because you've heard bad things about them. That being said, I plan to look into his history with the law and find out what I can. If he's a dangerous felon, we need to know."

"Noah has cerebral palsy. He manages with leg braces and crutches. He's in really good shape. He's pretty strong and nimble. But, Cal, he can't run away if someone is after him. He's smart and happy and otherwise healthy but he needs health care supervision, physical therapy and a medical protocol. It's amazing how well he's doing after just losing his mother. He has his moments," she added with a shrug. "His grief comes through, but Owen and Romeo help so much. . . The thought of him going to an abusive or uncaring home, even for a day or weekend, just fills me with panic."

"Given the facts and Erin's meticulous planning, I think we're going to avoid that. Let's save the panic for later. It might not ever become an issue. Are you still planning to stay the whole summer?"

"Of course. We'll talk about the next steps in a couple of months," she said.

"Are you considering adoption?" Cal asked.

"I am, but I don't want to rush Noah. I want to be sure he understands he's not giving up his mother. I also want him to know I want him forever. Before this complication, I thought we'd just take as much time as we needed to get to that conversation. Would it help if I —"

"I doubt it would make much difference. But unless you are subpoenaed or there's a warrant and extradition, which is almost impossible, stay here. If you need something from your house, do you have a friend who can get it for you?"

"Yes. I wasn't planning to go back before the end of summer."

"Good. If there's a court willing to hear Mrs. Addison's case for custody or visitation, we should get Mr. Tamaris to step in, given he not only represented Erin, he'd known her for a long time."

"And the court appointed an attorney ad litem to represent Noah," she said. "The name is in the paperwork."

"Excellent. Give me a few minutes to copy all of this. I'll have a conversation with Mr. Tamaris, tell him that I've agreed to represent you and I'll let you know where we are in a few days. I'll also do a background on both Roger and his mother. Meanwhile, it might be best if you told your Minneapolis contacts not to share your current whereabouts with the Addisons."

"Oh, believe me . . ."

"Try not to worry," Cal said. "If Mrs. Addison had been involved in Noah's life from the start, if she'd filed for her rights before the court granted your guardianship, she might have a case here, but if you've told me everything, I can't imagine what leverage she would have."

"Blood," Hannah said. "She's using the fact that she's his only blood relative."

"Hannah, the family court judge generally likes to keep families together when possible, but also does not hesitate to remove children from abusive or negligent homes to put them in foster care. How is Noah's grandmother going to care for him? Is she gainfully employed? Independently wealthy?"

"There's a trust," she said.

"Is it large?" Cal asked. "Substantial?"

"Depends on how you look at it," Hannah said. "When you consider what college might cost in a dozen years, when you consider any special needs he might have because of his condition, it's probably not enough. If I didn't have to think about Noah's future, it would seem huge. Over a million dollars."

Cal sat back in his chair. "Hello."

"That's what terrifies me," she said. "That she could somehow get custody, get control of that trust, ignore Noah's needs and —" She couldn't finish. "Over the years she's given her son a fortune to help him get out of trouble and I'm afraid that's all she wants. Erin used to say, 'If you met my mother, you'd like her. But she isn't really who you think she is.' Please help us, Cal. Noah shouldn't have to shoulder any more disappointment. He's been through so much."

"Don't worry, Hannah," he said. "We've got this."

"Have you known Cal a long time?" Hannah asked Owen.

"I met him shortly after he and Maggie married. We run into each other sometimes. He hangs out at Sully's with his daughter and I've seen him on the trail a few times. And in the way of this neighborhood, I know about him. People talk about him, about being helped by him, about helping him work on that barn. And there's this

218

understanding among the locals that Sully, while maybe the friendliest guy around, has an uncanny instinct about people and Cal wouldn't be married to Maggie if Sully had a bad feeling about him."

"He made me feel so much better," Hannah said. "Do you think he's actually a good lawyer?"

"There's been talk that he's a semifamous defense attorney from Michigan," Owen said. "Maybe we should look into that."

"After Noah goes to bed," she said. "How about some dueling laptops tonight?"

He pulled her close. "You really know how to turn a guy on."

After Noah had gone to bed, Owen and Hannah sat on the couch, each holding a laptop, researching California Jones. Before long Hannah was snuggled up against Owen, staring at his screen, and he was reading aloud to her. There was a bio online that either Cal or his firm had produced that listed his degrees and licenses, then there were a couple of articles written about him that were more human interest pieces. And there was an obituary — it seemed while Cal lived and practiced law in Michigan, he had been married to a woman, also a lawyer, who developed scleroderma and died. That had been about six years ago.

There were no details to describe how he managed to meet and marry Maggie Sullivan a couple of years after his first wife's death.

There were a few newspaper pieces about seemingly impossible cases he had tried and won in Michigan but nothing newsworthy in Colorado.

"I think we should have Cal, Maggie and Elizabeth to dinner," Hannah said. "I'd like to get to know them better and learn more about how Cal landed here."

"A couple of years ago when we first ran into each other at Sully's, he mentioned that once when he was going through a lot of indecision in his life, he did a lot of hiking and things started to shake into place. I told him the same had happened with me. Like men will, we got away from the emotional aspect as fast as possible and started to discuss whether the altitude was healing."

"Like men will," she said, just shaking her head. She ran her fingers through the longish hair at his temples. It was threaded with a little gray. No wonder Cal and Owen took to each other, seemed to be ready friends. They'd plowed their ways through difficult losses and not only survived, they'd come through very well. "I would love to have them to dinner but I can only seem to cook hamburgers and mac and cheese."

"I know," he said. "You're very good with salad. Maybe you can add that. And I'll do the rest."

Owen took it upon himself to choose a day with Cal that Maggie would be in Timberlake so the two families could get together. Until then, Hannah and Noah were resuming their schedule — four mornings a week. Twice they would go to Aurora to the physical therapist and twice to the counselor. With Hannah and Owen continuing the PT at home the rest of the week, the therapist thought Noah was in excellent shape for his condition. And the psychologist pronounced him to be very stable for a child who had just lost a parent a few months ago. Of course, he was still dealing with grief but he was doing so in a loving family.

It was not lost on Hannah that Owen was busy in his shop when she was returning with Noah. He always made time to play — to swim, hike, throw a ball, whatever activity Noah wanted. But clearly he had work to do.

"Let me see if I can help you a little, then we'll play," Hannah said.

"I don't think there's any way for you to help, but thanks."

"You never know," she said. "What's going on?"

"I'm transferring some photos onto other mediums for a gallery — canvas, wood, glass. And I'm going to try one large transfer that I'll do in pieces."

"Okay, I'll empty trash, clean up and do whatever you want me to do. Noah, come over here a little out of the way and go through your pictures or color on your computer."

"I've got a couple of transfers that are dry. I'll show you what to do and you can rub off the backings. It's very tedious," he said.

"Sounds like work I specialize in," she said with a smile.

At some point while they were working, Noah went to lie down on Owen's bed and Romeo curled around him. They both fell asleep. Hannah cautiously and meticulously rubbed the paper backing off a photo transfer onto canvas while Owen was going through photo collections on his computer. He asked her opinion a couple of times and she fearlessly gave it. Once he said, "Yes, right," and once he said, "Nah, not that one." Whether or not he took her advice, she was thrilled to be asked.

Later that night when they were watching the moonrise over the lake from the front porch, she told him how much she enjoyed working in his shop, helping him. "You must promise to tell me if I'm in your way and less than helpful. You're used to working on your own without anyone else in your way."

Then she suggested transferring one of his trees onto a tall, slim pottery vase and he loved it. The tree was black, leafless, spindly with branches like long fingers and it was stunning when finished. It was easy, inexpensive and very artsy. He signed it in black ink.

"I think I've been working alone just about long enough," he said.

And, with that, Hannah took her place beside Owen in his shop, helping. Not all day, of course. She had her own chores as well as tending Noah and his regular appointments. He brought her a picture he'd drawn in his counseling session — a very tall man, a woman, a child with crutches, an enormous dog and up in the sky, above a tree, a small, smiling angel.

"Noah, this is so beautiful," she said. "We're going to have to frame it, save it forever. Is that angel someone I know?"

"My mom," he said. "I think she's happy. I think Romeo is happy."

"I know I'm happy," Hannah said. "I miss your mom very much, but I'm still happy.

Because of you, I think. You make every day special."

"And Owen?" he asked.

"I'm sure Owen is happy. You can ask him, though," she said.

"No, you," he emphasized. "Are you happy with Owen? Because you guys kiss a lot."

She laughed. "I guess it's pretty obvious, isn't it? I'm so happy with Owen. He's a very good man."

"And a very good boyfriend?" Noah asked.

"He's an excellent boyfriend," she assured him.

"But, Hannah? Sometimes I want her to be here so much I can't even talk," he said.

"That's okay, buddy. That happens to me all the time, too. And sometimes I just talk to her anyway, like she's right next to me."

"Out loud?" he asked. "Right out loud?"

"Uh-huh. And sometimes right in my head. I think she is listening either way."

"I don't know," he said, shaking his head. "She doesn't talk back. She did that one time, but only that one time."

Hannah was taken by surprise momentarily but hoped it didn't show. "And when was that, honey?"

"Oh, it was . . . I was taking a nap with Romeo but I didn't get all the way asleep and she was sitting right on the bed, petting his head. And she said, 'I like this dog, Noah. I'm glad you're friends. Be very brave and remember to always be kind.' And then she said, 'I love you, close your eyes.' So I did and when I woke up, she was back in heaven. Is that okay, Hannah? That she was right on my bed?"

She fought tears. "I think that's wonderful," she said in a choked whisper. "I'm so happy for you."

"Maybe she'll come to your bed," Noah said.

A huff of laughter came through her tears. *Wouldn't that surprise Owen,* she thought. *Or maybe it would surprise Erin?* "I'll be sure to tell you if I see her or dream of her. I promise. And I have an idea! We should make some cobbler for dessert one of these days, just like your mom used to do. Mine might not be as good as hers, but I'll try. Would that be nice?"

"Peach?" he asked.

"I'll have to find peaches. It might be a little early for them, but I'll look."

"That would be good."

Late that night while they hovered under the covers, Hannah shared that conversation with Owen. He drew back and chuckled. "Maybe I should put my pants on?" he asked.

"Erin is very discreet," Hannah said. "She'd never peek."

A few days later they had Cal and his family over. They didn't talk about the custody issue during dinner but when Noah and Elizabeth, watched over by Romeo, were settled with a movie and they moved their party onto the porch with nightcaps, Hannah asked if he had heard anything.

"I haven't been holding out on you," Cal said. "Late this afternoon the judge in the Minneapolis family court threw out the custody case, dismissed it for lack of standing. What that means is he wasn't going to overrule another court, especially since you and Noah weren't present. That's done. This issue might not be completely resolved. Mrs. Addison asked how she was to go about finding out where her grandson was. The judge said her lawyer could walk her through that process. We'll face that if we have to. Meanwhile, do you know Roger Addison or his mother?"

"I met Erin's mother once, very briefly, years ago. I've never met Roger. And Erin's stepfather is deceased. Why?"

"I've been looking into Roger Addison's

criminal history and it's ugly, starting when he was a minor. He is a serial felon and has served time for battery, fraud, felony drug possession and theft. But his arrest record is worse — those are crimes he was indicted for but not convicted of. Armed robbery, more battery, rape, more theft. Young Mr. Addison, a mere thirty years old, is a criminal. And not a very good one. From the time he was fourteen till the age of twenty-six. He hasn't had any run-ins with the police in the last few years. He's either getting better at his crimes or has cleaned up his act. He's been steadily employed, though in a number of different jobs, and no recent arrests.

"I checked Mrs. Addison's background and she appears to have a clean record. That doesn't mean she's a good person, but if she has committed crimes, she hasn't been caught. And yes, she's been very supportive of her son, paying bail money, drug treatment, et cetera."

Hannah looked over her shoulder, making sure the kids weren't in the doorway. "She's not a good person," Hannah said. "She hasn't even asked about Noah. None of us have heard from her. I don't know how anyone can think she has Noah's best interests at heart. But it's Roger who scares me and I don't even know him. He's the main reason Erin moved to Madison—she was done putting up with him taking advantage of anyone when he was in trouble. She and her mother would fight when Erin refused to help him. It was a complicated family. Their last blowout was before Noah was born. Which is why Erin has always been so adamant about how Noah should live. And with whom."

"Roger Addison's name doesn't appear on Mrs. Addison's court documents, but given what Erin described about their relationship, he might be driving the notion of custody for money. If you hear from either of them, refer them to me and hang up. If you see either of them around, call the police and then me."

"I don't think I'd even recognize either one of them! And what am I supposed to tell the police they've done? Given me the willies?"

"I'll text you a couple of photos and I'll tell Stan I'm representing you in a custody case with a woman who has personal ties to a felon who has a long criminal history. Roger Addison might be hoping if his mother can get custody and control of that trust, the money will somehow flow to him. Or maybe he thinks he's smart enough to talk her out of it. It wouldn't be the first time a delinquent kid out-conned his parents. I'm just being cautious, Hannah. I've handled custody cases that involved people with criminal histories before and it can get treacherous. It's hard for me to believe that a woman who was completely estranged from her daughter and has no relationship with her grandson wants custody of him. There's more to it. I don't want to be right, by the way. I'd rather this just fizzle out."

"Me, too," Hannah said. "I asked Noah if he'd ever met his grandmother and he said he couldn't remember. There's obviously no history there."

"Enjoy your summer and pay attention to anything unusual. Let me know if you're contacted."

A couple of days later they were all together again when Owen, Hannah, Noah and Romeo went to the Crossing for a Fourth of July picnic potluck.

"I apologize for bringing a Great Dane to the party but Romeo doesn't enjoy the sound of fireworks when he's home alone. He's counting on Noah to protect him," Owen said.

"I'm glad you brought him," Sully replied. "The Fourth of July gets some of these animals all riled and sends them on the run. Connie and Sierra brought fireworks, like usual. The kids love 'em even if the dogs don't."

Cal's sister Sierra and her husband, Connie, also brought their two little ones, a little boy they had adopted and a little girl about a year old who had been their surprise biological baby. Hannah made a mental note to talk to Sierra about adoption when there weren't so many people around.

During the afternoon at the Crossing, Maggie and Hannah talked about Hannah's job and when her family leave would expire. Being a neurosurgeon, Maggie understood the role of a sales rep of medical equipment quite well.

"My leave expires in September," Hannah said. "The problem is sales involves a lot of long days and travel. As you would know, we spend a lot of time with radiologists, surgeons, ER docs and other MDs who use our equipment. We take them out to dinner to discuss how to better meet their needs, follow them into surgery and treatment, confer with them constantly and . . . Well, I don't think those long days and a lot of travel are going to work out for me. I'm no longer a woman alone."

"I was thinking about that," Maggie said.

"Have you thought about working in a hospital or clinic? It probably wouldn't pay as well, but you never know until you look around."

"That's an idea," Hannah said. "I'm looking for a change."

A few days later, Owen mentioned his upcoming trip. "It's time for me to get ready for Vietnam. If you're at all uncomfortable being here by yourself, just say so. I can reschedule."

"I can't let you do that," Hannah said. "Not only are you looking forward to the trip, I'm excited to see the pictures when you're home!"

"Things are a little rocky right now," he said. "It's uncertain with the Addisons."

"A bit, but so far Mrs. Addison has been taking her issues to court and for that I have Cal and Judd."

"I'm going to talk to Cal again before I leave," Owen said. "If there's any word from them, consider staying with friends for a few days. There are plenty who would welcome you — Cal and Maggie, Leigh and Rob, Helen and Sully."

"Please don't worry," she said.

"I'm not going to be able to be in touch when I'm in the cave."

"Owen, I'll be very cautious. And Noah won't be outside alone for one second. Not even on the porch. And by not alone, I won't leave Romeo in charge. But I bet he'd come in real handy if any uninvited guests showed up."

"He's never been put in the position of protector . . ."

"And hopefully he won't have to be the protector, but he looks huge without even trying." She reached up to palm his cheek. After his experience with his own son, of course he would be feeling nervous. "We're going to miss you but we want you to explore that cave."

"While I'm gone, think about something," he said. "I don't want to make you feel rushed or cornered or pressured but I want you to know, this works for me. I'm ready. Finally. Ready for a family. You don't have to worry about a job. Not for money anyway. If you want to work because it feels good to be productive, there must be something around here that can fill that space. I love you. I want you and Noah to stay."

"What about my house?" she asked.

He shrugged. "Rent it? Sell it? Let it sit for six months or a year while you give yourself time to be sure? While you see if

this is as good as it feels? I'll pay the mortgage."

"Owen, you're acting a little crazy . . ."

"Hannah, I'm pretty well-off," he said.
"It's meaningless without a family. Shit, I
was trying not to say anything that would
pressure you."

She laughed a little. "Owen, the last few
months have been lifesaving for me because
of you. I'm facing a whole new life with
Noah and because of you, it's been sane and
manageable. I worry about taking advantage
of you. But since I've been helping in the
studio a little bit, I'm less worried about
that."

"Will you think about this while I'm
gone?"

"As soon as you tell me what 'this' is," she
said.

He leaned down and kissed her forehead.
"It's whatever you want it to be. It can be
just like it is now, two people sharing a
house, a dog and a boy . . ."

"And having fabulous sex," she added.

He grinned. "It can be a commitment, if
you want. Or when you want that — I'm
not in any great rush as long as you're staying. It can be a commitment with an agree-
ment that Noah's trust will be managed
only by you — we seem to be up to our

necks in lawyers if we need documents drawn to protect you and Noah. 'This' can be us being a team that works together. Anything you say."

"I will think about all of that, yes," she said. "I want you to go to the biggest cave ever. And we'll work on this project when you're home."

"Will you be lonely?" he asked.

"I'll miss you just awful but I have PT, counseling, an active boy and dog and brand-new friendships. Maybe we'll finish reading *Treasure Island.* I'll be too busy to be lonely."

He pushed her hair behind her ear. "I think you belong here."

There is no doubt that it is around the family and the home that all the greatest virtues. . .are created, strengthened and maintained.
— WINSTON CHURCHILL

9

A feeling of belonging had long been an issue with Hannah, but she hadn't quite realized it until Owen said it. Was it a place? A person? Was it a talent or profession? A group like the First Baptist Church, AA or the Boston Pops? The first time she was conscious of not belonging had been when she was about six and her mother had the second of her two new daughters and someone said, "Hannah's not even the same color, is she?" Hannah's hair and eyes were brown to their white blond and blue. Her skin tone was slightly more tan and rosy than her sisters', who were ivory. And, of course, Hannah was adopted, but there were good records — she was supposed to be of French, German, Danish and Portuguese descent. Yet she'd always felt different. And why should she trust biological parents who gave her away? They might have tossed out some nationalities without knowing anything.

Owen wanted her to think about staying . . . with him. And she would. She couldn't help it; she could think of little else. But she was also going to think about belonging in a larger sense, like what she was committed to and what and who was committed to her.

Owen left early in the morning but even though the sun was barely up, he wouldn't leave without kissing Noah goodbye. "I'll be back in ten days," he said. "Will you take good care of Romeo?"

"I can do that," Noah said sleepily, rubbing his eyes.

"Remember, when you leave him home, tell him how long you'll be gone."

"Sure, okay," he said.

Owen rubbed the big dog's head. "You take care of Noah," he told the dog. "I'm counting on you."

"You excited, Owen?" Noah asked.

Owen shrugged. "I'd sort of like to put it off. I've been having too much fun lately and I think I'm getting lazy."

"Hannah says everyone has jobs to do," Noah wisely lectured.

Owen laughed. "She's a slave driver," he said.

"Am not," she said from behind him. She

stood in the doorway, watching him say goodbye to Noah.

"Are, too," he said, his lips lifting in a smile. "Noah, my car is packed. I'm going to say goodbye and get out of here before I talk myself into staying."

"We'll come on the porch," Noah said, giving Romeo a pat on the rump to get him up.

Noah reached for his crutches and Owen scooped him up. "I'll give you a lift," he said. "You can sit with Romeo on the porch and try not to get in my way while I say goodbye to Hannah. I have some serious kissing in mind."

"I'm starting to think you like all that kissing," Noah said.

"Me?" Owen asked. "Nah. I just don't want her to feel ignored."

"That was a total fib," Noah said and Owen tickled him.

Noah and Romeo waited patiently on the porch while Owen and Hannah kissed and hung on to each other beside Owen's truck. Owen lifted her chin and looked into her brown eyes. "I want you to have fun, stay busy, be around the people you like, fill your days and if you think of it, take pictures of Noah and Romeo. And listen, if there's Wi-Fi anywhere, I'll email, but I've been told that's unlikely. But I want you to have fun so it goes by fast."

She laughed at him. "I plan to. And yes, I'll be very careful and lock the doors. But we're going to be fine. I think we said everything last night."

"Last night," he whispered, pulling her close. "That was amazing."

"I think that falls into the royal send-off category."

"I will admit, I haven't been bid farewell like that before," he said. "It almost makes me want to plan more trips."

"Wait till you see the welcome-home party," she said, giving his lower lip a lick. "I'll miss you. Please go. You're wearing me out. And I have things to do."

He gave her a last quick peck, whacked her on the butt and climbed into the truck. Romeo let out a mournful yowl but he didn't move away from Noah's side. Once the truck disappeared down the road, Hannah turned to Noah. "Breakfast?" she asked.

He gave a nod. "Then what?"

"I have some ideas. Let me get some of my chores done and then we'll talk over all the things we can do while Owen is visiting the biggest cave in the world."

"Wish I could see that cave," he said.

"I think you're going to have many exciting travels in your life," she said. "We should look through Owen's books and make a list of all the places you'd like to go."

That first day that Owen was gone, Hannah and Noah went to town and met Leigh for lunch at the pub. Then they went to the firehouse — Connie Boyle was working and was more than happy to show Noah all the fun stuff. Noah sat behind the wheel in the big fire truck and Connie showed him how to turn on the lights. They spent some time in the kitchen, where one of the guys was making cookies. They went out to the Crossing and Helen convinced them to pluck some fresh fruits and vegetables from the garden but then talked them into staying for dinner, as well. Because Noah had promised Romeo they'd be back in two or three hours, first they had to go home and get him. "Because he knows the time," Noah said. "He could get upset." They got him and brought him back so he could have a nice romp with Beau.

The next day they went to therapy, then swam with Romeo. Sully came over and he and Noah fished off the dock for a while. They went shopping one day in Colorado Springs, then dropped by Cal's house for a visit and again stayed for dinner. "I guess the word is out," Hannah said. "If Owen's away, I won't be able to feed myself and Noah."

They swam and fished and kept their appointments all week. After almost a week, Hannah told Noah she had a surprise for him. They went to Colorado Springs to a place Connie suggested and Hannah got a tattoo on her right shoulder blade that said Noah; it was inside a heart that was inside a flower. She showed him the picture first to make sure he approved.

"It's kinda girlie," he said.

"I'm kinda a girl," she shot back. "It doesn't make *you* girlie!"

"Are you getting one for Owen?" he asked.

"I'm not quite ready for an Owen tattoo yet, but I'll think about it."

They read, watched movies, hiked the trail behind the Crossing, swam, fished, went into town for hamburgers and ice-cream sundaes, visited their friends.

One of the most enlightening visits Hannah paid was to Sierra Boyle, something she'd been meaning to do since first meeting her when the family gathered at Sully's place. Helen and Sully agreed to keep Noah for a couple of hours so she could have some adult time. She wanted to talk about Sierra's experience in adopting Sam but she got way more than she bargained for.

"We were fostering Sam, our adoption application pending, when Sam's grandmother suddenly changed her mind and asked for him back. She wasn't that old but she was beset by some chronic medical conditions and really in no shape to take care of a baby. She could barely lift him out of the crib. It was a nightmare. I found him sobbing, soaked and dirty in his crib. I was just about ready to kidnap him and run for my life, but I called Cal."

Hannah was stunned silent for a moment. "Sierra, have you perhaps heard? Noah's grandmother has recently turned up, looking for some kind of connection with him. She'd like custody but two courts have refused her so far. Cal is helping us."

"Us?" Sierra asked. "Does that mean you and Owen . . . ?"

"Owen is as invested in Noah's well-being as I am. He'd like us to be a family. I'm trying not to lose my head. It seems to make sense to take it slow. If it's the right thing to do, it'll soon become apparent, right? But tell me about your custody battle for Sam!"

"It didn't take long for Sam's grandma to realize she wasn't up to the job, but there were long days leading to that realization and I fell apart. It took me about one day to love Sam so helplessly that there was just no turning back."

Sierra told Hannah the whole story — Connie had responded to a vehicle accident and pulled Sam from the wreck that took his young mother's life when Sam was just four months old.

Then it was Hannah's turn to go through the events that led to asking Sierra about the minefields of adoption and how to handle the invasive presence of extended family members like Noah's grandmother. By the time a couple of hours had passed, what she would have described previously as a friendly acquaintance became a bonded friendship. Hannah couldn't wait to tell Owen all about it when he got home.

That night at two in the morning the phone rang, jarring Hannah awake.

"I had a signal," Owen said triumphantly. "I don't know how long it'll last. I may lose you."

"Tell me quick — is it wonderful?"

"It's unbelievable," he said. "When Noah is stronger and has more endurance, I'm going to bring you both here. I am getting some great pictures."

"We've been looking through your books, making lists of places we'd like to see. Most of them are shrines or temples that involve

243

steep climbs of millions of steps."

Owen laughed. "Incentive," he said. "How is he doing?"

"Fantastic," she said. "We've been busy every minute so we hardly miss you, but I promise when you get home, I'll make you feel welcome."

"Don't knock yourself out," he said, a laugh in his voice.

"I really do miss you very much," she said.

"And you haven't had any problems?"

"None," she said. "The weather is beautiful, high seventies, sunny, and there are a million people around. Vacationers, I think. Most of the long-distance hikers on their way to Banff have passed through, but there are a few stragglers. We've been spending time with all our friends. The one thing missing is kids Noah's age, but he doesn't seem to be bothered by that. He has Romeo, his best friend. And I have a nice surprise for you —"

The connection was suddenly lost. She had no way of knowing how much of that he might've heard. "Oh, Owen, you big tease," she said to the phone. "Only four more days . . ."

She was thinking about a lazy day around the lake anyway, but Owen's middle-of-the-night phone call made that even more desirable. She took her coffee onto the porch in the early morning and caught a couple of young deer grazing on the big lawn that separated the house from the barn. She'd been there only about three minutes before the sound of a car disturbed the deer and they scattered. She squinted. She didn't know the driver. She was just about to run into the house and lock the door behind her when the driver stopped in the drive, got out of his running car and stood behind the door. "Hannah Russell?" he asked.

"Do I know you?" she asked.

"I doubt it," he said. "I have something for you."

He held up a piece of paper. He didn't turn off his car but took several steps toward her. He mounted the porch stairs as she backed away. He held the paper toward her and she took it warily. He wasn't the post-man after all.

"You have been served."

He turned and bolted back toward the running car. To her relief he backed away, made a three-point turn and headed off Owen's property. She opened the paper and saw it was a summons to family court.

Mrs. Victoria Addison was suing for custody of Noah in Colorado.

■ ■ ■ ■

"Try not to panic," Cal said to Hannah. "I'll get in touch with her attorney and find out just what she's asking for. I can't imagine that she has a leg to stand on if she hopes to take Noah back to Minneapolis and raise him. First of all, custody has been established. The wishes of his mother have been carried out. Second, she has no history with the boy. Third, he's a special-needs child and she hasn't cared for him for even a day since his birth, so his routine must be unknown to her. Fourth, according to this letter Erin wrote before her death, Victoria has a biological son who frequently lives with her who could be a danger to Noah. I could go on and on, listing the reasons this seems like a preposterous request. Too little, too late on her part."

Hannah had called Cal immediately and Cal told her that Maggie was home, as was Elizabeth. Maggie offered to watch the children play in the great room while Hannah met with Cal in his office.

"Do I have to try to explain this to Noah?" she asked.

"Let me find out what I can from her attorney. He's licensed to practice here but

246

his office is in Minneapolis."

"Isn't that unusual?" she asked.

"Not so much. It's possible he has vacation property here and made sure he was licensed to practice law here. Or maybe he plans to retire here. I was originally licensed in Michigan, but Colorado has licensing reciprocity with Michigan, which means I didn't have to take the bar again to practice here, but I did have to apply, fill out a lot of paperwork, get credentialed here."

"So if I ran back to Minneapolis, I wouldn't escape this suit?"

"Her custody has already been denied in Minneapolis, remember?" he said. "That judge upheld the ruling in Madison. I highly doubt Judd Tamaris is licensed to practice here but the good news is we don't need him to practice. We can use him as a witness and he can work up video depositions from other close friends that we can use in court. Given that Erin worked for Judd for years, he was very close to her and her situation, is the executor of her will, and he explained he and his family considered her a close friend. But defending this custody is not what worries me. What I want to know is *why?* Why does a grandmother who never visited her grandson now want to raise him? Is it sentimental? Something like this happened to Sierra . . ."

"I know," Hannah said. "I had a nice long visit with her and she told me all about Sam's grandmother."

"For a few days, it was harrowing," Cal said.

"I think Victoria is about sixty-five," Hannah said. "I don't know anything about her state of health or fitness but Noah isn't very able. Owen had to install a shower bar for him and he still fell a couple of times. I'm strong and these arms have complained some at the weight when I've carried him from room to room but I'm getting stronger. If he's not that easy for a young, fit woman to manage . . ."

"That's what I mean," Cal said. "Something more might be going on here."

Later that evening when all was quiet and Romeo had had his romp around the yard, Hannah pulled Noah onto her lap. "I have a question for you. Do you remember your grandma?"

"No, but I think I have one," he said. "Do I have one?"

"Yes, you do. In Minneapolis. Your grandma and your mom didn't agree on much. I think it's safe to say they didn't agree on how to take care of a little boy.

That's why your mom specifically asked me to be your guardian."

"Okay, good," he said.

"I'm pretty happy that I got to be the one," Hannah said.

"Me, too. When is Owen coming home?"

"A few days. Are you excited?"

"I'm very excited," he said, grinning. "Is he coming home late or early?"

"I think he's coming late, like, after dinner. But he'll call and let us know when to expect him."

"Then I think we should wait for him to eat and make him something that's his favorite, like ice cream. He loves ice cream."

So much for the grandma subject. Noah thought he had one but hadn't seen her. He wanted to be with Hannah. Wasn't that good enough even though he was only five?

Owen texted Hannah that his initial flight out of Ho Chi Minh City had been delayed but they'd be taking off at the soonest possible moment. He had given Hannah his flight information so she could follow his progress on the computer. She texted him back, Get sleep if you can, be safe, we're waiting for you.

The whole way to Vietnam he kept thinking about canceling, going straight home.

While preparing for the expedition into Hang Son Doong cave, he thought about changing his mind and leaving. Once he started into the cave, he made a pledge that he just wouldn't do this anymore; no more long trips. He wanted his family — Hannah and Noah and Romeo. He missed them to distraction, finding it so hard to concentrate on his photography. He had to carry several extra battery packs for his cameras and tablet and was surprised at the end of each day to find some amazing shots. He couldn't wait to show them to Hannah and Noah.

There were about twenty civilians on the expedition, plus five guides, two park rangers, two chefs and a bunch of porters. Owen was the only American. Though there was a slight language barrier, he made friends with a Brazilian couple and a Chinese man. There was an Australian woman who must be independently wealthy because she'd been traveling the world for a couple of years, particularly taken with biking tours, yet she was in her early sixties and fit as a boxer.

The trek through the cave was safe but challenging. It took two days of jungle hiking to get to the cave, five days to get through to the end, then a turn that took them to the second entrance. They camped at night. Seven straight days of hiking and camping. Food and water was either carried or had been delivered prior to them entering. The cave had its own ecosystem. The Vietnamese guides spoke Vietnamese, Cantonese, French and some pretty impressive English. Hang Son Doong wasn't open to the public yet and it might be years before it would be, but these special expeditions, booked years in advance, were gaining in popularity.

The cave was incredible. There was a large lake and a sandy beach on which they camped two nights, parts that were dark and narrow, a rain forest, an area that was so high a fifty-story building could fit under the dome. A Vietnamese guide who Owen was sure had never been to New York City said that a New York City block could fit inside the cave. The flora was magnificent; there were exotic birds sighted.

When Owen was asked about his life at home, he said that he had a woman and her little boy living with him and he assumed they would be together forever. "Marriage?" they asked.

"I will do anything to make her happy," he said.

After emerging from the cave, he cleaned up in a visitor's center, showering and changing clothes. He headed straight to the airport. He carried on his camera and computer equipment, checked his backpack full of mostly dirty clothes. He was exhausted. Ordinarily he would spend a couple of days resting, hydrating, sampling local cuisine and getting back to his fighting strength, but he had pared this trip to the bone, so ready to be with his woman again. His woman and his boy. He sat on the plane during the delayed departure and plugged one card after another into his tablet — not the best viewing medium — and was amazed by the beauty of the photos. He had been so unfocused, they shouldn't be this good. He couldn't wait to show Hannah.

From Ho Chi Minh City to Denver was over twenty hours. They touched down at ten at night. He didn't text Hannah. He just got his backpack, his car, and headed home, knowing they would be asleep. But when he got to the house, all the lights were on even though it was midnight.

He went inside, dropped his duffel and backpack. "Honey, I'm home," he said quietly.

Hannah unfolded from the couch and ran into his arms. Romeo nosed open Noah's door and joined the party.

"Why are you up?" he asked, kissing her

whole face.

"I was watching your flight online and knew you were on your way. Noah couldn't make it. I carried him to bed a couple of hours ago."

"You feel so good," he said, his lips going to her neck.

"Did you have a wonderful time?" she asked.

"I'm having a wonderful time right now," he said. Romeo was trying to edge between them, pushing until Owen gave him some attention. That done, he was kissing her again.

There was the sound of *bump-shuffle-bump* and they turned to see Noah coming toward them on his crutches. "Hey, buddy, did I wake you?" Owen asked, bending to pick him up. Noah dropped the crutches and looped his arms around Owen's neck, hugging him tightly.

"It's okay," Noah said. "We got you some ice cream."

"Would you like some?" Owen asked. "Ice cream at midnight?"

"I could do that," Noah said.

Owen ruffled his hair. "I'm going to want something a little stronger. I'm not sure what day it is. I think it's yesterday." He maneuvered over to the couch, sitting with

Noah on his lap. "My legs are about a foot too long for sleeping on airplanes, even in first class. Hannah, will you play waitress just this once?"

"Gotcha covered," she said, heading for the kitchen.

"Was the cave good?" Noah asked. "Was it hard?"

"The guides and porters were outstanding but there were places we had to crawl or climb or even swim. It was like a difficult hike. One of the friends I made was a sixty-eight-year-old man from China and he was stronger and more able than I was."

"I won't ever be able to do that . . ."

"Actually, I think you will," Owen said. "It's going to take some more good muscle and training but you have time — that cave isn't open to the public yet and they're not letting kids go on that expedition. But you will do everything you want to do. I wouldn't be surprised if you climb Mount Everest someday. The way you're training and exercising now . . . Yes, sir, by the time you're grown a little more . . ."

Hannah delivered a bowl of ice cream and a Crown Royal on ice. Then she curled up on the sofa against Owen and just listened to him talk about the cave. They were a big pile—Noah on Owen's lap, Romeo's head on Owen's thigh, Hannah pressed against them.

"We'll look at the pictures tomorrow," Owen said. "And I think we're all going to have to sleep in. Hear that, Romeo? That means you, too."

"What was the best part of the cave?" Noah asked.

"There were lots of best parts. The cave is so big . . . There's a lake and a sandy beach inside. We camped on the beach. We had cooks making our meals and night on the beach was so beautiful. There were passages so tight we had to crawl and places so wide-open you could build a house in there."

"Did you have a boat on the lake?"

"No boat," Owen said. "Maybe it was too hard to get it in the cave. Or maybe they didn't want it in the cave. It was beautiful."

Noah asked question after question while he ate his ice cream and Owen sipped his drink. It was about fifteen minutes before Owen took the empty bowl out of Noah's hands and put it on the coffee table. Noah curled up, his head on Owen's shoulder, and yawned hugely.

"Someone is very tired," Owen said.

"It's me," Noah said, yawning again.

Owen shifted him a little bit, settling him against his chest, where he quickly fell asleep. He slid his other arm around Hannah, drawing her near. He proved very talented, holding Noah against his chest, his drink in that hand, his other arm embracing his woman. "Ah. It is so good to be home."

When Hannah didn't say anything, he just cuddled her closer. Then he heard a sound and looked down to see that her cheeks were wet. "Are you crying?" he whispered.

"I just wish it could be like this always," she said with a sniff.

"If we want to, we can make it so," he said, dropping a kiss on her brow.

She turned her dark, wet eyes up to his face. "Mrs. Addison," she whispered. "She filed for custody. Here. She's going to try."

"You called Cal?" he asked softly.

She nodded. "I went to see him. We're going to be gathering ammunition. Witnesses. There is going to be a hearing. He says a hearing is nothing to fear."

"We'll make this work," Owen said. "We won't let go. Don't worry."

She touched the angry muscle in his cheek with gentle fingers. "Owen, it's not your fight. It's mine."

He was quiet for a moment. "You know better than that," he said.

Owen held them both through the night.

Hannah could tell he didn't sleep much. He was still but there was a tenseness in his body that revealed a carefully concealed restlessness. She woke a few times and looked at him and he looked right back at her. "It's all right," he said. "Just sleep." Once she rose in the morning, he was up right behind her, but he tucked the covers around Noah before pulling on sweatpants and following her to the kitchen.

They were quiet while Hannah made coffee. When two cups were brewed, Hannah sat down at the table with him. "I can't lose him," she said in a whisper.

"You won't," he said, covering her hand with his. "I don't want to invade your territory but I want to help if I can. You have to speak up, Hannah. You have to tell me what you can allow me to do."

"I don't understand," she said.

"Well, I've been away. This has happened in my absence. I'd like to talk to Cal, ask some questions, find out what his strategy is. But you're the client. If you'd like me to do that, you'll have to tell him so."

"We can go see him together, if you want."

"Do you want my help? Is it all right that I'm involved?"

She thought about what he'd been through, losing his own son as he had.

Would he be traumatized? Could he be so over-protective that his rational thinking was slipping? Or would his own experience make him even more helpful? But the objective thinking was up to Cal, who had experience in this sort of thing.

"I would like your opinion but I don't want to be a burden," she said.

He shook his head. "You didn't bring trouble to my door, Hannah. You came here with your boy, I love both of you and I want to be part of your lives. Just tell me if I'm too involved. Tell me if I need to back away."

"I will," she said. "Right now I really do need your support. I'm scared, Owen."

"Is it all right to call Cal? I'd like to hear his ideas."

She nodded. "He filed for a continuance to gather together the people who knew Erin and Noah and Erin's plans for Noah. He said he also hoped to be talking to some people who know the Addisons. He should be in touch about the date of the hearing soon. Like within a day or two."

Owen talked with Cal but had very little additional information to report to Hannah. The court date was set for just three days later. There was a rush to get plane tickets for their witnesses. Judd was able to put together a deposition from the babysitter, Linda. Kate was on her way but Sharon had to be excused, as her due date was upon her. Sharon was deposed at home. Kate was bringing clothes from Hannah's house — business attire for her to wear to court.

Then there was Noah. Some kind of explanation had be made but she didn't want him to be worried. While they were reading in the hammock, she broached the subject.

"Aunt Kate is coming tomorrow for a very short visit," Hannah said. "I have to go to the court to wrap up a few loose ends about my legal guardianship of you. Just some minor legal details."

"Are you sure?" he asked. "Because you and Owen whisper a lot."

Oh, he was so smart. "I'm not worried about anything, but I do have to go to court and you really can't go. Court can be long and boring so Sully said you can spend the morning with him. And if it takes longer than the morning, he will bring you back over here to let Romeo out. We've been talking about going to court because Owen wants to go with me."

"Why?" Noah asked.

"Because he cares about you. And he cares about me, too," she said. "I bet you never

259

thought we'd go through so much legal paperwork just to be together, did you?"

"But it will be okay?"

"It will be okay because I love you so much and I'm so proud of you," she said. "I never thought it would be you and me, Noah. But now that it is I can't imagine it ever being any other way."

"Hannah? What if you die?"

She was stunned for a moment and just held him closer. She took a deep breath. "First of all, it's highly unlikely. But I understand your worry about that. Your mom planned carefully, Noah, so if I couldn't take you, Sharon or Kate could."

"And Owen? Could I stay with Owen?"

"I don't know the answer to that. That sounds like another question I have to ask a lawyer. And Owen. I would have to ask Owen."

"Will you, then? Ask him? I know he has a lot of trips and stuff but maybe I could stay with Cal or Sully when he has trips."

"Don't you want to stay with Sharon or Kate?" she asked. "This is silly — I'm never leaving you. Nothing will happen to me, Noah."

"I like Kate and Sharon a lot," he said. "But I don't want to miss Owen and Romeo."

That dog better live to be a hundred, she thought. "We will talk about all possibilities and make sure you feel happy and secure. Okay?"

"That would be good," he said. "My first choice is you." "And my first choice is you," she said. "I miss my best friend Erin every day, and every day I say a little prayer of thanks to her for giving you to me."

Try not to become a man of success but rather try to become a man of value.
— ALBERT EINSTEIN

10

Cal was pleased with their assigned family court judge, one Leonard Vincente, who had been on the bench for forty years. But Hannah was a little panicked. She looked at his picture online. He was ancient.

"He's sharp as a tack and has decades of experience," Cal said. "I've only been before him once but he has a very strong reputation. He's respected. He comes across as a kind little old man but he has a very sharp edge and nothing much gets past him. That was both my experience with him and what I've heard about him."

"Why is he still on the bench at his age?" Hannah asked. "Isn't he long past retirement?"

"He obviously loves his work," Cal said. "This is a small county and he's been around a long time. His record is exemplary. He's never been overturned in appeal. He appears to be a simple country judge but there's nothing simple about him. He has a sophisticated knowledge of the law and its applications. And he is fair."

The courthouse was small and newer than most of the other buildings in Leadville and yet it was probably fifty years old. The hardwood floors were scuffed, the spectator benches few. There weren't many cases being heard and Mrs. Addison was nowhere to be seen.

Hannah and Cal took their places at the defense table at the front of the courtroom. Kate and Owen sat in the spectator's section right behind them. There was a sheriff's deputy, a court stenographer, a clerk and a woman who appeared to be a security or corrections officer. Then Hannah saw Helen walk into the room. She gave a little smile and wave and took a seat next to Kate and Owen. They all chatted quietly for a moment.

Then Mrs. Addison and her attorney entered the room and walked down the short aisle to the front. Mrs. Addison smiled and nodded as if she knew the people around her. She did not look like her picture; her picture had not done her justice. She wasn't a little old lady by any means. She appeared much younger than her years and sophisticated. Her hair was short and stylish in a salt-and-pepper cap; her figure was fit and trim. Her makeup was expertly applied and her black pantsuit was runway perfect. She ran her fingers through her hair on one side, briefly drawing attention to diamond earrings. She smiled at Hannah. She stood out in the room because of her beauty and attire.

Her lawyer was young, perhaps around thirty, and he was very sharply dressed, as well.

"Do you know any more about her lawyer?" Hannah asked Cal very softly.

"No. But I looked him up when his name appeared on the paperwork. He hasn't had time to get much experience but he has a good record."

Hannah couldn't imagine this rich-looking creature wanting custody of a five-year-old on crutches, nor could she envision Mrs. Addison rolling around on the floor with Noah, fishing with him, piggybacking him along a mountain trail. It must be about the trust, Hannah thought. What else could it be? Erin said her mother would never see the truth about Roger. Could she want the inheritance for Roger? But surely no one could be that foolish, that cruel.

Everyone in the courtroom stood as the judge entered and settled himself behind his large desk. He was smaller in person than in his photo. She felt a rising panic. She wasn't sure what she had hoped for in a judge. Maybe a powerful Santa-like figure, someone who would be both kind and protective.

"Good morning, ladies and gentlemen," he said. "I've read through all the documents, the suits and countersuits, reviewed the in loco parentis petition, also known as grandparents' rights, the will, the bequests, and have listened to and read all the depositions. I chose a hearing this morning because it's a good opportunity to hear all sides of the argument in the form of a discussion, a conversation. Perhaps there's a solution that hasn't presented itself yet but once we hear each other, something will materialize. But let me begin this conversation by removing some of the suspense — I will not be reversing guardianship. The will and accompanying deposition are very clear and very reasonable. It was Ms. Waters's wish that in the event of her death her son be raised by Ms. Russell. It appears she had very sound reason for making that decision. I won't object to that."

Hannah let out her breath audibly, nearly collapsing against Cal. But Mrs. Addison broke down and began to sob. She cried against her folded arms, head down on the table. Her lawyer patted her back.

"Mr. Renwick, do we need a recess?" the judge asked Victoria Addison's lawyer.

"Please give me a moment, Your Honor," the young man said. He stroked her back and whispered to her.

Everyone in the courtroom seemed to hang in suspense, waiting. Finally, Mrs. Addison lifted her head very dramatically, dabbing her wet cheeks, giving her nose a dainty blow, sniffing back emotion.

"It's okay, Your Honor," she said, a quiver in her voice. "I apologize."

"Let me know if you need time to collect yourself," the judge said. "As I was saying, the issue of legal guardianship appears to be settled to the court's satisfaction. By my count, this will be the third court in these United States to settle it. Ms. Waters did an excellent job of seeing to her son's future welfare. I have learned that she was familiar with the law and she followed it to the letter."

Cal stood. "Your Honor, in that case, can we dismiss these proceedings so my client can get on with her life?"

"Not so fast, Mr. Jones. Not everyone here is satisfied quite yet. My primary concern is with our minor child. Five years old." He clucked and shook his head. "And he has suffered an enormous loss. If you'll indulge me, I'd like to hear from the grandmother. According to sworn testimonies, you have not been a part of this young man's life. Do I understand that correctly?"

Mrs. Addison nodded, eyes closed, her chin quivering. "I have so many regrets. And now here I am, begging. Noah is my last living family and I'm being shut out of his life . . ."

"I was given to understand you have a son . . ."

"We are estranged, Your Honor. He's a . . ." She cleared her throat. "He's been in trouble and he stole from me. The problem is drugs, I think. I had to cut ties for his own good."

The judge's face remained expressionless. He said, "First your daughter and now your son? What prevented you from being a part of your grandson's life before, ma'am?"

"My own shortcomings, Your Honor. My daughter and I had a falling-out over my son, her half brother. He was in trouble. He did not treat her decently. No matter what I did, he was always in trouble and I tried my best to help him. Erin, my daughter, she gave me an ultimatum, insisting that I cut all ties with him or with her."

"And did she give you a reason for that ultimatum?" the judge asked.

"The same reason I had for finally giving up on him. Roger was arrested a few times and even served time in jail. He called Erin for help a couple of times. She gave him money once and was never repaid and she was done with him. I can't say I blame her but at the time I begged her to be patient and generous. In the end, I suppose it was my mistake. But a mother is stubborn. I wanted to help him straighten out. His father was a terrible influence, Your Honor. Needless to say, the family is split apart. My ex-husband died years ago, my son can't be trusted and now my daughter is gone. And my grandson is being held away from me."

"And what measures have you taken to attempt a relationship with your grandson?"

She looked shocked. "He was given to someone else to raise, Your Honor. I filed a request for guardianship and was denied."

"Did you contact your grandson's guardian? Did you attempt any kind of reconciliation?"

"I don't know what you mean."

The judge sighed. "Did you ask to visit with your grandson?"

"No, Your Honor. It was made clear to me

by the boy's nanny that the boy was placed in the care of someone else, that my daughter stipulated he wasn't to be a part of my life. You can't imagine how that hurt. I regret not begging my daughter for another chance. I always thought there would be more time to make amends. I also thought Roger would grow up and straighten out but I was wrong about that, as well."

"Ms. Russell," the judge summoned, "does Mrs. Addison's story match what you've understood to be true?"

"Not exactly, no," Hannah said. "Erin didn't describe it as one falling-out that caused them to be estranged. Erin told us her mother was emotionally abusive and her brother was sometimes physically abusive. Before her death, even before her will was written, she was adamant that she would never be in the same town much less same house as her mother and brother. That's the main reason she made her home in Madison and not Minneapolis, where we all grew up. And it wasn't as though Roger was in a little trouble — he's been arrested and convicted on felonies and imprisoned multiple times. He's scary and dangerous. Erin didn't trust her mother to keep Noah safe."

"We?" the judge asked. "You said where 'we' all grew up."

"Yes, sir. There were four of us from Minneapolis in college together. Best friends and confidantes. We were very close. We all shared stories of our growing-up years. Erin's sounded especially hard." She took a breath. "We've been best friends for seventeen years, Your Honor. Our friend Kate came to Colorado to help with this hearing if she could, but Sharon is about to have a baby and can't be here. I believe you have her deposition. We were all together a lot. I've been close to Noah since the day he was born."

"You know Mrs. Addison, then?" the judge asked.

"No, sir. I think I met her once in college but since I don't recognize her now, I'm not sure I remember accurately. Even if we did meet once, I can't say I know anything but what Erin told us. She didn't come to the funeral."

"And you, young woman — Kate. Did you know Mrs. Addison?"

"I met her once when we were in college," Kate said. "We were all at the funeral, of course. We were pretty disappointed that Mrs. Addison didn't even come."

The judge frowned and looked at Mrs. Addison.

"I wasn't even informed until the day

before the event. I was completely devastated, Your Honor," the woman said. "I couldn't get out of bed for days."

"My deepest sympathy, ma'am," he said. Then he looked at Hannah. "Since her next of kin didn't even attend, who made the arrangements? You?"

"Of course," she said. "We — the three of us — planned it according to Erin's wishes, took care of the details and took care of Noah. Your Honor, Noah is doing well. He's in physical therapy for his cerebral palsy and in grief counseling and he misses his mother but he's coping very well. We're managing better every day. He didn't even know he had a grandmother."

"Oh, Your Honor, I would give anything for a second chance," Victoria Addison said tearfully. "Any kind of second chance! Please!"

"Mrs. Addison, it doesn't comfort me much to know you were so distraught over your daughter's death that you couldn't even attend her funeral. I would be concerned about a child in your care if your constitution is fragile."

"I was afraid to go," she whimpered. "They all hate me! My daughter told her friends that I was a horrible mother and I couldn't face them in a public setting. I admit, I made mistakes, but I loved my daughter. You can't imagine the pain of not having made amends and getting to know Noah before she was gone!"

"I'm sure you have many regrets," he said. "I have grandchildren and great-grandchildren and I couldn't bear it if they weren't in my life." He looked at Hannah. "Family is important. It's also complicated and sometimes difficult. I've seen some impossible situations in this court. Since none of you actually witnessed firsthand the relationship Ms. Waters had with her mother, my scope is limited. Would you consider visitation? Let little Noah have a chance to meet and visit with his maternal grandmother?"

Hannah shook her head and said, "No, Your Honor. Erin was explicit. She didn't want her son mixed up with her family. She didn't trust her mother or half brother."

"That's understandable, given the experience she described," the judge said. "She wrote a very detailed account of the difficulties she had with her mother and half brother. But I would suggest a couple of supervised visits. I can assure you, neither his safety nor custody are at risk, but he should meet his grandmother and she should meet her grandson. For all we know, that could be the end of it. Or they could form some kind of bond of friendship. Maybe something more positive than what we have."

"Oh, Your Honor!" Victoria said, clasping her hands in front of her. "Oh God!"

"The court can arrange for someone from Social Services to supervise, or if you have family or friends who —"

"I'd be happy to supervise," Cal said. "Mr. Renwick is welcome to join us if he'd like."

"Mrs. Addison, I'm going out on a limb here. I'm not sure exactly what kind of relationship you've had with your kids but it sounds as if it has been very troubled. I think everyone deserves a chance, however. A very limited chance. Not a reversal of verdicts, but a chance to get acquainted. Briefly acquainted . . ."

"Your Honor, I was praying for at least joint custody," Victoria blurted.

"Madam, I would appreciate it if you would not interrupt. There is one thing I will insist upon — this brief visitation is only for you. Your son isn't invited, is that clear? Your daughter was afraid of him and it sounds like she had good reason. He is not accorded visitation and you are not allowed to take the minor child out of this county. In fact, you can't take him anywhere without

Ms. Russell's and *my* permission. You can visit with him at a location chosen by his guardian and her attorney. Let's say two visits, not to exceed two hours each. Then we'll meet again."

"But, Your Honor, I live in Minneapolis! And Noah is here at some rented lake house with Hannah!"

"Very well," he said. "No visitation it is." He raised his gavel.

"No!" she said. "I'll stay. I'll stay as long as I can at least see Noah."

"There you go," the judge said. "Wasn't that easy?"

It didn't feel easy to Hannah. It was not her desired outcome. She wanted Mrs. Addison and her son to just go away and leave them alone.

The judge picked a date in two weeks and a second date in three weeks, a next court date in a month. Mrs. Addison tried to convince him to get it all done in a week and Judge Vincente said that wouldn't work for him. He stuck stubbornly to his dates. And he was firm.

Cal suggested a cup of coffee before everyone headed home. He whispered to Hannah that she could have anyone she felt comfortable discussing the court appearance with to join them. Hannah invited Helen and, of course, Owen and Kate were there, as well. Cal directed them into a coffee shop on the main street.

"Kate, I'm so sorry," Hannah said. "You came all this way for a hearing and it might've been a waste of your time. You were barely allowed to speak."

"I didn't have much to offer, but I think it's clear to the judge that we were all very close for years, that Erin's wishes are being followed and that Erin knew her son would be safe with you."

"But why did he order visitation?" she said.

"Two supervised visits," Cal said. "I don't have the court order yet — I'll pick it up on Monday. But it's a couple of short visits. Do you think a woman who couldn't even be bothered to go to her own daughter's funeral is going to hang around in a town where she has no job and no friends to have a few hours of supervised visits with the grandson she's never known? Judge Vincente might be making the idea of having a second chance with her grandson so difficult that she gives up. He was very straightforward — it will be brief, it will be supervised and it will not change the custody arrangement. On the other hand, he might be testing her — maybe she's seen the light and just wants a relationship with the boy and will make personal sacrifices to have that. The judge is crafty — I wouldn't underestimate him. I'm telling you, this judge's decisions stand. He might look like a sweet little old grandpa but he's tough. Respected. Beloved."

"Do you think it's possible Victoria really does have regrets?" Hannah asked. "What if she has turned herself around and has become loving?"

"Leigh and I are best friends and we are devoted to each other," Helen said. "But we've had a standoff or two. If I'd lost my niece before I had a chance to work things out with her, I'd be devastated. But that being said, it would never have taken me five years to work through a problem. Even if Victoria has somehow become a sweet and caring grandmother, you will still be Noah's guardian. I'm afraid the woman has given up her rights by staying away too long."

"That's right," Cal said. "You're a good parent and this arrangement was decided by Erin. It's very cooperative of you to put up with Victoria's visit, giving her a chance to know Noah. But that's all. We won't let you be coerced or bullied. You're going to be surrounded by people, including me, who watch every second of the visit. And I'm going to deepen my background check on her. Something is missing."

"She's a little too slick," Helen said, stirring cream into her coffee. "She doesn't have the look of a woman who wants to be a cuddly grandmother."

"She looks so young and beautiful," Kate said.

"That's not the look I'm referring to. Beautiful and youthful women can be loving and devoted grandmothers, fun grandmothers. I didn't buy the tears or the pleas of regret and I absolutely don't believe she was afraid to come to the funeral because she had a notion everyone hated her. Where would she get an idea like that? She didn't know you. You weren't in touch with her at all. If she wanted to know her grandson, why didn't she show up the moment she heard of her daughter's death and beg for a chance to see him, get to know him? She should have been at her daughter's house before the funeral. I would have been in the car and driving inside thirty minutes! What's the drive? Four hours or less? Yet she wasn't even heard from. I'll tell you why — because Erin's death was completely unexpected and I'd bet my next royalty check that when she heard Erin had died she was terrified she'd get stuck with a kid and that's why she hid out. A kid on crutches, yet. I bet she was worried about what Erin's death might've cost her. Then something changed. Could she have found out there was an inheritance?"

"The custody is a matter of public record but not details like that," Cal said. "For example, it is not accessible public record how much was inherited or how much insurance was paid. We can't look up each other's bank balances. But can that information be found out? When people talk, it can."

"None of us would."

"You told me there was a trust," Helen said.

"But I never said how much," Hannah said. "I just said it seemed generous unless Noah wanted to go to medical school or something."

"No worries, I haven't mentioned its existence to anyone," Helen said. "But we should all stretch our brains. Find out what the connections are between Victoria and Noah's future. The babysitter? Someone in Erin's legal practice? A neighbor? Because the one thing that is undeniable — Victoria Addison didn't come out of the woodwork until weeks after her daughter's death. Something changed. It's possible what changed is she found out there was money."

Cal looked at her and gave a sly smile. "Helen, would you like to work for me?"

"My mind just works that way," Helen said. "It frightens Sully to death."

Hannah knew all about Roger Addison's record in the criminal justice system but she knew next to nothing about Victoria. Cal thought it might be good for all of them to know more—like how she earned her money, spent her time and entertained herself — some of the minor details that wouldn't make it into legal documents that were a matter of public record. He and one of the freelance investigators who served his law practice were right on it, hoping to pull together a better profile before visitation began.

Hannah thought it would be a good idea to talk with Noah. As usual he was extremely mature and accepting. "I have a grandma, then?" he asked. "I thought so."

"And she wants to meet you," Hannah said. "In a couple of weeks we're inviting her over. You can spend an hour or two with her."

"Is she nice?" he asked.

"I don't know," Hannah said. "I guess we'll find out. It's for a short time, just because you don't know each other and she wants to know you. I'll be with you and Owen will be near. Maybe you can introduce her to Romeo and show her how to fish."

"What if Romeo knocks her in the lake?" he said, showing Hannah a devilish grin.

"Do you remember your mom saying anything about your grandma?" Hannah asked.

"I think they didn't like each other that much," he said. "But is she mean?"

"I only met her for a few minutes, Noah, and she seemed nice. But don't worry — we're all going to visit with her together. She'll be perfectly nice because if she's not, she won't be asked to stay for lunch. How's that?"

"Probably a good idea," he said. "Owen better show her how to fish. Maybe I can show her how I can swim."

"Your swimming is impressive, that's for sure," Hannah said. "Since she lives in Minneapolis, I don't think there will be many visits."

"But, Hannah, you live in Minneapolis," he said. "Hey, maybe we should just stay here!"

"Clever, Noah. I just haven't figured out how I'm going to support us if I don't go back to my job. If I don't work, how do I pay the bills and buy groceries? How much do you like food?"

"Not that much," he said, grinning.

Just a few days before their first meeting, the last week in July, Owen surprised them with news of visitors. "I hope this doesn't complicate an already complicated situation. Sheila, her husband, Lucas, and their daughters want to come for quick visit."

"That's great, Owen. I'll welcome the distraction, won't you?"

"I won't let it distract me," he said.

"This is new territory for me," she said. "I've never met an ex-wife before."

"No? Well, there's a chance you're going to like her more than you like me," Owen said.

"I promise I won't," she said.

But as the visit approached she found herself feverish with excitement. When they pulled up to the house, Owen and Noah were on the dock. Owen secured their lines and poles and followed Noah safely off the dock. Romeo was barking at the car and dancing around in excitement because he believed anyone who was coming to the house was coming to see him.

It was Sheila who jumped out of the car

first and ran to Owen, throwing her arms around his neck and hugging him closely. She was so beautiful. Hannah wasn't surprised by her appearance — she'd googled the heck out of Sheila Abrams and had watched a couple of YouTube videos of her on talk shows so she already knew she was breathtaking and extremely well-spoken. The sight of her in the flesh did bring a few surprises — like her height. She was probably six feet tall. Her hair was strawberry blond, her skin pale and freckled, and even from a distance Hannah could see Sheila's green eyes dance. Owen whirled her around, apparently not the least intimidated by Sheila's husband getting out of the car. Nor by Hannah standing nearby.

Then Sheila looked him over. She put her hands on his trim waist, measuring. She said something that made him roar with laughter. Then she bent at the waist to look at Noah.

"Well, hello there," she said. "You must be Noah."

"I am. Owen said it's okay to call you Sheila."

"Indeed it is, that's my name. And may I call you just Noah? Or should it be Mr. Noah? Or Sir Noah?"

He giggled. "Just Noah. I haven't been

knighted yet."

"A real smarty-pants, aren't you?" she said. "I'm sure if being a knight is your goal, you will have no trouble achieving it. And where's Hannah?"

"I'm right here," Hannah said, coming up behind her. "It's so nice to meet you, Sheila."

"Oh, sweetheart, it's so nice to meet you!" And she opened her arms and enfolded Hannah in an embrace. Even though Sheila was tall and slim, her embrace was warm, soft and filled with affection. Hannah didn't want her to let go. It was hard to reconcile, this brilliant attorney who could live in the cold world of fighting human trafficking and yet be so gentle and filled with love.

"Well, old man, looks like you're surviving," Lucas said, stretching out a hand to Owen.

Hannah peeked to find Owen and Lucas were shaking hands and grinning like old friends. They each clapped the other's upper arm, making it almost a man hug. She realized she'd never seen any pictures of Lucas. He was Latino with thick black hair and the slightest touch of gray over his ears. His complexion was tan and showed the evidence of earlier acne, yet he was ferociously handsome. Unlike the slim Owen and Sheila, he was a man with muscles — broad across his chest, strong in the shoulders, legs like tree trunks and big hands.

"And you're Hannah," he said, taking her hand and giving it a squeeze.

"Oh! You must have sisters!" Hannah exclaimed, letting him hold on to her hand. His handshake was firm but gentle.

"Four," he said, grinning. He had a lot of large straight white teeth. "They made sure I was educated in how to never crush a woman's hand!"

The little girls, occupied with Romeo, slowly made their way over. Introductions were made. Jenny was six and Amber was seven and both of them had their father's dark good looks and black hair. After having seen pictures of Brayden, it was obvious that he had inherited a lot of his mother's fairness. But these girls favored their father. They had an exotic beauty.

There were suddenly a million things Hannah wanted to know about these people. How had they managed to keep their relationships in the right spaces and remain close after all they'd endured? How had this couple managed to divorce and recouple on such lovely terms? They carried on without jealousy or misery, without longing or anger, yet they'd been through so much hardship. Hannah had never seen the like.

"How about something to eat? To drink?" Owen offered.

"We stopped for snacks for the girls and they've been eating nonstop since we left the airport, but I will arm wrestle you for a cold beer."

"No need to get physical, Lucas. I'm all stocked up. And, madam?"

"Any cold and very expensive woody chardonnay will keep me from complaining," Sheila said.

"She's always had expensive taste," Owen told Hannah.

"I hope you're prepared," Hannah said, looping an arm around his waist.

"I have a wine cellar!"

"I hope it's full!" Sheila said. "I'm on vacation."

"Let's get your stuff," Owen said. "Work before pleasure."

It was as though they'd all known each other for years, Hannah thought. Well, in fact they had, except for Hannah and Noah, who were newcomers. Sheila and Lucas put their things in their room and then, while the adults settled on the porch, the kids were all over the place. Noah was keeping up, though he used his crutches. They were inside, outside, they even tried going onto the dock until the adult voices yelled, "Hey! Off the dock!"

"Noah can't be on that dock without an adult. With his braces and heavy shoes — he'll sink like a rock," Owen said. "And he has. Romeo knocked him in the first day he was here."

"Jenny and Amber can swim. A little," Sheila said.

"I've got plenty of life jackets. And fishing poles. When the weather warms up tomorrow afternoon, we can all fish and get wet," Owen replied.

Owen had been thinking ahead and had a spaghetti casserole ready for dinner. Kids always loved spaghetti. By the time that was devoured, all three kids were in need of baths or showers, so dirty and gamey from play. By the time they were in pajamas, the dishes were done and Owen had lit the fire in the yard. The three kids were inside sharing the couch in front of a movie.

Now the conversation among the adults was quieter. Relaxed.

"I love this place so much," Sheila said. "Owen, how do you get any work done?"

"Living like this is the only way to get anything done. There's no unnecessary pressure, the weather cooperates more than not, it's moderate year-round and there aren't a lot of people to distract me."

"And you enjoy your own company," Sheila reflected.

"Lately I just put up with my own company. Hannah has been helping me mat pictures and frame and even do some photo editing and I've found working with someone is pretty great, too."

"But how does Hannah like that?" Sheila asked, looking at Hannah.

"It's fun," she said. "It gives me something to do. I have to think about working again. I've been on family leave since March."

"And what's your line of work?" Sheila asked.

"Sales," Hannah said, then went on to explain her product and territory. "I like sales and I'm good at it, but I'm a little bored with it after a dozen years. I'm a sales manager now so I'm not in the field as much. I manage sales reps."

"What's that like?"

"They're all young men so it's a little like herding cats. And a whole lot of paperwork," Hannah said. "The upside is I don't have to constantly worry about my commissions and sales figures, but the downside is I have to worry about the sales figures of the whole team. I make more money on a salary than

I did as a sales rep. But I have to run herd on a bunch of men with a lot of personality."

"Are they successful?" Lucas asked.

"They are," Hannah said. "And also rambunctious. I feel like a housemother sometimes."

Sheila laughed. "Great training for inheriting a son!"

"I guess so," she said. "I hadn't thought of that."

They had three days of fun before Victoria's visit. When the men had the kids in the lake, Hannah and Sheila went into town for a little tour and lunch. Hannah asked Sheila if she was up to company and Sheila said she was, so Hannah called Sierra and Leigh and they all met at the pub. When Sheila explained who she was and the reason for her visit, Sierra and Leigh were fascinated that exes could be so friendly.

The next day Hannah took Sheila on a hike and they visited Helen at the Crossing. Helen quizzed Sheila more about her work. The kids swam and caught fish, ran and played all day and ended each day with dinner cooked by Lucas and Owen, then a movie for the kids and a fire for the adults.

"And tomorrow is Victoria," Hannah said.

"Even though the judge promised her visit would have no impact on our custody arrangement, I'm nervous."

"And I have some news," Owen said. "My sister called and when I told her Sheila and family were here, she invoked sister rights. Mary is coming the day after tomorrow. Just for the day, with at least the kids and maybe her husband, too."

"That will be wonderful," Sheila said. "Have you met Owen's sister yet? She's fantastic!"

"This family," Hannah said. "You are so remarkable! I have two half sisters I can't even get along with and rarely even talk to. And the reason I have Noah is that Erin and her mother had been estranged for years. Yet you guys — after all you've been through . . ."

"We're very lucky to be good friends," Sheila said. "Maybe it's because of losing Brayden. We couldn't waste energy on divorce squabbles. It was like that was the least of our problems. We had more serious concerns. We had no idea what our lives would look like without being together, without Brayden. What will your life look like, Hannah?"

She closed her eyes to think. "I keep trying to see it and all I see is sunshine on the lake, snow on the mountains, deer in the yard." She opened her eyes. "I can hear Noah and Owen laughing together so I know they're part of my new life but I don't know what work I'll do or where I'll find the instincts I'll need to raise Noah, but he's there in my future everywhere I look.

"When I think about Noah facing Victoria, I feel a lot of warrior tendencies."

Sheila laughed. "That's a good sign. For you, not necessarily for Victoria."

"I can't fail Noah now," Hannah said.

"You won't. Listen to that quiet inside voice and trust it. If you start to smell an ill wind, wrap your strong mother arms around him and keep him safe. When and if that time comes, you'll make all the right choices." She smiled and squeezed Hannah's hand. "I'm so glad Owen found you. And I can't wait to meet Victoria," Sheila said. "Are you sure it's all right that we're here? We can take the kids on some outing for a while, just to give you privacy."

"We don't want privacy," Owen said. "It's a supervised visit. The lawyer will also be here. We'll make sure she gets her time with Noah, but not be alone with him. If Noah's mother didn't trust her, neither should we."

Sheila smiled. "Oh, my. The grandmother has no idea what she's gotten herself into with you."

"And that suits me fine," Hannah said. "I can be very brave when I have to be but I'll be the first to admit, I haven't always been skeptical enough. I'm inclined to be too trusting. Not this time, though."

We are all travelers in the wilderness of this world, and the best we can find in our travels is an honest friend.
— ROBERT LOUIS STEVENSON

11

Victoria Addison arrived at Owen's house at ten in the morning, looking fresh for a day at the lake. She wore denim capris, a sleeveless shirt with a sweater over her shoulders and a straw hat on her head. She carried a large canvas beach bag.

Hannah had been waiting on the porch with her gallery of friends — Owen, Cal, Sheila, Lucas, Jenny and Amber. Cal explained that for the visit to be useful, someone had to be with Noah and Victoria, listening to their conversation and observing their behavior. To that end, Hannah went down the porch stairs to meet her as she approached the house.

"Hello, Mrs. Addison," Hannah said, sticking out her hand.

In her head she was pretending Victoria was a difficult manager from the human resources department — that was the only way she could work it out in her mind.

When someone from Human Resources visited you at work, they might be wearing a pleasant expression but something was up — like maybe you were getting fired. Or maybe just disciplined or warned of a complaint directed at one of your staff. On the other hand, they might be coming to tell you about a complimentary letter from a customer that would go in your file. "It's nice of you to visit. This is Noah."

"Oh, Noah!" Victoria said, a little surprise in her voice as she took in the crutches. "I'd know you anywhere," she said, bending at the waist even though Noah was still on the porch.

"You would?" Noah asked. "I wouldn't of knowed you."

"Of course," she said. "Your mother used to send me pictures."

"She did? You never came to our house," he said.

Hannah thought, *I don't even have to be sneaky.* Noah didn't even realize it but he was astute. Nothing got by him, including the lovely Mrs. Addison.

"Well, that's a complicated story," she said. "But I'm happy to be able to spend time with you now. I've brought some things for you." She looked around with a slight frown. "Where shall we go to have our visit?"

Right at that moment Romeo loped down the steps to the yard and nosed right up against Victoria. She gasped and retreated, giving the big dog's head a shove away from her. Romeo sat, looking dejected.

"This is Romeo, Mrs. Addison," Hannah said. "He's very sweet and friendly."

"And awfully big!" she said.

"We don't ever push him or hit him," Noah said. "He's a little clumsy but he doesn't have a mean bone."

"Of course he doesn't," she said, stretching out a hand to tentatively pat the big head. "He startled me, that's all."

"Wait till he knocks you in the lake," Noah said. "Then you'll be surprised for sure."

Victoria laughed uncomfortably. "You have quite a gathering. Am I imposing? I could reschedule our meeting when there aren't so many people."

"You're not imposing. These are our friends. You've already met Mr. Jones. Lucas is going to take the girls inside. The rest of us are going to play a game of cards at the table out here while you and Noah visit on this end of the porch. You have the chairs and the swing. Can I get you something to drink? Coffee? Tea? Soda?"

"Are we to get acquainted with an entire crowd observing us?" she asked as she came up the steps.

Cal stood. "Give it five minutes and you won't feel awkward at all. The whole point is that you and Noah will be observed. I suggested your lawyer join us."

"And I suggested he not," she said. "I wasn't prepared for this . . . this . . . gallery!"

"It's a long porch," Cal said. "We won't interrupt you."

Lucas hustled his girls into the house while Sheila and Owen walked to the table at the far end of the porch.

"This is the only option," Hannah said. "Are you sure you wouldn't like something to drink?"

Victoria ignored her and just put a hand on Noah's shoulder. "Let's go sit on the swing and let me show you some of the things I brought. Can we do that? Is that all right?"

"I guess so," he said.

"Come on, then. I've looked forward to this for a long time."

Noah said nothing. He crutched his way to the porch swing.

Hannah felt as if her heart was being torn from her chest. She could feel the ache penetrating deep; her throat hurt from fighting the urge to cry. She was probably going to spend a long afternoon talking with Noah, trying to sort things out with him.

"This is a very beautiful place, Noah. I can see why Hannah wanted to bring you here for a vacation," Victoria said.

"We might stay," Noah said.

Hannah stifled a gasp. She had tried not to give him false hopes about staying; that decision was between her and Owen. She had been honest about needing to go back to work but that was as far as the discussions had gone.

Sheila put on a cheerful smile and sat down at the table. She shuffled the cards, dealt and made a little quiet small talk. She asked Hannah if she'd been to her friend Sully's garden lately, asked what he was growing, asked how long she'd known him. Owen and Cal were stoically quiet. Hannah was just nervous, trying to hear what was being said between Noah and Victoria.

She picked up little things. *It's all right if you want to call me Grandma,* Victoria said. *I'll just call you Mrs. Addison,* Noah replied. *Maybe when we know each other better,* Victoria said. *Look here, I brought you an iPad that you can play games and watch movies on. I already have one,* he said. *Maybe you can give it to some poor kid.*

It took about twenty minutes to realize Sheila and Cal weren't missing a word and they were purposely keeping their small talk quiet and superficial, not naming any full names, not giving away any information, talking about their cards, the weather, the lake, possible fishing later.

"Tell me things about my mom," Noah said.

"Well, when she was little, like your age, she had blond pigtails and liked to climb trees. She didn't want to wear dresses or fancy clothes. She was very smart in school." On and on she went. Hannah frowned. Victoria could have been talking about any pretty little child. Then Victoria began pulling things out of the beach bag — she had brought him clothes, a couple of baseball hats, some books, a few games and shirts emblazoned with the logos for the Minnesota Vikings and Twins, football and baseball teams.

"Tell me some things about my mom when she was older. Like, before she was my mom," Noah said.

"Well, she loved cookies and candy. She loved to bake pies, cakes and bread. Since she worked all the time, she wasn't able to do it too often, but when she felt like it, she baked up a storm. She loved to go to the state fair — she loved the rides, especially the scariest ones. She used to love all the food at the fair — corn dogs, cotton candy, barbecue and popcorn. She liked to stay up late and watch scary movies, and I remember she used to love to dress up for Halloween — a witch or a wizard or Alice in Wonderland."

"Did she have pets? Like Romeo?" he asked.

"She had a little dog when she was in high school but when she went off to college, she left him behind. She didn't have a pet after him, at least not that she ever told me about. She was independent. She liked being alone. Until you came along, that is. She loved being a mom."

"She did?"

"Oh, she did!" Victoria said. "She used to brag about you all the time! But, Noah, tell me more about you. What do you want to be when you grow up?"

"I'm planning to be a photographer," he said. "Or a doctor. Or I'd like to be a firefighter like Connie."

"Connie?" she asked.

"He's our friend," Noah said. "He's a mountain climber and a rescuer. He's the coolest guy."

Victoria was quiet for a moment. "Would you like me to read to you for a while? I brought some books."

"What was my mom's favorite color?" he asked.

"I'm not sure. When she was a little girl she liked pink and then blue later. She loved puzzles and music. You know, rock music, like all teenagers do. Let's read, okay?"

"Sure," he said. "Go ahead."

He settled back to listen and Victoria pulled out a pile of large picture books and asked him to pick one, which he did. Victoria began reading a picture book that might have been sold to her as appropriate for a five-year-old, but Victoria had no idea Noah was reading much of *Treasure Island* on his own, very seldom stumbling on words.

Hannah lost five games of hearts in a row because she just couldn't pay attention. Owen and Cal tried to engage her in conversation but she just couldn't focus. Her ear was turned to Noah. Finally, after what seemed like an eternity, Noah said, "Thank you. Hannah, can we be done now?"

Hannah looked at her watch. It had barely been an hour. She turned her questioning eyes to Cal, who gave a slight nod. "Okay." She got up and walked to the other end of the porch. "Thank you for coming, Mrs. Addison. And thank you for bringing all these nice things for Noah."

"Our time can't be over already!" she said.

"I guess our little guy is worn-out," Hannah said. "Maybe next time will last a little longer."

"Is there going to be an entire congregation for our next visit? Because that would make anyone uncomfortable, and I don't know how I'm expected to make a good impression with everyone staring at me."

"That's all right, Mrs. Addison. You were very nice to all of us and we didn't have any expectations. I guess we'll see you at your next scheduled visit. Thank you for everything. You were so generous."

Victoria merely grunted. She stood, leaned over to put a gentle kiss on Noah's head and briefly patted his hair. "I'll see you next week."

Romeo stood and stared at her. He didn't growl or snarl — he was not imposing — he just stood and stared as if making certain Noah was safe.

Victoria departed without another word of goodbye to the adults present. She got in her car, backed out and drove away.

"Can I go see if they're having snacks in there?" Noah said, referring to the girls and

Lucas in the house.

"Of course," Hannah said. "Try not to stuff yourself with snacks. I'm planning some gourmet peanut butter and jelly for lunch."

"Right, like you ever do that," he said. He grabbed his crutches and headed inside. Then he turned. "Does she have to come back?"

"We'll see," Cal said. "The judge wanted her to have a chance to meet you, get to know you. You didn't like her?"

He shrugged. "She's okay. But she shouldn't make up stories. My mom said that's the same thing as lying."

"And what did she make up?" Cal asked.

"My mom didn't like scary movies at all. She didn't like movies that much. Just the ones we watched together. When the commercial for a scary one was on she used to cover her eyes and say, 'No way.' She didn't watch TV hardly ever and I was only allowed one hour, except when we watched a movie. She liked quiet. She loved her books. And my mom hates rides — she threw up on the teacups at Disney. And she'd never let me go on hardly anything cool. And what's a corn dog?"

"A hot dog on a stick, sort of."

He just made a face and shook his head.

"I didn't never get hot dogs till I came here," he said. "My mom was a vegetable nut. She put spinach in everything — she said it was good for my muscles. I been to McDonald's, like, *once!* Here is better for food, but for everything else I still want my mom."

"I want her, too," Hannah said. "Thanks for doing that, Noah. I am very impressed by your manners."

"And we know what her favorite color is," he added. He crutched his way into the house.

Hannah sank into a chair, exhausted. "God, that was interminable." Owen and Cal wandered into the house, leaving the women on the porch.

"But he did all your work for you," Sheila said. "He brought her out. She's a fraud. She knows nothing about her daughter or her grandson."

"Erin had a dog — a little mutt, part Yorkie. While she was at school, living with us in our little duplex just off campus, her mother had him put to sleep. Victoria said he was old and sick, but she never even called. Erin went home to her mother's house and the dog was just gone. I hope Noah doesn't know about that. He's just a little boy."

"That was a good first visit — you learned things in a safe setting," Sheila said. "The judge will want to be told if the visit doesn't go well. And it didn't go well from the standpoint of making Noah quite sad because his mother was so erroneously remembered. What was her favorite color?"

"Variations of purple or violet or lilac. She wore it constantly. She painted her bedroom pale purple. We teased her about it. It was so gaggy. But she didn't force it on Noah . . . And Victoria read him baby books. What a trouper — he sat and listened. First time I pulled a little-kid book off the shelf in Owen's house, Noah informed me that he already knew that one, that it was a baby book. I started reading him bigger stories — we're working on *Treasure Island.* He can read a lot of it himself. He doesn't know what all the words mean but he can sound them out."

"At five?" Sheila gasped.

"He doesn't play outside as much as the other kids . . ." Hannah said, repeating what Noah had told her.

"He sure plays outside here. The three of them have been running wild."

"Since we've been here, he's been very active."

A glass of wine appeared before Hannah

and she looked up into Owen's eyes. "What's this?"

"A little sedative," Owen said. "Noah is already bouncing around, yelling and laughing with the girls, evidence he's not at all traumatized. They're playing Uno. And he's eating all their pretzels. Want wine, Sheila?"

"Of course. I'm on vacation."

"What did you think of the visit with Victoria?" Owen asked Sheila.

"It doesn't really matter what I think," Sheila said. "But it matters what Noah thinks and what Hannah thought. I didn't get a good feeling from Victoria. If she really wants a relationship with her grandson in spite of the fact that her daughter was opposed to that, then she'll accept the judge's decision and ask permission to phone him or text him or email him. She could get to know him a little and send appropriate gifts for his birthday and Christmas. Did you notice she seemed surprised by the crutches? It kind of looked like Victoria didn't know about his CP or what it meant. Just another little piece of information."

Owen put a glass in front of Sheila and the other men joined them at the table.

"I'm anxious to hear what you thought, Cal," Hannah said.

"Well, she didn't do anything wrong or

even suspicious," he said. "I had a case a long time ago in which a young child's mother died prematurely and the divorced father had returned to Mexico. The judge wasn't going to send a small child to a country he didn't know, to a language he didn't speak, but the father wanted his son and was entitled to him. The judge set up a series of supervised visits between father and son over an extended period of time and eventually the boy and his father were well acquainted and returned to Mexico, where the man's parents and siblings lived and were anxious to help out. A visitation schedule with his American grandparents was worked out. I don't know how they're doing now, but it was a very rational plan at the time.

"But the circumstances are a little different in this case. Erin went to a great deal of trouble to select the guardian she preferred and in addition, went to a lot of trouble to be sure Noah wouldn't go to his grandmother. She made her reasons clear; she explained in detail why it wasn't a good idea. Clearly Hannah has been closer to Erin and Noah the past five years than Victoria was."

"Did you ever find out more about her?" Hannah asked.

"I learned a few things, and not at all what I expected. First of all, she's a cancer survivor . . ."

"Wait. What?" Hannah asked.

"She told a neighbor and a coworker she'd been cancer-free for seven years, but neither knew what kind of cancer."

"But Erin never . . . Erin would have known. Even though they didn't have a good relationship, even though — Erin said she called her mother periodically, just to check on her, just to make sure she was okay. They didn't see each other for years, but they were somewhat in touch. Erin made that dreaded phone call every now and then — I got the impression it was a couple of times a year or once a year — but said that her mother never called her. She once told me her mother hadn't called her in four years. I'd known Erin for so long, I can't remember how often she said she'd talked to her mother after Noah was born. Maybe never. She said every phone call ended in an argument — either Erin wasn't doing enough for her mother or there was some issue with Roger, like he needed help or money. But if you'd known Erin . . . She was too tenderhearted to have ignored something like cancer. She would not have risked having her mother die without seeing

310

her. And from what she said of Victoria, she would have asked Erin for some kind of help." Hannah shook her head. "She couldn't have known."

"But if they were estranged . . ."

Hannah shook her head. "There were at least a few times Erin talked of being tempted to go see her mother or give her mother money after she moved to Madison. She said she had to be very careful. She said her mother wasn't above using her."

"I guess that doesn't matter much now. I'll see if that matter comes up again. She's currently unemployed," Cal went on. "She's had a variety of jobs, many of them in the human services area. Apparently she was known to be giving. Generous. She worked for a consulting business that provided seniors' services—they offered health care options, financial services like reverse mortgage, financial planning, long-term care insurance, investment counseling. They went out of business about six months ago so follow-up there was impossible. She has also worked in nursing homes, as a volunteer and in hospital administration. A long time ago she was in property management, in sales for an extended care facility, in a rehab facility. If that didn't tell me much, add to that her volunteerism — she obviously has accounting skills because she's worked for several nonprofits in that capacity. She's also been a companion to a few elderly people. She's dabbled in real estate, possibly for supplemental income. At first glance, it appears she enjoyed helping people."

"At first glance?" Hannah said.

"We haven't turned up many personal contacts. She's moved a lot, renting places around Minneapolis and Saint Paul for a couple of years or less and it seems she either wasn't close to her neighbors or they've moved just as much. There have been very few references — only a couple of coworkers who said she was very nice and well liked. She's a single sixty-five-year-old woman and yet I can't seem to find her friends. But a couple of neighbors from years past seem to know all about Roger. And while they didn't know Victoria very well, they were sympathetic. She had a troubled adult son who took advantage of her."

"That's a tad unsteady," Sheila said. "No long-term commitments. Who does she shop with? Play canasta with? Go to water aerobics with?"

"And she's a liar," Hannah said. "She told the judge she wasn't contacted about Erin's passing until the day before the funeral and that's not true. Noah knows she doesn't remember the true facts about her daughter."

"I did learn that Roger Addison is still in Minneapolis but there's nothing to indicate he was staying in Victoria's home, according to a neighbor. He hasn't lived with her recently, though he has visited for a couple of hours occasionally. Apparently he cut her grass a couple of times. He has a noisy truck, distinguishable by dents and peeling paint," Cal said. "I'll do a little more research. Maybe I can file an injunction, bringing this visitation experiment to an end. On the other hand, we might want to ride it out, then meet with the judge again."

"Before you make a final decision, let me have a talk with Noah," Hannah said. "If he's upset, we might need to step in."

In the early morning, Owen was holding Hannah closely. "It's our last day with our extended family," she said with a sigh. "How do you like the idea of establishing a commune? I think we could pull it off."

"What if I want you all to myself?" he countered.

"Don't look now but I think that ship has sailed. It's you, me and Noah. What are we going to do on our last day together?"

"You've already forgotten," he said. "It's going to be a warm, sunny day. There are fish to catch and swimming to do. And my sister is coming."

"That's right! Do you know when?"

"Before noon, I'm sure," he said. "Sheila and my sister remained good friends."

"You were right," she said. "I really like Sheila. I hope we can also keep in touch as friends."

He pulled her on top of him. "She's remained friends with her ex-husband all these years so I like your chances. She's obviously very tolerant. Let's put the coffee on and see what kind of a day we have."

Owen got busy in the kitchen. Hannah and Sheila took their coffee to the front porch and let Romeo wander around the yard. The kids were soon making noise in the kitchen and Lucas escaped to the porch. He informed them Owen was making pancakes and eggs. "There's food coloring involved," he said.

It was ten o'clock before everyone had eaten, showered, dressed and was ready to talk about the day ahead, but a car drove up and gave a horn a toot. Hannah just watched as Sheila recognized the occupants at once and let out a shriek of joy, covering her face with her hands. She ran to the vehicle as people started to emerge. An elderly lady, a woman about Sheila's age, and three kids embraced Sheila, then raced toward Owen. They were sidetracked by the dog and hugged him instead. Then Sheila's kids rushed to the kids from the car. Lots of hugging followed — it was clearly a reunion.

Owen put an arm across Hannah's shoulders. "The rest of the family," he said. "My mom, Janet; my sister, Mary; nieces, Susanne and Korby; nephew, James. My brother-in-law wasn't able to come, but you'll meet him soon, I promise. They're just here for the day. I wanted you to meet them and they all wanted to see Sheila, Lucas and the kids. We're a very strange and large extended family."

She looked up into Owen's eyes. "You're magical, that's what you are."

It was a very full day of storytelling, eating, playing, getting acquainted and general catching up. For much of the day the women were either sitting on the porch talking or in the kitchen putting together potato salad, deviled eggs, a veggie platter and condiments while Owen and Lucas had the kids either fishing or in the lake swimming. It was still pretty early when Owen and Lucas lit the grill and a feast of hamburgers and hot dogs was served. Everyone crammed around the big dining table.

The sun had barely begun its downward path when Mary rounded up her mother and kids to make the drive back to Denver. The day quieted quickly after that as the exhausted kids got showered and settled in front of a movie, Owen and Lucas sat at the dining table and played cribbage, and Hannah and Sheila sat outside in the deepening shadows.

"Full disclosure, I suggested to Owen that we invite you to stay and we could form a commune," Hannah said. "I'm really going to miss you. How crazy is that? My guy's ex has become one of my favorite people?"

Sheila laughed. "And you're one of mine, but a commune is not in our future. Please don't say anything in front of the kids, but we're going to make a change. It could take as long as a year, but we'll be relocating the foundation and the advocacy to DC. I've been asked to serve on a national council for children's safety. It'll give us a greater reach into the national network of child advocacy and it will make me a full-time activist. I'm ready. Plus, all the national lawmakers are there and I plan to be their worst nightmare."

"That's so exciting! Are you looking

316

forward to moving?" Hannah asked.

"I am. Lucas has a lot of family around Southern California so he's a little unsure, but he wants to grow the foundation and this is the most practical way to do it. I'm sure the girls will have trouble with the change but in the end it will be good for them. It will add experiences to their lives. But what about you, Hannah? What are you and Noah going to do?"

"I've never been happier than I have been since we've been here and Noah is doing so well, but my work is in Minneapolis. And even though Owen wants us to stay and says he isn't worried about whether I work, I don't know what I'll do without work. It's not just the income, it's the feeling that I'm doing something useful, that I'm contributing. Not that being Noah's mother isn't useful . . ."

Sheila laughed. "You don't have to explain to me of all people. Mothering is a blessing and rewarding, but you should have something to give yourself to. Something you're not giving to someone else but filling your own well."

"Owen talks about his well a lot," she said. "I've been helping him in the shop — transferring pictures onto other mediums. It's fun but I don't know if it would keep my interest over the long term."

"You know what Owen really needs? A business manager," Sheila said. "Someone with PR experience who could set up shows for his work, keep the books, write press releases, make his travel arrangements, interact with his agent and publisher, help him sell his work. I bet his financial books are a wreck by now — I used to take care of all his billing and receivables. He used to keep everything in a leather binder, completely disorganized . . ."

"He's almost paperless now," Hannah said. "I'm a little reluctant to get into his personal business."

"That's not personal," Sheila said. "It's his business and it has many very bothersome details from his corporation to his taxes and pension. And he hates it. Owen was made to wander with a camera and dream. He's not practical and he doesn't like practicality. He'd be happiest if he could just take pictures."

Hannah was quiet for a moment. "I was in sales, then I was a sales manager, which put me in charge of several salesmen. But I would never presume . . ."

"Maybe the subject will come up and you can let Owen know that you're qualified, if he's interested." She smiled coyly. "You wouldn't be the first family business on record."

"You are an amazing person," Hannah said. "How did you do it? How did you divorce, keep a great relationship with Owen and build yourself a new life? I think you still love him and it seems perfectly natural."

"I will always love Owen," she said quietly. "But we were bonded by tragedy and then, in order to survive, we moved in opposite directions. I threw myself into child advocacy, my role growing by the day. Owen just wanted to be out of the public view, to find his peace. His own peace. He's great with people, he's a fantastic neighbor and a good friend. He was a wonderful husband and father. But I went to one of his shows in Denver a few years ago and a lot of strangers looking and judging his work put red splotches on his neck. He's not a hermit, but being the center of attention doesn't really sit well. Me? I'm okay with being the center of attention! Ha!" She laughed. "I've testified before Congress, though I was terrified. The high I was on after doing a good job kept me afloat for days. Owen would have to sleep for a week just to recover after something like that." She smiled. "We each have our own gifts. We're better with people who understand and are a little like us. The secret is learning to accept people as they are, not as you wish them to be. You and Owen are good together. You seem to be a lot alike and just different enough to balance each other out."

I haven't had the best of luck in relationships, she thought. *But none of them were anything like Owen.*

The next morning there was a lot of commotion getting Sheila, Lucas and the kids breakfast, the car loaded and on the road back to the airport. There was a lot of hugging and promises of future visits. And when they were gone, trundling off down the road in their leased van, Owen, Hannah, Noah and Romeo just stood in the yard watching them go. A bird tweeted and a fish jumped.

"Sure is quiet," Noah said. He looked up at Hannah. "What are we going to do now?"

"We're going to have a day of rest," she said.

Victoria Addison fixed herself a drink and phoned Roger.

"Mother. Are you all right?" he asked by way of a greeting.

"I'm doing all right — I'm in Colorado. I tracked down my grandson, Noah. This Hannah, newly appointed guardian of my grandson, is going to be difficult. And she has hooked herself up to a man. A man who is emotionally connected to the boy. Do you remember Hannah?"

"I'm sure I never met her," Roger said. "It's not as though Erin shared her friends with me. Do you intend to make trouble for her?"

"Don't be ridiculous!" she snapped. "I only want to help her out. And get to know my grandson. I should have known Erin would do something like this — give my grandson to someone outside the family."

"I can't believe you want to be tied down to a child . . ." Roger said. "You don't actually like children. But then, you've tied yourself down to old people and you don't like them, either . . ."

"What is that noise?" she asked him.

"The radio . . ."

"Where *are* you?"

"At home . . ."

"You're lying to me! Where are you and what are you doing?"

He sighed into the phone. "I'm at home. A couple of friends came over. I'm not out. I'm not at your house. I was last there a month ago to cut your grass and I haven't been back since. I'm at my place. I have friends over. We're playing poker."

"Get yourself and everyone else out of my house! What did I tell you? I'm not supposed to have any contact with you! I've told everyone I haven't seen you or let you stay with me for a long time!" Then she disconnected.

If Roger was in her house with friends, word could get back to the landlord and she was dodging the landlord.

She took a sip of her drink. She knew this day would come. She would be officially breaking ties with Roger. Never mind she'd already told the judge they were estranged and had been for a long time. But this was inevitable; Roger was no longer of any use. Their relationship had always been stormy, fluctuating from highs to lows. There was a time she could count on Roger to listen to her. Now they managed best when he was in jail because when he wasn't, he struggled with drug and alcohol abuse, and when he was using, he made foolish mistakes.

He denied he was using; he claimed he had to take regular tests while he was on parole. He said he went to AA. But he was a perpetual liar and couldn't be trusted.

In earlier days, Victoria had much better control over Roger. Lately he'd become defiant and she couldn't fathom it — he owed her. She stood by him through every piece of trouble he'd gotten himself into. Well, she wasn't about to tolerate this now. She had no margin for error at the moment.

She had learned her last place of employment was being investigated, that most of the employees were being questioned by police, even those who had resigned before they went out of business. A couple of former employees had been indicted for fraud, embezzlement and theft, accused of taking advantage of their clientele, mostly elderly people who needed help with their insurance, benefits and finances. They hadn't gotten around to her yet.

It wasn't the first time there had been suspicion surrounding a business or charity she'd been involved with but it was by far the most serious. This time the attorney general was involved. And also for the first time she could be in serious trouble.

Victoria was good at winning people's trust. She'd learned most of her techniques from a man she'd been involved with when she was much younger. There was good money to be made from people who needed her caring and expertise. There was a reason she'd been named beneficiary in two wills. She'd been very careful before accepting any inheritance — those dear souls had no family and it hadn't been much that they'd left behind. She couldn't be named as a beneficiary in a lot of wills without raising suspicion because it was a suspicious world; people would just believe the worst.

But then she'd had a slip. She became the guardian of a rich old man, another man without a family, and she stood to collect $800,000 of his money when he passed. That was when she worked at her company, doing what they did, submitting invoices for her management of his property and care-taking, paid out of his bank account. Everything from lawn care and pool service to chauffeuring to medical facilities to scheduling him for screenings and health care providers' evaluations, none of which she actually did. He passed at home, the dear old soul, and she was just waiting for the paperwork and probate to clear when there was a hitch. It wasn't a family member, but a library. The man was a patron and had given a copy of his will to the librarian saying all of his money would be left to the library. They objected to this guardian stepping in and claiming to be the new beneficiary, even though she had a copy of his will, one that had been hastily written while he was in hospice care.

A public library. That began a lot of poking around so she quit her job and made herself scarce. She needed money but was afraid to show her face while the authorities were questioning the validity of the will.

Erin had not been deceased long and all she could learn was that everything had been left to Noah. She had no idea how much but Erin was stingy and clever with her money. Victoria made a bold decision — she would argue for custody. If there wasn't much inheritance, she could make the magnanimous gesture of letting Hannah keep the boy.

She didn't have a lot of time and she had ideas, but no plan. And so far, it wasn't going well. This Hannah had surrounded herself with lawyers and protectors.

Victoria moved what liquid assets she had, not nearly enough to retire on, sold a few things, packed up and headed south to Colorado. It was time for her to move on anyway. She left her house and stopped paying rent, having convinced the owners she'd been ill and was in recovery.

It was her plan to seek custody and with that, gain at least a large share of whatever inheritance belonged to Noah.

But then she discovered Owen. Not only was he clearly well-to-do, he was fond of the boy. She researched him and learned he had lost his own son years before, a fact that would make him much more vulnerable. Hopefully he would be very helpful in making Victoria go away. All it would take was money.

Of course Victoria would have to have some leverage. She was pondering which of her many talents she would employ.

She had one more supervised visit with the boy. After that the judge would rule on what kind of relationship she would be allowed to have with him.

*Love is composed of a single
soul inhabiting two bodies.*
— Aristotle

12

The first week in August brought the second visit from Victoria. It was not as tense as the first, though Hannah, Owen and Cal were all on hand. Noah made it two whole hours before complaining, but he did ask Owen if they could show Victoria the dock so she could see the fish swimming and jumping.

Victoria was full of questions for Noah: What was his favorite thing to watch on TV? What was his favorite thing to do in school? What did he want to be when he grew up? What did he read? Were there any sports he could play even though he was using crutches and braces? "Sometimes I pole vault," he said.

When Victoria said, "Really?" Owen snorted a laugh.

Hannah was not going to relax until their next visit with the judge was over, even though Cal continuously tried to reassure her that her guardianship was not in jeopardy. But this time the judge wanted to meet Noah prior to their hearing. The attorneys were present for the ten-minute meeting.

"What did he ask you, Noah?" Hannah asked when he returned to her. "Was it okay? Were you scared?"

"No, I wasn't scared. He's old like Sully. He has pictures of kids all over his office and he said he has about a million grand-kids. He asked me if I enjoyed seeing my grandma and I said it was okay. I told him I used good manners."

"You were exceptional," Hannah agreed. "Anything else?"

"He asked me if I'd like to see her again and I said . . ." He stopped and hung his head. "I said it wasn't that much fun. But he laughed so I think we're okay. Then he said it was very nice to meet me and asked, 'Was I looking forward to school?' and I said I didn't know because it would be a new school. Have you decided yet, Hannah? Because I know what I want to do."

She laughed. "I know what you want to do, too," she said. "Don't put pressure on me yet — it's a hard decision."

So the day came that they went back to court. There were only the original com-plaints — the suit for custody and motion to dismiss. Judge Vincente's courtroom was pretty low-key and casual.

"Did you have a couple of nice visits with your grandson, Mrs. Addison?" he asked Victoria.

"I tried," she said. "It was a little difficult being watched as if I'd steal something or beat my grandson."

"I hope you're satisfied that he's happy, healthy and in good hands. Here's where I'd like to leave the whole issue, unless your attorneys want to throw a lot of paper at me. Hannah Russell will retain sole custody, just as I told you would happen. Ms. Russell will provide her cell phone number to you and you may use it to inquire about Noah. Not to harass her but to politely inquire. Perhaps you'll even want to say hello to him. Maybe you'd like to see him sometime in the future, but that is at the sole discretion of his guardian and under only the conditions in which she feels comfortable. Be sensitive, Mrs. Addison. Ms. Russell also needs time to bond with Noah.

"I've been in situations like this before, Mrs. Addison. Different details in the circumstances, of course, but similar in many ways. If you tread carefully and respect the boundaries Noah's guardian has established, there may come a time you can see or talk to Noah more often and establish some rapport. Remember him at Christmas and on his birthday. Have you done that before?"

"Of course!" Victoria said. "But my daughter was angry with me and probably didn't tell him I sent gifts."

Judge Vincente frowned. "I see," he said. "Well, that takes care of our business. Sole custody to Ms. Russell, supervised visitation upon approval by Ms. Russell. Have a good day, everyone."

Hannah almost collapsed in relief.

It was no surprise that there were others waiting for the news. Cal had calls from Sully and Maggie; Hannah had turned off her phone during court, and when she turned it back on, there was a message from Leigh Shandon.

Noah had stayed at the Crossing with Sully and Helen, so by the time Hannah, Owen and Cal got there, an impromptu party was just getting started. Leigh and her baby showed up after her clinic hours were over. Cal called Maggie and she came with Elizabeth. Sierra came with her children, and Connie and a couple of firefighters came by. Owen drove around the lake to his house to fetch Romeo, the only guest who couldn't get there on his own. Everyone gathered around the front porch of Sully's house, leaving the porch at the store for the campers. The store was being tended by a couple of the Canaday kids who often worked there, with Sully popping over often to make sure they were doing all right.

Everyone decided simultaneously they could throw together dinner from what was on hand. Helen brought out some burgers and chicken breasts. Maggie and Hannah raided the garden and steamed vegetables and created an enormous salad.

"Is it really over?" Sierra asked Hannah.

"Cal said Victoria would have to have a profound reason to revisit the issue, like if Noah were being abused. Even if Victoria lied, Noah wouldn't let her get away with it." She shook her head and laughed. "I knew Noah was smart, but you have no idea how intuitive he is. He pretty much trapped her in lies during their first visit. It took me a second to realize he was actually testing her, asking her questions about his mother. She didn't have the right answers and he was done."

"How do you feel now?" Sierra asked.

"Like all my bones are made of tissue paper! Noah and I have been a team for five months now. I still miss Erin so much but every night I say a little prayer of thanks, hoping she's on the party line and can hear me. I will fight for Noah to the death."

"Welcome aboard, Hannah," Sierra said. "You're a mom."

After Noah went to bed that night, Hannah and Owen snuggled up on the couch and whispered about their relief.

"There's really nowhere else for her to go to attempt getting custody. But we're going to have to pay attention. Even if she does just want a chance to be a grandmother, I'm planning to give her a wide berth, I think," Hannah said.

"She doesn't look at all like what I was expecting," Owen said. "I guess I'd built her into some kind of monster in my mind. She looks harmless. She's attractive and well-spoken. She did some convincing crying in the courtroom during that first hearing."

"I had a friend in high school who could do that," Hannah said. "She could turn it on and off at will. I lost track of her. I bet she shows up on the Oscars someday."

"I think you're actually lighter," he said, giving her a playful jostle. "Not a tense muscle in your body weighing you down."

"I'm floating . . ."

"And by the way, it's August. We have gotten through two custody scares and school starts in less than a month."

She bit her lip and turned her head to look up at him. "I'm pretty nervous. Is it me or is it Noah? Because it's understandable that you'd feel protective of a lost little boy after losing your own son."

He bent to press a kiss on her lips. "I need to sharpen my skills if you think it's only about Noah. Yeah, I already love the kid. Anyone who doesn't should have his head examined. But I love you in an entirely different way. Level with me. Are you afraid to quit your job?"

"Oh, yeah. And move out of my house. And live off you. And all of it. The only thing that no longer scares me is the idea of being Noah's mother. I could never go back. It's what I want to be."

"Can you ask for an extended leave of absence?"

"To keep a job but not to keep my position. I've used up almost all my leave, remember."

"Can we take small steps that might turn into bigger steps? For you. I understand your uncertainty and I also understand that I don't have to quit a job or move, so I'm not risking as much."

"What kind of small steps?" she asked.

"Rent out your house. Ask for an extended leave even though it won't secure your position but it would ensure you a place of employment in a company you understand. It's a little safety net. It won't come to that, I bet. But one step at a time."

"I have a lot of stuff in that house . . ."

"Let's go empty it out. Bring what you want here, store the rest."

"It should be painted. Carpets cleaned. Repairs made. I've had a neighborhood kid cutting the grass but everything else is a mess . . ."

Owen laughed. "Everything except the sorting can be done by phone. Since you're not living in the neighborhood, you'll need a property manager. They get about ten to twenty percent. You'll pay the mortgage with the rent money. Maybe you'll like having a rental. Hannah, Noah has to go to school somewhere. You don't have much time to decide exactly where."

"This is such a small town," she said. "It's not like Minneapolis, where I can find so many specialists . . ."

"And yet we're friends with a semifamous criminal defense attorney and a well-known neurosurgeon. I think Noah will get what he needs. I think you know I would move heaven and earth to help you do that for him."

"He wants to stay here . . ."

"I want him to make friends his age here, and for that he needs school," Owen said. "I'd love to spend every second with him but that's selfish. He needs to be with kids. He can't spend his whole life with some guy and his dog. Have you seen him lately, the way he runs? With those crutches that he can manhandle? He's like a pony, loping across the yard. I don't think he even needs them anymore but he uses them so he doesn't have to contort his body to walk. Yeah, he needs more time with kids his own age."

"I feel a little safer at the idea of having him go to school in a nice little town like Timberlake," she said. "I'll feel even better when Victoria goes back to Minneapolis. Do you think she'll know when we're there, cleaning out my house? Because I can't leave Noah behind. I can't. Our whole custody thing has felt so slippery."

"She won't know. Maybe her flying monkeys will find out, but how would she? Unless she has a spy on your house. And if we're clearing it out, we won't be staying there."

"We could stay with either Sharon or Kate."

Owen smiled. "That sounds like you're willing to give it a try."

"Are you sure?" she asked. "We've only known each other a few months."

"I knew in a few weeks," he said.

"I'm afraid of being wrong again," she said.

"Aren't you afraid of walking away from something that's right? I am," Owen said. "Don't panic, Hannah. Just don't give up on us too soon."

The next day while Hannah took Noah to his therapy appointment, Owen gave Cal a call and asked him when he could get together for a talk. "I'm working at home all day," Cal said. "Stop by anytime."

Owen drove over right away so he could be back by the time Hannah and Noah were home. Cal let him in and gave him a cup of coffee. "What's on your mind, Owen?"

"Hannah has decided to stay on," he said. "She's going to enroll Noah in school here. We're making a quick trip to Minneapolis, clear out her house, set up some repairs and she's going to rent it."

"That's fantastic news," Cal said. "She and Noah will make a wonderful addition to the area."

"She hasn't told Noah yet, but she will real soon."

Cal frowned. "Why don't you look as

happy as you should?"

"I have a bad feeling," Owen said. "We don't really know where Victoria is. Is she staying around here? Where is she living these days? Does anyone have an address? Is she going back to Minneapolis and how can we find out? I know we settled the court issue, but I just have the feeling the woman wants something. And I don't know what to do. I can't just hover over Noah 24/7 without spoiling his life. I mean, we'll stay close, but I'd like a guess at what might be coming."

"This is when a crystal ball might come in handy," Cal said.

"You said you did an extensive background check on her. How'd you do that?"

"I used private investigators," Cal said. "At times, when there are crimes involved, I can get help from the police. It won't be too much of a challenge to find out where she is. But what good is that going to do? It won't tell you anything except where she is."

"I thought maybe you'd be better at telling me what good it could do. I think we should know where she is and what she's doing. I'd feel a lot better if I knew she'd accepted the ruling and was moving on. Can you help me with this?"

"Good detectives command a high price, but they're thorough."

"Of course," Owen said. "This is unknown territory for me, Cal. But don't you feel something is missing here?"

"Well, that's not uncommon. Whatever motivates Victoria is her secret, I'm afraid. After seeing her with Noah, it's hard for me to be convinced she wants a close and loving relationship with him. I suspect it's about money, but unless Erin told her mother about the trust she'd leave behind in the event of her untimely death, there's no way for her to know. From what I've learned about their relationship, that seems unlikely."

"I don't even know," Owen said. "I just know Hannah doesn't want to use it for living expenses. She wants it available to Noah. She said, 'What if he wants to go to medical school?' She's thinking way into the future. So this makes me wonder about this brother — he's a felon. He could be dangerous."

"But he's in Minneapolis. He's on parole. If he leaves the state, he'll be put back in jail."

"Can you arrange to take a closer look at this dysfunctional family until it feels like there are no questions left to ask?"

"Do you feel threatened, Owen?" Cal asked.

Owen took a breath. "It could be paranoia. Of course, I wouldn't break the law or ask you to break the law, but . . . Well, there's something we've never talked about that I should tell you. Just so you know I'm not really overthinking this. I'm cautious for a reason. You see, I had a son . . ."

After Owen and Hannah had discussed all that had to be done, they told Noah they had decided to continue living together in the house on the lake.

He had a stunned expression. "For real?" he asked.

"We both decided we want a little more time together," Hannah said. "Do you agree?"

"Oh, I definitely need more time!" And then he hugged Romeo.

"It's going to be a very busy couple of weeks. I have loose ends to tie up in Minneapolis. We're all going together. We'll get to see Sharon's new baby and visit with Kate and her family. We'll be counting on a lot of cooperation from you."

Noah hugged Romeo tighter. "I can do that," he said. "Is Romeo coming?"

"I'm afraid not," Owen said. "He'll take a

340

little vacation with Aunt Mary."

Hannah was feeling some anxiety about Victoria, wondering if she had returned to Minneapolis, if she'd be lying in wait for them, but his grandmother apparently never crossed Noah's mind. He didn't mention her even once. And while Hannah had complied with the judge's request to share her phone number, she had not heard from the woman.

Hannah and Noah went to visit the local elementary school when she registered him. They looked around a little bit and visited with the office staff but since classes were not in session, there wasn't much to see. The teachers weren't even present to set up their classrooms yet. The principal invited them back the week before school was in session to meet the teacher and see the classroom.

They began organizing a move long-distance. Kate was able to recommend a good property manager and Owen lined up and scheduled packers and movers. The property manager offered to arrange for the repairs, cleaning and painting once the property was empty of furnishings. Plane tickets were purchased, lists finalized, appointments made.

One of the first appointments that Hannah scheduled was with her boss, Peter. She didn't talk to him personally but rather made the appointment with his secretary. Once they had arrived in Minneapolis, that was the first thing on her agenda. And she dressed for the occasion, wearing her business attire.

Peter stood from behind his desk as she entered the office. Then he smiled and came around the desk to give her a hug. "Hannah, you look great."

"Thank you," she said. "A lot of sun and summer fun."

"Sit down. I'm glad to see you but I'll be honest, I'm bracing myself. Hoping you're here to tell me you're ready to come back to work . . ."

She smiled at him. "I'm here to ask if you would consider an extended leave of absence. My life has changed so much, so fast. I'm not ready to take on a full-time job yet but I love this company and hate the idea of giving it up."

"First, tell me everything," he said.

Peter knew about her reason for taking family leave and then extending it, but she was happy to have a chance to give him all the details anyway. And then there was the fact that she rented the Airbnb for a two-week vacation and hadn't left yet.

"I think you met someone," he said, grinning at her.

"The most wonderful man and his big dog. Noah has been thriving there, become so healthy and strong. We talk about his mother a lot but he's happy. I'm happy." Then she went on to tell Peter all about Owen, his work, his travels, his lifestyle. Next she began to mention Timberlake and the Crossing and some of her new friends. Then she glanced at her watch. "Oh my gosh, I've kept you so long!" she said, though if memory served, Peter was never one to rush a meeting. He was focused, very present in the moment. Despite his addiction to executive retreats, he was a very good boss, and working for him had been pleasurable.

"It wasn't just the sunshine that has you looking so healthy," Peter said. He moved some papers around on his desk. "You know our policy as well as I do, and extended leave except for medical situations is not something we do. But in this case, I'm going to agree to it. You know why?"

"I can't imagine," she said.

"You're not going to use it. I might never see you again after today. I think you've found your place and your people. Maybe you're just a little reluctant to cut all ties with the nine-to-five world —"

She burst out laughing. "Who are you kidding with that nine to five? We worked late every night and traveled all the time! But I love this company. This company gave me so many opportunities."

"And you will be greatly missed, I promise you. You were always one of our shining stars. But, Hannah, success in business isn't everything. It's one thing, that's all. Finding that thing you love to do is the first thing, but finding the right person to share it with — that's everything."

"I honestly had begun to think I never would."

"I remember — you had that lousy fiancé," he said. "Good thing you found out before he morphed into a lousy husband." Then he laughed. "Listen, you ever want a job, call me. No matter where I am, just call me. You were one of the best employees I had. And if you ever want a letter of recommendation, I guarantee you a good one."

"Thank you, " she said, standing and stretching her hand toward him. "I'm very grateful."

"You earned it. Now, enjoy motherhood — your little guy sounds amazing. Your older guy sounds pretty interesting, too."

"I'll send you one of his books," she said.

"You'll be enchanted."

Hannah dropped by the offices of people she had worked with, saying proper good-byes. She told them she'd be away from the company for an indefinite period of time, thanks to becoming a mother and relocating to Colorado.

Then she sat in the parking lot in the rented car she and Owen were sharing. Owen was at her house with Noah and it was time to take a last look at her old office building, knowing in her heart she wouldn't be back. Her phone twittered in her purse and she grabbed it.

It was a hang-up after two rings. The number was Wyatt's.

This was amusing and also it was getting a little old. If it was an accident he should have deleted her number after the first couple of misfires. She decided to return the call.

"If you want to talk to me, you should leave a message," she said when he answered.

"I didn't think you'd call back," he said. "I've wanted to talk to you for months."

"And yet you hung up every time? You used to be so bold."

"I used to be so stupid."

"What did you want to talk to me about, Wyatt? Hurry up now. I don't have much time."

"I wanted to apologize, though I don't expect it to do much good. I treated you badly, Hannah, and I know it. Of course I heard about Erin's death, about you taking on her little boy. I sent flowers . . ."

"Yes," she said. "I saw. Thank you."

"I wanted to call then but I also didn't want to make things worse for you."

She sighed. "I miss Erin more than you can imagine. But I've never been happier than since Noah came to live with me. He's a gift and a joy. And I think we're going to be happy."

"I heard from one of the guys in your sales department — you moved to Colorado . . ."

"I'm actually in Minneapolis right now, closing up the house. Noah and I like Colorado. I registered him for school and he has new doctors. And new friends. It's a big change, but a positive one."

"You sound . . . good. You sound good. Listen, I have to say something — I made the biggest mistake of my life. I cheated on you and I lost you."

"Apology accepted, but there's no going back. I'm in the right place now. I met someone and I realize, you and me, that was

346

my mistake, too. We obviously weren't right for each other."

"Hannah, you didn't do anything wrong. It was me — impatient and maybe a little bored and completely immature."

"I can't argue with that," she said, but she added a little laugh. "You and Stephanie?"

"That didn't last. Of course. Is there any chance I can . . . see you?"

She was shaking her head at the phone. "No, Wyatt. That part of my life is over. I'm not looking back. I'm certainly not going back."

"I don't blame you," he said. "But I wanted you to know, I regret my actions. I'm really sorry."

"Forgiven," she said. "I think this is where we say a friendly goodbye and you stop calling me. I'm committed. I don't want calls from old boyfriends."

"Committed so soon?" he asked. "It's only been a few months. We were together over a year before —"

"Like I said, this time is different for me. Plus, I'm a mother now. Noah is my first priority."

"Okay, then," he said. "I want you to know, if I could get a do-over, I'd take it in a heartbeat."

"There's no do-over, Wyatt. Just so I'm

clear, I hold no grudge, but it's all behind me. I wish you well. The right woman will come along. Here's a tip. The next time you make a promise to a woman, just keep it and see if your boredom or whatever it is doesn't just pass."

"I look at things a lot differently now," he said.

I wouldn't believe that for one second, she thought. "Goodbye, Wyatt. Go ahead and delete my phone number. It'll be simpler that way."

"I guess I should be grateful you aren't blocking my calls."

"Ah, that's a good idea, thanks! When you run into our mutual friends, please say that I'm quite well and very happy. Bye, then."

And she clicked on her directory and blocked his number.

When she got back to her house she found that Noah and Owen were packing up Noah's toys.

"How'd it go?" Owen asked her.

"Very well," she said. "My old boss was supportive and gave me an extended leave that he doesn't expect me to use. And I got an apologetic call from the ex-fiancé. He's called a couple of times and left no message so I thought it might have been an accident, a pocket dial. Working up his nerve, I guess.

What a gutless wonder."

Owen grinned. "Did he ask for another chance?"

"He did, but that's impossible. I told him he was forgiven, told him better luck with the next one. And blocked his number."

He put his arms around her. "Poor dope," he whispered.

Hannah and Owen worked like farmhands, getting the house all packed up and shipped. One load was delivered to a storage facility not too far from Kate's house, and she was given the entry code. A crate full of Hannah's favorite things and the lion's share of Noah's toys, bedding his mom had gotten him, pictures and other odds and ends were shipped to Timberlake.

Hannah gave away a lot of clothing, furniture, kitchenware and linens, but the pile of things to throw away grew larger by the day. During the whole process Noah stayed with either Kate or Sharon. They spent a few evenings with their friends. Although the work was hard and dirty, the reunion was excellent and the prospect of a fresh start was delicious.

It was their last day in Minneapolis and Owen was taking one final load of junk to the dump. Noah begged to go along and Hannah stayed behind to sweep out the garage, her last chore for the day. The property manager had been given a list of things that still had to be done and Hannah was very pleased with the rental price she'd be asking. It looked as if everything was going to be fine.

She was almost done sweeping out the empty garage when a small bruised pickup truck pulled up right in front of the house. There had been so many laborers dropping by to give her estimates on cleaning, painting, repairs and landscaping that she just leaned on her broom waiting to see who this could be. The minute he got out of his truck and began to walk up the drive, she knew.

Roger Addison. Cal had texted her pictures of Roger and Victoria weeks ago, just as he had promised.

She kept a firm grip on her broom. "Can I help you?"

He pulled the cap off his head. "You moving out?" he asked.

"Do I know you?" she returned.

He shrugged. His hair was thinner than his picture showed and he was short of stature, but his shoulders were broad. "Just looked like you was moving out. I've been looking for a place."

She didn't let on that she knew who he was. "It's been sold," she said. "I'm just doing a final cleanup."

"You don't know who I am, do you?"

"Should I?"

"Maybe. I'm your best friend's brother. Erin's brother." He looked around. "I wanted to check on my nephew. He okay?"

"I think you better go now," she said. "I'm busy here."

"I thought I should come over and at least say hello to you and my nephew," he said. "I don't know if we met before. I sure never expected you to be my nephew's mother."

"Roger, you have to go," she said, pulling out her phone. "Or I'm going to call the police."

"The police? For what? For me being friendly? Saying hello? Asking how my nephew is getting along? Listen, there are a few things you should know."

"How did you even know I was here?" she asked.

"I knew this was your address," he said. "I asked one of the neighbors if he'd seen you around and left my phone number with him. Mr. Handelson, down the street? I asked him to call me if he saw you."

She shook her head. "I don't even know him."

"Listen, there are a couple of things I want to tell you, since you're raising the kid now," he said. "I was in trouble a lot as a kid, Erin pretty much hated me and I don't blame her. But we're still family and I always meant to make amends. I guess I just ran out of time."

"No, I think she did," Hannah said.

"Yeah, I feel terrible about that. I didn't even know about her until about a month after she was gone. I'm sorry for your loss." His hands were tucked in the pockets of his loose jeans as he just watched her. "I didn't treat her right. I didn't treat a lot of people right. And I would never hurt the kid."

Just then, Owen's SUV turned sharply into the drive. Owen got out and slammed his door. "What do you want?" he said, recognizing Roger at once.

"Oh, man, you people are not friendly at all," he said, backing away a little. "I guess you probably heard all the bad stuff about me. But I wanted to tell you, that was a long time ago . . ."

God bless Owen's tall frame, all six feet five inches of him. He looked down on the much shorter Roger. "You have no business here," Owen said. "You were not invited. You'd better leave now."

"I just came by to see if you needed any

help," he said, holding up his hands, palms toward Owen. "I drove by a few times and I can see you're moving out. I just thought I'd check on my nephew, see if there's anything I can do. Maybe I should take him for a McDonald's or something. You know, a little family time . . ."

Owen got very close. "You listen to me. We're not family, all right? You don't go near the boy under any circumstances. In fact, stay away from all of us. If I see you again, you're going to be sorry."

"You threatening me, man? Because I didn't do anything to you! But I thought, since you have the boy, maybe we should talk. Maybe there are some things I could tell you that will help you."

"Hannah, call the police," Owen said.

"For what?" Roger asked.

"For harassing us," Owen said. "You're a felon on parole and you've been told to stay away from us."

"I wasn't told no such thing!"

"You're being told now," Owen said. "When the police come, they're going to hold you long enough to find out what your purpose in coming around here is. I'm willing to bet they find you guilty of something. Just go away before there's trouble."

"I don't know what your deal is," Roger

said. But he turned to go.

"Did your mother send you here?" Hannah asked.

He whirled around. He scowled. "My mother doesn't tell me what to do," he said. "I told you, I thought I'd check on the kid. With Erin gone, I don't have much family."

But Erin hated him, Hannah thought. "Erin said she hadn't seen you in years," Hannah said.

"That was her choice," he said.

"And now it's mine," Hannah said. "I want you to stay away and let her little boy recover and build a new life. He just lost his mother. He doesn't need more trauma. He has no idea who you are. That's the way it has to be. Good luck to you, and please, don't harass us."

"Listen, I know I deserve that cold shoulder — I earned it. But I haven't been in trouble in a long time. I'm in a program. I'm turning my life around and making amends. I just wanted to check on the kid. Noah. Is he okay? He lost his mom. Is he doing okay now?"

"He's okay. So there, you checked," Hannah said. "He's adjusting pretty well, considering. It was Erin's decision that he be placed with me and not her family. Please don't push it."

"Okay, but there are a couple of things you should know. Important things."

"Like what?" Hannah asked.

"Hannah, let him just go," Owen said.

"I'm going," he said. "Be careful of my mother. She isn't who she seems." Roger backed away while he talked, then turned toward his truck. "I'm not going to bother you."

If you met my mother, you'd like her, Erin had said. *But she isn't really who you think she is.* It rang in Hannah's memory.

Roger got in his truck and drove away.

Hannah ran to the SUV and opened the back door. "Where's Noah?" she shouted.

"I took him to Kate's," Owen said. "He was dirty and tired and I wanted to get back here to pick you up. We'll have dinner with them, then head back to the hotel. I think we're all done here. Let's lock up."

"Owen, what was he doing here?" she asked, tears in her voice.

"I have no idea," Owen said. "But damn, doesn't he just look like trouble? I'll be glad to get us back on home turf. Romeo might not be mean but he knows how to look scary."

*A coward is incapable of exhibiting love;
it is the prerogative of the brave.*
— MAHATMA GANDHI

13

It was a great relief to get back to Colorado. Hannah took Noah to check in with the doctor and physical therapist, both of whom said he was doing great. They shopped for some school clothes and a few supplies, went to Meet the Teacher Day before school started and got back into their routine.

Victoria called and asked when it would be convenient to see Noah, and Hannah politely told her it was much too soon, that Noah was very busy getting ready for school.

"But it's been a couple of weeks!" Victoria said. "And I miss him!"

That just plain rang false to Hannah. She hadn't seen him in his life till now. How could this have suddenly become so important? She knew the excuses — regrets, mistakes, et cetera. "I'm sorry, but we can't fit you in just now."

"I'd love to hear about his first week of school," she said.

"I'll give you a call and let you know how it goes," Hannah said.

"I was hoping to hear it from him," she replied.

Hannah paused dramatically. "We'll see," she said tiredly.

Hannah was trying to get her things settled into Owen's beautiful house and she ran into even more things she didn't need. Her giveaway pile grew as she let go of things that really had no place in Owen's house. But that locked trunk in the master bedroom closet was emptied of Owen's things and Hannah was invited to use it for her sweaters or wraps. It took her the better part of a week to settle in.

"This is as lived-in as my house has ever felt," he said. "I love having your clothes in the closet and your pretty soaps and lotions in the bath."

"I have work to do in Noah's room," she said.

"I saw. I think that room needs another bureau and some shelves."

"Don't you have work to do?" she asked.

"I'm planning a big catch-up once Noah is in school. For now, helping you make this your house is a priority."

Through the last dog days of summer, late August, there was a lot of time in the lake swimming. There were fishing and reading and visiting friends and neighbors. Then first day of school finally rolled around.

And Noah couldn't eat his breakfast.

"You really need a little something in the tummy," Hannah said. "It's going to be a long day."

"I don't feel like it'll fit," Noah said.

"Are you nervous?" she asked.

"No," he said. "I think it's way worse than that."

"And you know what? That never changes. First day of kindergarten, first day of junior high, first day of high school, first day of college . . ."

"First day of a new job," Owen said, coming from the back, rubbing a towel over his wet hair. "First days have a reputation that way."

Noah promptly leaned over and threw up on the floor.

"Well, that should take care of an immediate problem," Hannah said.

Noah looked up at her with watery eyes. "Hannah, what if I throw up at school?" he shrieked.

"A lot of that stuff happens in kindergarten," Owen said, bringing paper towels to the table, wiping up. "You're not the only nervous one, Noah. I promise."

"I'm the only one who can't walk," he said.

"Are you kidding me?" Hannah said. "You get around as well and as fast as Romeo. All I have to say is, please be careful until you get the lay of the land and find out where all the bumps and holes are in the play-ground. Try not to crack your head open on the first day."

"Maybe I shouldn't go today," he said. "I don't know anyone there. I don't feel scared when I have Romeo but when I don't have no one, I could fall or throw up or . . . What if I . . . Hannah, what if I cry?"

She pulled him into her arms, kissing his cheeks. "Noah, there isn't anything you could do today that the teacher hasn't seen a lot of times before. The best thing to do is get that first day out of the way. Let's get your teeth brushed and get your backpack. Let's do this!"

"Ohhhh," he said. But he crutched off to his bathroom.

And Hannah leaned against Owen and said, "Ohhhh."

"He's going to be fine," Owen promised. "We'll take Romeo."

The atmosphere around the school was festive and charged with excitement of all sorts — kids running, reuniting with friends, small children clinging to their mothers or fathers, older kids walking younger siblings to the door, teachers waiting near the doors to welcome children.

Owen parked in the lot and got out of the car with Romeo on a leash. He bent down to kiss Noah on the head. "Knock 'em dead, Noah." Then, to be manly, Owen gave him a fist bump.

"'Kay," he said. Then he gave Romeo a loving stroke.

"Hey, that your dog?" someone said. A child of about seven or eight came over and got close. "He bite?"

"Nah, but he sometimes steps on people," Noah said.

"Can I pet him?"

"Sure," Noah said. "He doesn't have a mean bone."

The boy started running his hand from Romeo's head, down his back. Romeo obediently sat. "He's cool. What teacher you have?"

"Mrs. Dempsey," Noah said.

"I had her! She's cool. Now I'm in second grade."

A young couple migrated over and introduced themselves as Rick and Lydia. Then suddenly a firefighter they knew stopped by with one of his kids. "Hey, Noah," Rafe Vadas said. "First day, good for you." Then Rafe shook hands all around.

A couple of other kids approached, making a fuss over the dog, and Romeo was in his element. It clearly gave Noah some confidence.

"Let's get going," Hannah said. "I want to walk with you to the classroom, make sure you find your seat and cubby for your backpack. Did we forget anything?"

He shook his head. "Can Romeo come?"

"Not in the building," Owen said. "I'll wait here. But I'll bring him this afternoon when we pick you up."

"'Kay," he said, then bravely started off toward the doors.

Children poured in. It was noisy and disorganized. A couple of little ones cried noisily and begged their mothers not to make them go. There were women with babies bringing their older children to school. Older kids who knew the routine jumped out of cars that were dropping them off. Some rode bikes to school and they were stowed in a long bike rack. Some women were dressed for work; Owen spied a woman in hospital scrubs taking her son into the building.

Lots of passersby stopped to say hello to Romeo and he thanked many of them with a face wash using his oversize tongue. Owen opened the back door of his car and asked the dog to get in, but he stood by the car waiting for Hannah.

Then he saw her on the other side of the parking lot. Victoria. She stood outside her car, hands clasped in front of her. She lifted one hand in a brief wave. Owen didn't return the wave. He watched while Victoria slowly got in her car to leave. He watched her drive away.

That was intimidation, plain and simple. He knew she had called Hannah, asked to see Noah, and Hannah told her they had too much going on.

Damn, he hated to do this to Hannah, give her any more cause for worry than she already had after dropping Noah off for the first time. When Hannah finally arrived at the car, she was wiping the tears from her eyes.

"Is he okay?" Owen asked.

"He's fine! He made friends instantly! The boy sitting next to him wanted to try his crutches."

Owen smiled. "I'm afraid there's a small complication. We're going to have to take Romeo home and come back. It's too hot to leave him in the car. Maybe things will quiet down by then."

"Why?"

"Victoria was standing on the other side of the parking lot watching."

"Why would she do that? I told her it wasn't convenient to see Noah right now. I didn't make plans with her for another time."

"She knows what you want," Owen said. "I don't know what she's trying to do. Wear you down? Show how determined she is? It doesn't matter. We need to have a talk with the principal and let her know we have a custody issue with his biological grandmother. Even though we were very specific about who he could be released to, we didn't tell the principal there's one person who might be a danger to Noah."

"A danger?" Hannah asked. "What in the world . . ."

She got in and Owen started the car. "Anyone who tries to spend time with Noah without your consent is suspicious and could be dangerous. Would she try to check him out of school and take him? I can't answer that."

"Stop! Stop the car!" She jumped out and ran over to Rafe Vadas, who was just leaving the building. Then both of them came back to the car together. "Go ahead and park. Rafe said he has time to stay with Romeo while we talk with the principal. I'm not leaving Noah here without doing that."

"Everything all right?" Rafe asked. "Is Noah okay?"

"Oh, yes, he's fine. But there's a grandmother who met Noah for the first time a few weeks ago and she tried to get custody. She's been granted supervised visitation at my discretion, and the last time she asked I told her we were too busy. She doesn't know him, he barely knows her, and Owen saw her standing in the parking lot, watching the children go into school. We really should tell the principal."

"You really should," Rafe said.

"This is so uncomfortable," she said, waiting for Owen. "She's probably harmless, but I'm not willing to take any chances."

"Hey, don't let that worry you," Rafe said. "I'm sure they hear about these issues with noncustodial family members all the time."

By ten in the morning, Hannah was stir-crazy and bound to drive Owen crazy, as well. She finally decided to go see Helen and Sully. Helen was so calming, so worldly.

Labor Day having passed, the campgrounds at the Crossing didn't seem to be very busy. The weather was still warm and a couple of campers were sitting on Sully's dock, soaking up the sun. Helen's laptop was open on the table on Sully's porch, so Hannah went to the store first.

Sully was putting up stock, wiping the shelf clean of dust as he went.

"Hey, Sully," she said.

"Hey, girl! I haven't seen you in about two days."

"Today is the first day of school. We dropped Noah off and he made a friend before I even left the classroom."

"And now, doesn't that make you happy?" he asked.

"Sure, I'm just so nervous. Do you think I'd be a huge pain in the butt if I interrupted Helen?"

"Might cost me the Pulitzer," Helen said from the doorway. "Come over and I'll put on some water for tea. It's just finally cooling off enough."

"I promise not to stay forever," Hannah said.

Helen slipped her arm through Hannah's. "Stay long enough for me to get an idea, will you please? It's been sheer drudgery this morning. It feels like I have a rock in my head, not a brain."

"I don't know how you do it in the first place," Hannah said.

Once they were seated at Helen's table on

the porch and her laptop was closed, tea in front of them, Helen pulled the trigger. "Something's bothering you."

Hannah took a sip of her tea. "Today is Noah's first day of school. He was so scared to go but he sucked it up and off he went. By the time I left him, he'd already made a friend, and the teacher is a dream. But I'm a wreck. I realized that Noah hasn't been away from me unless he's been with you and Sully, Owen or one of my two best friends, who have known him since he was a baby. I thought you, being a teacher, could talk me through it."

"Oh, my. I remember being a little distracted when Leigh started school, but I was much too busy to let it bother me. How's Owen holding up?"

"Very well for someone who should be paranoid. Do you know about Owen's son?"

"I didn't know Owen had a son," Helen said.

"He died twelve years ago. He was only seven." Then Hannah proceeded to tell Helen the story. By the time she got to the end, Helen was wiping away tears. Hannah, already in a sentimental and emotional mood, shed a couple herself. "Owen admits he doesn't talk about it. I can't blame him for that. It's not a secret, though. I was researching Owen when I first met him and I found only one brief mention that he'd lost a son but I didn't see many details. However, if you were to look up Sheila Abrams, his ex-wife, you'll see that she has been an advocate and activist for over ten years. And she's the most wonderful woman."

"She must be! And I already know Owen is an amazing man. I can't imagine one ever gets over something like that."

"I'm sure he'll never be over it," Hannah said. "But you know what's so powerful about Owen? His understanding! I'm sure the temptation to hover over Noah is there but he said, 'Why should I make Noah's life difficult because I'm a little crippled?' He encourages Noah's independence, though that must come at a price. I think if it hadn't been for Noah getting Owen's attention, he'd never have noticed me."

"Oh, now, I've seen the way Owen looks at you, Hannah. I guarantee it isn't because of Noah. Even though Noah is irresistible. I'm sure if I were in his position, I'd be volunteering at the school every day."

Hannah tilted her head. "There's a thought. Do you think they'd let me?"

"Now, you don't want to be *that* mother," Helen said. "I'll see if Sully will do it."

Hannah laughed in spite of herself. "I know Sully is great with kids, but I doubt he's going to fall for that one. He has too much to do and too many little ones in the family."

"I don't usually advocate for hiding your feelings from your children — they always figure you out anyway. But in this case I think it's admirable to encourage Noah's independence. Teach him safety but push him to rely on himself. It's essential for every child, but more so for Noah. He'll need the confidence going forward if he's to overcome his limitations."

"I know. That's what keeps me from running back to the school and guarding him. It doesn't help that even though Victoria has been told she can't see him right now, she turns up in the parking lot, lurking, watching the kids. I don't know what's going on with that woman but she sure knows how to make me uncomfortable."

"Wait . . . What?"

"I said, she really knows how to make me un —"

"Not that! You say she was lurking in the school parking lot?" Hannah just nodded.

"That's creepy and suspicious," Helen said. "I heard the judge's instructions to her and Victoria isn't stupid. I wouldn't be surprised if she did that deliberately to make you uncomfortable!"

"Owen said something to that effect," Hannah said. "It's so frustrating — I keep fluctuating between feeling sorry for her, deprived of her only grandchild, and angry with her for the confusion she's creating. If Erin hadn't been so adamant, I might be more flexible, but . . . Oh, Helen, why do I feel guilty?"

"You can stop that right now. I don't know why Victoria and her daughter were at odds, but Victoria had plenty of time to make amends. Five years since Noah was born and quite a few years before that!"

"What do you suppose she wants?" Hannah asked.

"I don't know, but I'd be wary, too. Humph, loitering around an elementary school, snooping. How inappropriate! You'd better tell Cal about that. Cal might want to tell the judge."

"Owen said he was going to call Cal while I was over here."

"Good. She's a grown woman and Noah is a little boy who lost his mother! She should be ashamed of herself, making his life complicated just because she wants something!"

"What do you suppose she's up to?"

"I don't know but I bet we find out. Watch your back. Maybe talk to Noah. Just tell him that the rule is Victoria can't visit with him unless she has permission and you and Owen are present. That way if she shows up at school or something, he can tell her that's not allowed. And don't worry too much as long as he's in school. The Timberlake schools are wonderful. I've met a few of the teachers around town. And having been a teacher, I can assure you, they've come up against custody issues before. They know what to do."

"We had to fill out paperwork naming *exactly* who would be allowed to pick up Noah. They were very serious about that."

"You better believe it. That kind of interference has a name, you know. It's called kidnapping. It'll get you up to twenty years!"

"You know that, right off the top of your head?" Hannah asked.

"Darling, you'd be amazed at the things I have stored in there!" Helen grabbed Hannah's hand. "Apparently the judge's orders haven't really sunk in. Maybe it would be a good idea to be very firm and very frank with Victoria and make sure she understands your boundaries. If you think about it, you'll find a way to be both sympathetic and understanding and leave no room for doubt."

After Hannah left, Helen got on her computer. Hannah didn't remember Victoria's exact address but she did remember from court documents that Victoria was staying on Butler or Baxter Street in Leadville. Helen looked it up. It wasn't a long street.

She went over to the store. "Sully, I'm going to go out for a little while. A change of scenery could jog the ideas."

"Have you had lunch?"

"I had a little something at the house. Want me to pick up anything while I'm out?"

"I want you to tell me how Hannah's getting along," he said. "She seemed a little ruffled."

"She's fine. Just first-day-of-school jitters. It'll be okay."

"She did seem better when she left," he said.

"Sometimes all a person needs is a little empathy. I think I'll poke around Leadville for a while, see if I can clear out some cobwebs."

He frowned at her. "Why do I think you're up to no good?"

"I haven't the first idea. What a crazy thought. I'll check the bookstore, see if they have my new book on order. And what should we have for dinner?"

"I don't care," he said. "But I bet it'll either swim or cluck."

"How are the tomatoes? Have you picked them clean yet?"

"There's plenty but could you get a couple of big onions and some mushrooms?"

She sniffed the air. "You going to eat both of those onions?"

"It's the only fun I have, Helen. Are you going to tell me what you're really going out for? Because you don't like to poke around. You like to eat, drink, write and write and then read."

She sighed. "I wasn't going to tell you. You can't keep your mouth shut."

"Yes, I can!" he protested. "I do it all the time! What's up?"

"Noah's grandmother is behaving strangely. She wasn't invited to see him this week so she turned up at the school on the first day, watching from the parking lot, setting Hannah's nerves on edge. That's very inappropriate, don't you think?"

"You're going to make trouble."

"For Pete's sake, I wouldn't make trouble for those sweet kids," she said. "But I might check out this Victoria Addison."

"And do what?" he asked.

"I might find out what she's up to lurking around the elementary school."

"You think she's going to tell you?"

Helen smiled. "You'd be amazed at the things people tell me."

*Don't go around saying
the world owes you a living.
The world owes you nothing.
It was here first.*
— ROBERT J. BURDETTE

14

After spending some time talking with Helen, Hannah began to think about how she might shift the axis of power. By being unpredictable, Victoria had taken control of their lives. They were scrambling around trying to anticipate her and how to make sure they were making the rules for their family. Or more specifically, how Hannah could be sure she was protecting Noah. And on her terms.

Noah had a successful first day of school. He was very happy with his new friends and didn't sit out, even when they had playground time. He could maneuver expertly and, with the assistance of the crutches and braces, he had no trouble keeping up. He said people wanted to know what happened to him, so he told them. "I said I had a little cerebral palsy and that I was hoping to grow out of it."

"Excellent answer."

"And there's only one kid who reads as good as me. The rest of them are way behind."

"I think it's more likely you're way ahead," Owen said. "Because you got lots of special attention from Linda and your mom."

"I want to tell Linda about school," he said.

After dinner they called Linda on Face-Time. Noah was so excited, yammering a mile a minute, telling Linda everything he could think of. But when he went to bed that night, he cried. "How long do you think I'm gonna miss her?"

"Linda?" Hannah asked.

"Well, yeah, because I know I'm gonna miss my mom forever, but Linda isn't gone. She just isn't here."

"When I was a little girl, the phone was just voices, no FaceTime. I think we should make it a point to call her anytime you feel like it," Hannah said. "I think that would help."

His second day was also very good and though he seemed tired, he bounced out of school with a smile on his face. He wanted to call Linda, which they did. On Wednesday of that first week, Victoria showed up in the parking lot again. Hannah and Owen, still delivering Noah to school as a team, did not wave. "I'm going to be having a stern talk with her," Hannah said.

Hannah walked across the parking lot and stopped Victoria just as she was opening her car door. "This better stop," Hannah said.

Victoria turned. "Whatever do you mean, Hannah? I only wanted a glimpse of him since I can't have time with him."

"It's intimidating. Rude and invasive. You have definite boundary issues."

Victoria actually chuckled. "Why in the world would you be intimidated by me? I lost my case. I have no place in my grandson's life! I'm just a grandmother standing on the sidelines, out of the way, hoping for a glimpse of my grandson. The only one I will ever have!"

"We both know you're pushing it. If I see you here again, I'll talk to the judge. I've already warned the school principal to watch out for you."

"Now, that was rude!" Victoria said, but she got into her car.

Victoria didn't show up the rest of the week, and Noah's first week was very positive. On Friday night when Hannah was snuggling him at bedtime, he said, "I wish I could tell my mom."

"I wish we both could," Hannah said.

"But I always feel like she's near. When I start to think about her, I feel her. My heart feels a little bigger." She smoothed back his hair. "I get the feeling that she's kind of happy about the way things are going— we're all happy, healthy and trying hard to live the kind of life that's good for us. This was what she wanted for us."

"I miss my mom, but I never had anything like this," he said. "It's kind of like a family with a mom and a dad. I know you're not really my mom and Owen isn't really my dad . . ."

"And Romeo isn't really your brother," Hannah said with a laugh.

Noah giggled. "But it's like he is," he said.

"We're doing all right, aren't we? We're making the best of things."

"I like it like this," Noah said. "Even if it's not really . . ."

"Noah, if it's really a family to us, then it's really a family. I love our family and Owen loves our family. We'll stick together, the four of us. That's how we'll be okay — we'll stick together."

"My mom would like it," he said. "It's what she wanted. That's why she wrote it down. I just can't figure out how she knew about Owen and Romeo."

Hannah felt a catch in her throat. "Those

darn angels," she said. "They know everything."

"Noah said the sweetest things at bedtime," Hannah told Owen. She buried herself in his embrace. "He said this was what his mom wanted and that's why she wrote it down."

"Sometimes that kid baffles me with his understanding."

"I know. He said he liked our family even if we're not really one."

"We are as far as I'm concerned," Owen said. "We might not have the usual documentation, but it couldn't feel closer to the real thing for me. And maybe, when you and Noah are ready, maybe we'll make it legal. It might give us that extra solidarity we need when someone like Victoria comes along."

"Is that what you want, Owen?" she asked.

"As long as I can lie beside you every night, I have my first wish. I believe in us, Hannah. You, me and Noah — we'll be okay together. Anything I can do to protect us, that's what I want. I love you."

"How did I find you?" she asked. "You have been so good to us."

"I think the house and the dog found you," he said. "Thank God."

■ ■ ■ ■

On Saturday morning, Victoria called. She wondered when she could see Noah. Hannah had been expecting this. "There's a coffee shop not far from the courthouse in Leadville," she said. "Let's meet there for pie and coffee this afternoon at two. My treat. We should have a little visit before you see Noah again."

"Is something wrong?" Victoria asked.

"Are you free to meet?" Hannah pushed.

She asked Owen if he could keep an eye on Noah while she met with Victoria, and he nodded but lifted an eyebrow in question. "I think it's time Victoria and I have a discussion about what will and won't be tolerated."

Owen just smiled, but his eyes glittered.

At two sharp, Victoria showed up at the coffee shop. Hannah already had a cup of coffee and greeted Victoria with a smile, though the older woman didn't reciprocate. "Thanks for coming, Victoria. Let's get you some coffee or tea . . ."

Victoria seemed a little stiff. She knew something was coming and that was another thing that bothered Hannah — Victoria somehow seemed one step ahead of everyone.

When coffee was served, Hannah spoke. "We'd better have a talk about your expectations, Victoria, because it's already very clear that your plans and mine are not even barely similar. Noah agreed to a visit with you because I asked him to. He's so polite and he likes to please, but he was very honest — he didn't enjoy it very much. He was obviously uncomfortable, as was I. Not that you did anything wrong, just that he doesn't know you and doesn't understand why you suddenly want to be a part of his life. And lurking around the elementary school when you don't have permission to see him — that has to stop. Fortunately Noah didn't notice but frankly, it creeps me out. It's like you're stalking this innocent little boy."

"I only wanted a glimpse of the grandson who has been denied me."

"Well, it has to stop. I don't know when you last had a friendly relationship with Erin, but I know you hadn't seen her in years. She said she called you now and then and that's all. Noah is the priority here. He's recovering from his loss, but —"

"I lost my daughter!" she exclaimed hotly.

"And I lost my best friend — and we were best friends up to the day she died, never an unkind word between us! But Noah is a child! And he's the priority! If you'd like to call me to ask how he's getting along, I'll be happy to take that call. No more than once a week."

"When can I see him?"

"I don't know yet. Maybe in a few weeks, provided you don't try anything tricky like stalking him."

"What a ridiculous thing to accuse me of! I stayed here to see my grandson! It's very inconvenient!"

"Then go home. It could be months before we're ready to have you to lunch."

"You can't do this to me! I have rights."

"Not as many rights as you apparently believe. I am not opposed to letting you see Noah, but you have to be patient and appropriate. He's grieving. He's coming along but we still have rough patches. If you care about him, you'd better give us time. His birthday is coming up in a couple of months — send him a gift. Call to wish him a happy birthday. Be gentle with your approach. Be understanding. He wasn't even sure he had a grandmother until you took us to court. You'd better lighten up. I will not hesitate to go back to the judge if I feel pressured or harassed or threatened."

"Now you're being paranoid! I haven't done anything to —"

"Victoria, I don't know you. I don't know

you at all. I only know that Erin didn't want you involved with Noah. Your pushy and inappropriate behavior makes me nervous — if Erin didn't trust you, why should I? I'm not completely closed to the idea that you might have seen the light and hope for a good relationship with Noah, but I'm also not completely convinced. When you refuse to respect my boundaries, I grow more resistant. The judge was specific. I think I can count on his help."

"There's nothing you can do and you don't scare me."

Hannah leaned back. "There you go — that was threatening. I will see the judge. I'll file for a restraining order."

"I haven't threatened or assaulted you. You think you can just have a restraining order because you don't like someone? No, you can't. Besides, you can't prove I said anything!"

"Why are you so angry?" Hannah asked.

"How would you feel if your only grandchild was torn away from you?"

"You didn't care about him before. The choice was made by his mother, and it was very carefully thought through. Erin knew the law and she planned meticulously. Now, Owen and I are willing to work with you, but —"

"He's not your husband! Erin didn't give him permission to be guardian."

"He's my partner and Noah loves him. Noah trusts him. I thought maybe we could talk this through and that you'd be reasonable about your expectations, but if that's not going to work . . ."

Hannah pulled a few bills out of her purse and put them on the table.

"I will deny we ever met!" Victoria said.

Hannah slid her phone out of the pocket of her light blue cotton shirt. "Good luck with that."

"You've recorded us? Oh, how conniving! How could you? All I want is a chance to get to know Noah! I won't try to take him away from you. I just want to see him regularly!"

"And I'm telling you, from everything I know, his mother would not be in favor of that. But I'm willing to be flexible—every few months, maybe. You can go home, we can stay in touch by phone, arrange a visit now and then, and maybe later when there's more trust between us . . ."

"I worry that I won't survive that long. I'm not young and all I want is that he remember me," she said, tears coming to her eyes.

"What are you talking about?"

"I haven't been feeling the greatest. It's probably just the stress. The doctor suggested some tests. I'm seeing a doctor in Denver so I'm not going anywhere until I have some answers."

"Not feeling well how?" Hannah asked.

"Don't worry. It's probably nothing. Women my age have complaints, you know. I'll have a few tests, get some answers and go from there."

"I'm sorry to hear that, Victoria. But I won't change my mind about the boundaries. I'm trying to parent a little boy and it's my job to protect him, help him get through it as best I can. You're going to have to be cooperative or I won't make any further effort."

Victoria narrowed her eyes. "I really hadn't figured you as someone who played hardball."

That's where we differ, Hannah thought. *I finally realized you would.*

Helen didn't know that Hannah and Victoria would be meeting for coffee at the café in Leadville, but she recognized their cars parked outside. She'd been haunting Leadville for the past week, looking for an opportunity to run into Victoria. A chance meeting.

Oh, Sully might be right — she might be making trouble! But she was going with her gut instinct. Her gut was going with the obvious. Any self-respecting grandmother who longed for her beloved grandchild began that longing when he was a baby. A new baby.

She browsed in the bookstore, near the front window, watching the coffee shop. Hannah left first and didn't notice Helen or her car. Victoria left second. She drove a few blocks to the market. This was perfect. Helen could kill two birds with one stone. She needed a couple of things for dinner.

Inside the market, Helen grabbed a small cart and crept down the aisles like the super sleuths she was always writing about. When she saw Victoria poking around the produce, she made a sharp turn, drove her cart around an island piled high with fruit and melons and smashed right into Victoria's cart. "Hey!" Helen fairly yelled. "Oh! Mrs. Addison! Excuse me!"

Victoria glowered at her.

"What an oaf I am! I'm so sorry! You're all right, aren't you?"

"I'm fine," she said. "Do I know you?"

"I'm sorry, it's Helen Culver. I'm a friend of Owen Abrams and I was in court the day you argued for time with your grandson.

Oh, I wanted to reach out to you just then, but you seemed so upset. I'm so sorry that didn't work out better. I'm a grandmother myself. Well, not technically — it's my niece, who I raised, who just had a baby. And I know only too well how difficult it can be, wanting more time with your grandchild."

"Do you now?" Victoria asked, clearly cynical.

"Well, let me rephrase. My niece would have me take care of the baby full-time if she could, but that wasn't exactly on my agenda. But if anything happened to my niece, I can assure you, I wouldn't want my great-niece given to another family. Are you doing all right, Mrs. Addison?"

"I've been better," she said. "What did you say your name was?"

"Helen," she said. "I know Owen because he's a neighbor. I live on that same lake." She looked at her watch. "You know what we should do? Maybe get a coffee. Or better still — a glass of wine! I hardly ever meet women in my same generation."

"I don't know," she said. "I just —"

"I have to grab some broccoli and onions for dinner, then I'm free for a couple of hours. I'm taking the afternoon off from work and I admit — I wouldn't mind a little gossip time with a woman. What do you say?

Coffee or wine?"

"I suppose. But I don't have much time."

"Let's finish up here and meet at that little pub across the street. How's that?"

"All right."

Helen quickly tossed some broccoli and onions into her cart. She was momentarily at a disadvantage — she had expected Victoria to know who she was. Helen was not universally well-known, but in some circles she was a bit impossibly well-known. At book fairs, conferences and conventions, people sometimes stared and were afraid to approach her. When someone knew she was a moderately famous author, they were anxious to talk about themselves.

Oh, well, she'd have to prime Victoria a bit. All she really hoped to get out of this meeting was a clue as to who this woman really was and what motivated her. It was impossible for her to believe that all Victoria's maternal feelings suddenly bubbled to the surface a few months ago. Even more important, Helen wanted to know what kind of mother Victoria had been. Things must have been quite awful for Erin to go to such lengths to be sure her child wasn't raised by his grandmother.

Victoria was already settled into a booth in the pub when Helen walked in. Helen slid in opposite her.

"Just what I need," she said.

"Me, too," Victoria said. "I'm sorry if it sounded like I wasn't very grateful for the invitation. I'm in a mood. I've just come from coffee with Hannah. A meeting, if you please. Where she dressed me down and told me what my boundaries had better be if I hope to ever see Noah again."

"Hannah? She doesn't seem like the sort," Helen said. "What's that all about?"

"I'm not sure," Victoria said.

The waitress was at their table and they each ordered a glass of wine.

"You were saying," Helen urged.

"That's all there is to tell," Victoria said. "I've been asking permission to see him for an hour here or there and so far, the answer is no. Today she told me it's going to be no for some time and suggested I just go back to Minneapolis and wait to be summoned." She laughed hollowly. "I was laid off last year and haven't worked in a good while. I don't have money to fly back and forth. I wonder if it's worth it to stay on here if Hannah is just going to prevent me from seeing my grandson."

"Oh, Victoria, I had no idea . . ."

"Well, it's something I'm going to have to think through, make a decision. I suppose I should accept the inevitable. I thought she would be more understanding . . ."

"If you don't mind me asking, what in the world happened between you and your daughter?"

"Well, it's not easy for me . . . Erin was a vicious daughter. I couldn't please her no matter how I tried. She had a falling-out with her brother, moved away and stopped talking to both of us. Roger is no angel — I'll be the first to admit that — but he tried. Tried and failed. But for Erin to stop talking to me, for her to make me out to be some kind of monster . . ."

The wine arrived and Victoria took a sip.

"I was so shocked and ashamed by the things she said about me in some letter her lawyer produced. She called me abusive, claimed that I never protected her, that I allowed her brother to physically abuse her, that I was cruel. I don't know where that came from. I didn't have an easy life and I did my best to be a good mother."

"Of course you did," Helen said.

"And I'd do my best to be a good grandmother. But Hannah has hooked herself up to a rich man and she won't budge. She isn't going to give me a chance and her rich boyfriend is going to back her up no matter the legal cost."

"Owen?" Helen asked. "Oh, Victoria, I'm sure Owen isn't rich."

"I saw that house," Victoria said.

"Yes, it's something, isn't it? He rents it out when he travels on photo shoots. You have to understand about writers — hardly any of them make money. Most barely squeak by. Owen has made a comment or two about spending too much on that house and wondering if he should sell it."

"Is that a fact? What do you know about writers? And I thought he was a photographer, not a writer."

"He publishes photo essays. Coffee-table books. They're beautiful and he's well-known for them but they're not runaway bestsellers. They sell a respectable number to libraries. The real money is in popular fiction."

"Huh," she said. "How does he get this fancy Wikipedia page and everything? If you google him, he's all over the place!"

"That doesn't cost anything," Helen said. "You can put yourself out there in a big way, too. Just by spending some time on the computer and generating some photos and content. I do it all the time."

For what?"

"I'm a writer, too. A little luckier than Owen — I've been at it a long time and lucky for me, my books are popular. But don't get me wrong, I love Owen's work. He's very gifted. I just don't think he's rich, that's all. Maybe he will be one day.

"Now, tell me, Victoria. What kind of work were you doing when you were laid off?"

"Oh, that. I've done every kind of work imaginable. I've worked in real estate, in mortgages, home health care —"

"You're a nurse!" Helen said.

"No, not that kind of care," she said with a laugh. "I don't like to mop up. I'm more of a counselor, the kind of overall care needed by the elderly or disabled — everything from arranging long-term health care to reverse mortgages, that sort of thing. I'm best at helping people. I'm good at taking care of the details so these poor folks with no one to help them aren't completely abandoned. It's all very ordinary and doesn't exactly pay well, but it's satisfying. But tell me about your writing? I can't believe I know a real writer!"

Helen wasn't above laying it on a little thick, glamorizing her profession more than was accurate. The truth was she pulled on jeans and a top, sat on the porch and typed every day, had a light lunch with Sully, had a little exercise, messed around in the garden, had dinner, read in the evening and then repeated. She'd never spent so much time out of her routine as in the past week, stalking Victoria. It was frankly driving her bonkers. Sully was right — Helen didn't like to poke around.

She did like research, however.

So she told Victoria about her travels and vacations, the few famous people she'd met and plans she had for renting a condo in San Diego for a few months come winter. And she thought it might be about time for a new car.

Victoria chattered on about how much she liked Colorado but wasn't sure she could afford to stay and then she asked Helen a lot of questions. Helen was looking for important talking points. Victoria wanted to know more about Helen's travels, like where and when and what hotels she stayed in. She asked about Helen's books, of course, and asked where she got her ideas. They talked about the Crossing and Sully and his garden. Victoria wanted to know where in Chicago she had lived and whether she had any good friends besides Owen. "I'm very close to my niece," Helen said. "But she's married with a baby and quite busy with her husband. I'm something of a loner while I'm here. It's when I travel that I see my women friends, and I have some wonderful ones in the writing community. It's nice to have met you! Finally, someone closer to my age I can talk to."

Victoria asked if Helen had a secretary and who managed all her business details. She said she hoped Helen had experts to help her protect her assets. "That's what I did for a living, you know. I connected people with the right agents and managers to make sure they got the most out of their retirement or disability funds."

Every now and then she'd turn the conversation back to herself and drop in something a little emotional — with Erin gone and Roger pretty much out of the picture these days, she felt she had no family at all. She longed for her daughter's company, but it had been so long since they were on good terms. She'd had a hard life, twice widowed — though Helen knew that would actually be divorced — and struggling to raise two children alone.

Sully called her cell phone and Helen sent him to voice mail. "I'll have to go soon. Sully's probably restless and hungry. But we'll have to do this again. Let me give you my number."

"You don't feel awkward, do you?" Victoria asked. "Hannah and Owen are trying to keep me as far away as possible."

"If we're friendly, it has nothing to do with them, does it?" Helen said. "An occasional coffee klatch or glass of wine, that's just what the doctor ordered."

"Don't even bring up doctors," Victoria said. "That's a particular problem right now."

"Oh?" Helen asked.

"I need to see my oncologist," she said. "It's a long story. We'll talk about it next time."

"But you know my niece is a doctor, don't you? Family medicine and emergency medicine. She runs the urgent care in town . . ."

"Unfortunately, that's not the kind of doctor I need. Let's put that subject on hold for now."

"Of course," Helen said. "But where is your doctor?"

"There's more than one. Primarily, the Mayo Clinic. Now, when can we get together again?"

"I absolutely must work the next couple of days. How does Tuesday look for you?" Helen asked.

"What on earth do I have to take up my time? Tuesday would be perfect. Same time, same place?"

"Three thirty right here," Helen said. "See you then."

They hugged in parting, girlfriends. Helen went to her car. Now Victoria had a couple of days to research Helen. She called Sully from the car.

"I'm on my way. Did you think of anything else you need?"

"Not a thing, my dear. Have you caused any trouble?"

"Not yet, I haven't," she said.

Helen did a lot of writing about heroes and heroines, but she also had to write about the bad guys and gals. Over the years she'd learned a lot about how they played out. She'd studied interrogation techniques and body language. Victoria hadn't said or done anything obviously suspicious and her body language was appropriate to their discussion, except those few times her eyes strayed, as though looking up or askance in search of the next comment or answer to a question. And it was the weirdest thing — her damn ears got a little red when she lied. Helen was going to have to look that up. When she said her daughter was vicious, pink ears. When she said she would be a wonderful grandmother, she pursed her lips. When she was asking Helen questions that directly related to how much money she could spend, she got a hungry look and crossed one arm over her chest protectively.

Helen didn't know much, but she knew Victoria was lying and she was after something. She wondered about her work as a counselor for seniors, but Hannah said Cal had learned that. And this business about an oncologist? When a woman of a certain age had a condition that required a cancer doctor, it was usually impossible to shut them up, yet Victoria wanted to save that conversation for later.

When she got home, Sully was marinating some chicken breasts in the kitchen at the store.

"Oh, you sweet man, you couldn't wait for me. I brought us some broccoli."

"Why do you have such a satisfied look on your face?" he asked.

"I finally ran into Victoria Addison. Literally. I took her to a pub for a glass of wine and the story of her life. It's a bit different from the story Hannah told us."

"If you think she's not a good person, should you be spending time with her?"

"Someone she doesn't suspect has to, Sully. Besides, there's an old saying — keep your friends close and your enemies closer."

"And what is it you hope to gain?"

"Her motivation," Helen said. "It's exactly the way you'd construct a novel. The villain can't just be bad for no reason, they have to be driven to be bad for a very specific reason. Hannah and Owen can't very well protect Noah from harm if they don't know what they're dealing with."

"Is it not possible she just wants to spend time with her only grandchild?"

"Anything is possible, darling. We're going to find out."

"Helen, do you do this sort of thing regularly?" he asked.

"Oh, a time or two I've dug around in places I should stay out of, but nothing terrible ever happened. Oh, there was that one time . . . I called the police department and after explaining who I was and what I did for a living, I asked them how a person would dispose of a lot of heroin. This was before Google, you know. They referred me to the information officer who never returned my call. But I did have an unmarked car in front of my house for a long time. And an excessive number of patrol drivebys. Why they didn't just ring the bell and ask me why I wanted to know is beyond me. But see, nothing bad —"

"Jesus," Sully said. "You're lucky the SWAT team didn't kick in your door and cuff you!"

"I don't think there's any danger of that

here. Do you?"

"No, but you could piss someone off!"

"Somehow, I don't think so. I think she's dirty. All I'm lacking are the facts."

However mean your life is,
meet it and live it.
— HENRY DAVID THOREAU

15

Hannah watched as September gently settled over the land just as she settled into her new life. The leaves were just starting to turn and Sully's campground had fewer campers.

Noah had come a long way since that first day of school when he thought he was too sick to go. Now he was happy each morning and even wanted to see some of his friends outside school. That presented a new challenge to Hannah — she wasn't sure how to verify that the homes he'd be visiting were safe for him without looking like she was paranoid and overprotective. She decided to admit her doubts and wear them like armor. His first playdate was just after the first week of school at his friend Seth Loughlin's house. She decided to be up front about everything when she dropped him off.

"Mrs. Loughlin, I don't know if you know

this, but I'm a new mother. In fact, I'm not an official mother, but have been Noah's guardian for the past few months and we're a forever team."

"I didn't know," Sue Loughlin said. "Please, call me Sue. I guess that explains why he calls you Hannah. My daughter went through a phase of calling me by my first name, so you can never tell about things like that."

"I'm pretty inexperienced at this but I feel like I should ask a few questions before dropping Noah at your house to play."

Sue laughed lightly and said, "The house is safe and child-proofed. My husband's hunting rifles are locked in a gun safe in the garage and there are no guns in the house. If Noah has any food allergies, just tell me and I'll be sure he doesn't get any of those foods at our house. And I will absolutely be supervising. They can play in the rec room or the fenced backyard. There is no pool, and they aren't allowed in the front by the street unless I'm out there with them."

Hannah smiled. "Do I have any other questions?" she asked with a laugh.

"If you think of something, call. You plan to pick him up after two hours, right? And tell me, does Noah need any kind of assistance?"

"No, he's as fast on those crutches as I am on my two legs. But watch your shins — those shoes are hard."

"Thanks for the tip."

"And please don't let anyone but me pick him up."

"Would someone else try?" she asked with a look of concern.

"We have a slight issue. Noah's biological grandmother wants to see much more of Noah than I would like, though I can't imagine how she would know he's here. But to be safe . . ."

"I will stand guard! Have a nice two-hour break!"

Hannah's nerves over being away from Noah or sending him off for a playdate began to calm and she enjoyed helping Owen in the shop. One problem, working together like that with Noah at school led to hanky-panky. She would feel his hand on her butt or his lips on her neck and the next thing she knew she was sprawled naked beneath him, shuddering with a mind-blowing orgasm.

"Next summer I'm going to plant a garden like Sully's, but on a slightly smaller scale," she said.

Owen raised up on an elbow and smiled down at her. "You're still all pink from sex and you're talking about digging up my yard."

She giggled. "This isn't good for your career progression," she informed him.

"It's good for my life, though."

"It's a honeymoon," she said. "No interruptions, no kid calling out every five minutes . . . Oh, Owen, what you do to me."

"I know — I make you think of dirt. I'm not letting you dig up the yard unless you marry me."

"We don't have to do that . . ."

"We could get married and adopt Noah — then we'd all have the same last name and be a real, legal family. It could give us a little extra protection against the Rogers and Victorias of the world. Want to think about it? Talk to Noah about it? Want to ask Cal if it would make your position more secure?"

"Is it too soon after Erin's death?" she asked. "I don't want Noah to feel like we're ignoring his mother. She'll always be an important part of our lives and I'll do whatever I can to keep her memory alive . . ."

"It might make him feel more secure. I'm in for the long haul."

"Are you sure? Because I love this life with you but I haven't really figured everything out yet. I have no job."

"You don't? For someone with no job, you sure seem to be busy all the time. Do you worry that if you find something you'd like to do, I'd try to stop you?"

"You might, once you get used to my help in the shop."

"Nah. You've called off two weddings, saving yourself for me. Do you have your heart set on a big wedding? If so, we have to start planning. And we have to get Cal to work us up a pre-nup. Not for me, for Noah's trust. Did you say yes yet?"

She put her arms around his neck and rolled with him, ending up on top, her hair falling like a curtain around his face. "I think we should let Noah decide if he wants us to be a forever family. I know he'll say yes, but I want to reassure him."

"Okay," Owen said. "Let's do it. And then I'll help you dig up the yard next spring."

"Don't you have trips planned?" she asked.

"I'm not going anywhere until we're all buttoned-down here." He gave her a little kiss. "Thank you for taking a chance on me."

"I thought it was the other way around."

Helen was feeling a little guilty. She wondered if she should tell Hannah or at least

Cal that she was sticking her nose in Victoria's business. But she wanted to have more information to present before doing that. On three different days over two weeks she'd had three more casual glasses of wine with the woman and really felt she was getting to know her. Well, getting to know the person Victoria wanted her to know.

In the couple of weeks since their first glass of wine, Victoria had read some of Helen's books. She had a lot of questions about how many books Helen had written and how many copies she had sold. Helen was devilishly tempted to ask her if she wanted a calculator. She had no proof but it seemed as though Victoria was trying to estimate Helen's net worth.

Victoria raved about Helen's writing for a good fifteen minutes — it appeared she had read at least three or four books. Helen found it hard not to be charmed by her. In fact, if Helen weren't inherently cynical and suspicious, she would make Victoria her best friend.

But Victoria's conversation was punctuated with heavy sighs and a bit of nervous twitching. "Victoria, is something wrong? You seem not quite yourself."

And then Victoria dropped the bomb. "Oh, I haven't been feeling well. I've lost a few pounds, my lymph nodes are swollen, I'm fatigued. I'm afraid my cancer is back. Hodgkin's."

"Oh, no!" Helen said. "When did you have it before?"

"A few years ago. Five years now."

That was a different number. Cal had been told seven years ago.

"What will you do?"

"I'll go back to the Mayo Clinic in Rochester. That's where I was treated before."

"Will you stay in Minnesota, then? To be closer to your doctor?"

"I don't think so," she said. "I let my house go. I think I'll stay somewhere near the clinic for tests. I might come back here. I do have my grandson here. I'm going next week — there's only one way to know for sure — biopsies and blood work."

"We can keep in touch by phone."

"I'll try. It's an insidious disease," Victoria said. "It couldn't come at a worse time. And, of course, my insurance was canceled. Fortunately I have enough saved to get through the biopsy."

Helen could see where this was leading and she was very cooperative. "But what about the treatment?" she asked. "How will you pay for that?"

Victoria shrugged. "I'll manage somehow."

"You said you were afraid your cancer is back. How did you manage before?"

"I had insurance then," she said. "And a couple of coworkers held a fund-raiser for me and that covered the copay and my rent while I couldn't work. I don't have any coworkers here. Very few friends at all, for that matter. And aside from a couple of distant cousins, no family."

"But you must have dozens of friends in Minneapolis. Haven't you lived there forever?"

"Yes, I have a few friends, most of them live from paycheck to paycheck, like I used to. And the truth is I feel closer to you than most of my other friends, and in such a short time, too. But thankfully I've stopped worrying so much about Hannah and Noah. I think I have a more positive attitude toward the whole affair. I have a feeling if I'm patient, I'll have a future with my grandson. How much of a future, only God knows."

So Helen went home and made a call to Cal. "Do you have an address for Victoria Addison? I've been poking around in her life a bit."

"What are you looking for?" he asked.

"I'm not sure," she said. "Lies, I suppose."

"I hate to break it to you, but everyone

411

lies. And it's not illegal." But he did give her the address. Victoria was not his client; it was the same address his private detective had discovered.

Helen looked up the county assessor's website in Minneapolis. She found the name of the owner of the home Victoria rented was Gerald Sudmeyer. She googled his name and got a phone number. Then she walked over to the store to borrow Sully's phone.

"Why?" he asked.

"I want to call someone and not have my name pop up on the caller ID. I'm being clandestine."

"Oh, brother. I think you're butting your nose in."

"A little bit, but for a good cause."

"And what good cause might that be, madam?"

"I don't want to divulge that information just yet," she said. "I'll bring your phone back when I'm done."

"And then you'll tell me?"

Helen grinned. "You play all innocent but you're just as nosy as I am. Yes, I'll tell you after I make a call. I might not have much to tell."

She got comfortable on the porch and went over everything she might say in her mind. Then she dialed.

And, of course, she got the voice mail. *This is the Sudmeyer residence . . .* What a buzzkill. She thought the chance was slim that anyone would return her call but left a message anyway. "Hello, my name is Jane Sullivan and I'm calling about a woman who might be a mutual friend of ours — Victoria Addison. Would you please call me back at this number? I'd so appreciate it." Then she put the phone down on the table in disappointment. She opened her laptop and attempted to set her brain to her story in progress.

It was barely ten minutes later that Sully's phone rang and she looked at the caller ID to see if it was one of Sully's friends or family. The name on the ID was Sudmeyer. "Hello?" she answered expectantly.

"Hello, this is Gerry Sudmeyer. Is Jane there?"

"Speaking. Thank you for getting back to me, Mr. Sudmeyer. I'm trying to locate Mrs. Victoria Addison. Do you happen to have a number for her?"

"I have a number but it doesn't appear to be working," he said. "Do you mind if I ask — how do you know her?"

"Oh, we go way back, but I haven't spoken to her in quite a while and frankly, I've gotten a little worried. I sent last year's Christmas card to an address that appears to be your house." Helen recited the address. "I was hoping she was staying with you."

"That's a rental. We haven't seen her in months. I don't know how to tell you this but . . . Well . . . she's sick. I thought maybe you were a relative calling to give me the bad news . . . Her son stopped by to cut the grass a few months ago but I don't have any contact information for him and I don't know his first name. I've called several hospitals . . ."

"Sick?" Helen asked. "Oh, my, that's not good news. What was the matter? Was she terribly ill?"

"I'm afraid so," he said. "Cancer. Lost her hair from the chemo and she was looking pretty bad. She'd lost weight and had dark circles under her eyes. You called just in time — I'm going to have to put her things in storage and clean out the house."

"You haven't heard anything from her?"

"No, ma'am. Like I said, she's been sick. She wasn't able to pay the rent for months and we let it slide as long as we could. If she had at least called . . ."

"If she's too sick to call, I suppose she's too sick to make the rent," Helen said.

"I have a storage locker — large. I can

hold her things for six months. That's in the lease, by the way. But I can't hold it any longer than that. Our rentals are for our retirement."

"I'm sure she'd understand. How long has it been since you've heard from her?"

"At least three months. But she was sick a lot longer. We worked with her, you know. I wouldn't turn out a sick woman. I'm afraid she might've . . . You know, it's possible she passed."

"Mr. Sudmeyer, births and deaths are public record. You can look at the obituaries . . ."

"Oh, I did. But she said that she'd lived in Minneapolis for ten years but wasn't from Minnesota. And I'll be damned if I can remember if she even said where she was from. I suppose I could search all fifty states but the wife and I — we're not that slick on the computer. I could ask my granddaughter . . ."

She hasn't passed, Helen thought. *And she's a master with makeup.* She was a petite woman and it was possible she wore clothes a size or two larger than she needed so it looked like she was wasting away. But what was the point? You can't make a living by dodging the rent.

"Oh, dear," Helen said. "It's been almost

a year since I talked to her and she promised . . . I'm ashamed, it's just plain selfish
of me to think of that loan when poor Victoria might've —"

"You loaned her money?" he asked.

"It's been quite a while ago now," Helen
said.

"We loaned her money, too. A good
amount. She needed it for medical expenses.
Not that we really had it to spare . . ."

Pow, Helen thought.

"I'm sixty-five," Helen said. "And not
made of money, either." "Well, we're in our
seventies and our whole plan was to live off
the rent on a few houses. But she was in
need. What're you gonna do? I want to sleep
at night."

"Would you mind taking down this number, and if you hear anything at all about
Victoria, would you give me a call?" Helen
asked. "I'd so appreciate it."

"I will. And if you hear anything . . . ?"

"I'll call you, of course. And, Mr. Sudmeyer, I hope everything is all right and you
get your money back."

Helen sat for quite a while with Sully's
phone in her fist, thinking.

She wondered if lots of people dodged
their rent. She had acquaintances who had
rental properties and about half of them

complained that their property was damaged or their renters ran out in the night, owing them money.

Helen had a thought. She looked up the cost of chemo and the range was wide, depending on the specific cancer and the drugs required. It was all over the place — from ten grand to five hundred thousand dollars. There were dozens of programs that could offer help, depending on the patient's financial status.

Victoria really didn't seem like the kind of person who would take money from a landlord who didn't have much to spare. Sure, she'd given Hannah and Owen a little trouble, but once the judge and then Hannah stood up to her, she backed off and seemed happy to have someone to share a glass of wine with.

Someone whose net worth she was working out in her head.

Then she chuckled, not because anything was funny. Victoria had worked in a seniors' services center. Nursing homes. Real estate. Mortgage companies. Oh, my.

She took Sully's phone back to him at the store.

"Well?" Sully said.

"After some novice investigating I might have figured out Victoria Addison, but it will take a lot more to be sure. I think maybe she's a grifter."

Victoria called Helen just to say hello, her voice sounding weak and thready. "It's just the pain medication, Helen. That's all. I'm really doing just fine. I don't have the results just yet."

"Oh, drat," Helen said sympathetically. "And when do you suppose that will happen?"

"Tomorrow or the next day," she said.

"So, did you have to stay overnight in the hospital?" Helen asked.

"Yes, I've been here two days but I'm very sure I'll be discharged right after I see the doctor tomorrow. Tell me, Helen. Do you think Hannah is a good person? Kind?"

"Sure," Helen said. "She's very sweet . . ."

"Bit of a tiger about keeping me away from Noah," Victoria said. Then she coughed dramatically.

"I think she's just trying to honor her friend's wishes, and I am sorry about any misunderstanding between you and your daughter. But that's not Hannah's fault. You know I speak the truth."

"It's such a strange feeling being here, waiting for test results and feeling, oddly enough, that because of Noah, Hannah is like my nearest relative. I wonder if she'd take pity on me now."

"Hmm," Helen hummed, saying nothing more.

"I wonder, Helen. If it turns out I need a little help, would you consider a loan?"

"Hmm," Helen said again. "I could look into it, depending on the circumstances. Shall we wait and see what happens?"

Victoria coughed again and then said she'd better say goodbye and get some rest.

Helen went to the internet again, looked up every hospital within a hundred miles of the Mayo Clinics in Rochester and Minneapolis. She asked to speak to Victoria Addison, a patient. They had no such patient.

She told Sully she was going to dash over to Cal's and visit with him a bit.

"Do you mind running by the store in Timberlake and getting us some batteries?" he asked. "We're running low and I still have some hikers coming through. Just get a couple of big packs of AAs and Cs and I'll order a larger supply."

"Be happy to, Sully. In fact, I'll do it on my way to Cal's. Anything else?"

"Pie?" he asked.

"I think you know better. Maybe some frozen yogurt," she said.

But when she got to the store, she was unable to pay for her batteries or yogurt. Her wallet was gone. Other than slipping her phone in and out of her purse, she hadn't been in it once since she met with Victoria for wine several days ago. And Victoria had paid the wine bill.

"I'll be damned," she said. "Who *is* that woman?"

"I think your detective might have missed a few things," Helen told Cal. "Or maybe he didn't come to the right conclusions. I can't say I understand Victoria's plan, but I'm getting a pretty clear picture of who she is. I got a very clear picture when I noticed my wallet was missing from my purse and the last time I had it I was with her."

"You think she's a pickpocket?" Cal asked, eyebrows raised.

"More of a petty thief with the occasional windfall. I've learned she can get by faking illness and dodging rent. She probably has a lot of scams she was never arrested for, large and small. I talked to her last landlord and he said he believed she was very sick and didn't evict her, but you can't make a living that way. That's pocket change. But she also got a loan from him and, of course, she hasn't attempted to repay him. Or even call him. Remember when you learned she was seven years cancer- free? She told me it was five years and she's afraid her cancer is back. She also mentioned friends held a fund-raiser to help her with the bills. I bet that's happened more than once, the poor darling. She thinks I'm wealthy and asked me if I could float a loan if she needs treatment. She assumed Owen is wealthy, and I played him off as just getting by as a writer, but she was calculating the value of his house.

"Here's the thing — I'm very good at snooping, but just along legal channels. And I think I'm clever about figuring things out — like what she might be up to. Like we've thought all along, I think she wants a piece of Noah's trust. But here's what I'm not good at — getting the proof."

"Banking records might help," Cal said. "For that we need a warrant. I don't think any judge would give me a warrant because she lied about when she had cancer."

"Is it possible she's been ripping people off for years and hasn't been caught even once?"

"It's possible she has no arrest record in Minneapolis," Cal said. "And if the police have looked at her, questioned her, watched her movements, there wouldn't necessarily be a record of that. And some records are expunged, if there's no action. But usually people who make a living stealing are very well-known by police even if they aren't formally arrested or indicted. We always look first at public records — warrants, arrests, convictions. We like a snapshot — where she lives, what she drives, where she works, divorces or deaths, approximate income level, credit scores. We also like to know who her friends and family members are."

"She called me and told me she was hospitalized for tests at the Mayo Clinic. I called every hospital within range of the clinic — she was not a patient. Cal, I think she might've stolen my wallet out of my purse but other than that suspicion, she hasn't really done anything wrong. Yet I feel her continued presence in the area is suspect. I could be wrong, but I think she's targeted Noah and Hannah. I think she's setting up a plan to fleece them. I just don't know how."

"I think we're going to have to open a dialogue with Hannah and Owen about what you've learned and I'll have to deepen my investigation. When are you free?"

"I'm at your disposal," Helen said. Then

she clapped her hands together. "I love this stuff!"

"We might be disappointed, you know. She could be a curious woman who is not above taking advantage of a little boy and his trust fund if she can. And if she can't, she might move on," Cal said.

*In life you are either a passenger
or a pilot, it's your choice.*
— AUTHOR UNKNOWN

16

Roger Addison entered the police department in Minneapolis, the place he hated the most in all the world. His AA sponsor had offered to go with him but he went alone. It was important that he go alone. This would be the hardest thing he'd ever done.

His mother had called him a few days ago and asked him to come to Colorado. She said she had a job for him, an important job, and if he'd do this one last time she'd never ask another thing.

He had argued. "I can't leave the state. I'm on parole!" he had said. "I'm in a good program and I'm not using and I'm done with crimes. I can't."

"You're not wearing an ankle monitor," she said. "You can slip away for a day or two and no one will ever know as long as you don't miss your appointment with your parole officer. Just come. I'll make it worth your while."

"Tell me what you want me to do," he said.

And she had laughed. "You think I turned stupid? I'll tell you when you get here."

"It doesn't have anything to do with Erin's little boy, does it? Because I'm not getting in the middle of that. There's no reason to do anything bad to that little boy."

"I never do anything bad!" she snapped. "It's all perception. It'll be fine."

But he knew better, he'd been down this road before. He told her he'd have to think about it for a couple of days. Rather than thinking about it, he told his counselor in his rehab program. His counselor already knew about his twisted relationship with his mother, and in rehab that wasn't a rare story. His mother was a thief. She'd been the one to teach him how to get a wallet out of a pocket or purse. He'd never been as good as she was, but it had gotten him by a few times when he needed drugs. He and his boys used to steal just about anything they could get their hands on.

He escalated his thievery as his drug habit had grown until he was arrested for armed robbery and was facing twenty years. He got away with only three and parole, and that was where he got cleaned up, in a program in prison. It was a miracle, really. It wasn't at all hard to get drugs in prison, but he got the right cell mate and tried the program.

The police had talked to him about his mother several times but he couldn't turn on her. Not because she was so good and not even because he cared about her, but she was his mother. She'd been involved in shady real estate deals, in fraudulent guardianship situations. Victoria could smell a potential scam in so many situations and it wasn't unusual for her to recruit Roger to help out in one of her business deals. Her last project was the guardianship of an elderly man with dementia. She took care of his bills and living expenses out of his account. There appeared to be no will so Roger held the smartphone and recorded the old guy saying that he was so grateful to Victoria that he wanted her to inherit his estate. His assets were valued at around $800,000.

But there was a will executed before the man entered into a guardianship arrangement with Victoria. His original will was drawn when he was lucid and in control, and given he had no family, he had bequeathed his estate to the public library. And the library had a copy of the will and contested Victoria's claim.

As it turned out, Victoria was part of a small group of guardians headed up by a crooked attorney, and one by one they were going down. And that was when Victoria decided she *must* find her grandson. She suspected Erin might have left behind at least a good insurance policy. Then Victoria found Noah in the custody of Hannah and a man she described as rich.

"Well, Roger," Detective Wilhelm said. "I have to say I'm surprised to see you here. Have you decided to talk to us about your mother?"

"I might want to talk about possibilities," he said. "I don't know. I don't want to roll over on my mother. But I might have to. Depends."

"She's a person of interest but her status is rapidly changing as witnesses talk to save themselves. And, of course, we know where she is," Bruce Wilhelm said.

"Do you know why she's there?" Roger asked.

"I think we're up to speed, but why don't you tell me why you're here?" the detective said.

"My sister," he said. "I never treated her right. At first because I was a spoiled kid and later because I was a delinquent usually on drugs. I've been clean a few years. Well, three and change. And my sister is dead. I wasn't able to make amends."

Wilhelm frowned. "What's that got to do with anything? You know what I want to know. I want to know about that crooked guardianship con your mother was running with her crew."

"It wasn't her crew," Roger said. Because, as Roger knew, she liked to work alone.

"Okay, she was recruited or she heard about their con and got on board — doesn't matter which. Does that conspiracy have something to do with your sister?"

"No, I can't tell you about the guardianship thing — I wasn't involved. Since I've been in a program, I keep a safe distance. Really. But something might be happening that would be bad for my sister. My dead sister. See, she had a kid. She had a kid and a will that said to keep that kid away from her family, specifically me but also my mother. The reason my mother's in Colorado is to see if she can get custody of the kid. He's just a little boy and he's on crutches. I guess he's got some kind of disease or something. Like I said, my sister didn't talk to me. But my mother wants me to come to Colorado and do a favor for her."

"What kind of favor?"

"She won't tell me till I get there but I know her — it has something to do with the kid. She wants custody for my sister's insurance money or whatever is left to the kid. If she wants me involved, she plans to do something not good. She'll want me to do it because she doesn't like to get her hands dirty. Maybe I can keep something bad from happening to my nephew. That would make my amends with my sister."

Bruce Wilhelm folded his hands on his desk and looked directly at Roger. "I'll be honest with you — I want your mother for fraud in the guardianship scam. I think she got away with some serious money and she can witness against the others. I can't arrest her for what she might want to do."

"Well, I could go to Colorado like she wants. I could find out what she wants me to do."

"You know you can't leave the state under your parole conditions. Unless," he said, drawing out the word. "You talking about a sting?"

"I'm not going to testify against my mother. I can't, that's all. But if I have a chance to stop her from robbing my dead sister's kid . . . That's another story. It would be the first time I did anything for my sister." His eyes grew moist.

Bruce Wilhelm was quiet for a long moment. "Give me a few hours to think about this. Can you hang around?"

"Here? Come on, man. This place gives me hives. How about the Starbucks down the street?"

Bruce looked at his watch. "Four o'clock."

One of Cal's favorite PI's from the Twin Cities called him. "Something popped. We have an extraditable warrant, which means they might be looking to arrest Victoria Addison and extradite her back to Minneapolis. I have the name of a detective in the fraud unit. You might want to speak to him."

"I might want to, yes," Cal said.

Victoria wasn't surprised when Roger agreed to come to Colorado. She gave him her address and asked him to meet her at her little rental.

She gave him the details of her plan as soon as he sat down. "I need your help on a project and then I will never ask you for anything again. And you'll be paid very well. I have been observing my grandson and his new family so that I know their habits well, and the schedule they keep is very routine. You're going to snatch him."

"What?" he said, shooting to his feet.

"Oh, relax, we're not going to hurt him. Just borrow him for a little while. He goes to school every day, has regular trips to the physical therapist, likes to visit a little campground across the lake, but the best part is — he lives in a large house in the woods on the lake. There is a long drive around the edge of the lake that runs through the woods. The best time and place to catch him alone is when he's playing after school in the big yard. He plays with a dog — big dog, but very friendly. You should have some hamburger or something for the dog to lure him. The boy will follow. You can just scoop him into the car. A rented van would be better."

"You have completely lost your mind," he said. "This is too much. You get twenty to life for something like this."

"Well, I have to. But that's just part of the story. I admit, that's the hard part. But when that's done, you take him to Colorado Springs, call my cell phone and I will go to them — Hannah and her artist boyfriend — I will be stricken, but I'll tell them I know where the boy is and that I can safely retrieve him for five hundred thousand as long as there are no police. I'll explain you just want some money to get away and you'll never be back. I'll give you a hundred."

Roger just smirked. "They'll never go for it. They'll call the police before you even get there."

"If it doesn't work, we'll both make tracks out of here. But I think they'll go for it. See, the man — Owen is his name — he had a son who was kidnapped years ago, and he didn't get him back. I have a feeling he'd like a second chance."

Roger shook his head. "I think you've finally lost your mind. You do know the police want to talk to you about the guardian thing you were involved in . . . ?"

"Ach, I had very little to do with that."

"That's not what the other people are telling the police."

"I knew I should have talked first. I should have known they'd say it was me. I had that one case. That woman lawyer in charge must have had twenty cases. Well, I'll be out of that business for good. But I do have to get out with a little money."

"I can't believe you're broke," he said.

"I have a little stashed away. Not enough to retire on. I'm thinking Florida. I've always had good luck in Florida."

"Fleecing old people?" he asked.

She didn't answer. "Are you going to do

this for me, Roger? I swear it's the last thing I'll ever ask of you."

"You say that a lot. I could get three years just for being here. I have a program back in Minneapolis, one that puts me on the right track."

"You're using again, aren't you?"

He just shook his head. "I don't know if I can do this. I'll have to think about it."

"Listen, I'll give you directions to the place on the lake. You can drive out there and look it over, see how isolated it is. This is like taking candy from a baby and I promise you, I'd never hurt anyone. I'll come and get the boy and you'll take off, never to be seen again. You can go some-where, find a new program, ditch parole and change your name. It's easy. At least look at the place before you say no."

"I'll think about it. But I'm not staying here with you while I think."

"Probably best," she said. "We really don't want anyone to see us together. I might still have a little time to further endear myself to family and friends. How much time are you planning to take?"

"Prepare yourself for me to say no. I'm not sure I'm willing to take this kind of risk. But I'll think about it. Maybe have a look at the property and the dog."

While she was waiting for Roger to come around, she phoned Helen and invited her to meet at the pub for a glass of wine.

"I didn't realize you were back!" Helen said. "And how are you feeling?"

"Splendid!" Victoria said. "I'll catch you up when you get here! Same time, same place?"

"I look forward to it," Helen said.

As she was leaving the store, Helen called Cal to tell him she was meeting Victoria. "I'll tell you if I learn anything." Then she gave Sully a kiss on the cheek.

"Helen, this sets my nerves on edge," he said. "You playing detective."

"I'm just going for a glass of wine," she said. "There's really nothing to worry about. We'll be in a public place. Nothing can happen to me."

"I know she's not a serial killer or anything, but I also know you think she's trouble. I know that's why you're going. Not because you like her but because you don't."

"I'm doing it for Noah," Helen said. "For Owen and Hannah, too. She's a con artist. And you don't have to worry, Sully. I'm very cautious and I'm very smart."

"Smart women always have scared me to death," he admitted. And Helen laughed.

Helen really expected Victoria to be wearing her sick makeup and clothing, acting out. But she wasn't. Just the opposite. Helen hoped her surprise didn't show. "You look wonderful! You look the picture of health and vitality!"

"Thank you, I'm feeling okay. I'm afraid there's a little more treatment ahead, but not nearly what I worried there might be. And I have good news about that — the doctor says that while I'm going to have to suffer through some chemo, this is not likely to be as bad as the last time. We caught it early! My doctor has a treatment plan and says I'm going to be fine."

"You look better than the last time I saw you," Helen said.

"Well, I wasn't sick the last time we had a glass of wine so I think that was just stress and fear. And when I last talked to you, I wasn't sure of the diagnosis. I admit, I was weak with worry. The doctor was very successful in putting my mind at ease. He's seen this before. The cancer coming back, you know. That's why they check so often so they can catch it early."

"What about your insurance?"

"Nonexistent, I'm afraid."

"But I thought it was against the law to

cancel insurance because of recurring illness."

"Someone must've forgotten, but there are alternatives. First off, I have a little savings. Not much, but a little. And the hospital will help with some financing. I'll soon be healthy and have enough energy to work. It's just a matter of finding a job. Any kind of job. This little duplex I'm renting is cheap and the landlord is nice. Of course I'm staying here. I'll find some sort of work."

"Staying here?"

"I may not be invited to see Noah much yet but he's the only family I have. I think if I'm careful not to be pushy, eventually Hannah will give me another chance. For now, while I'm recovering from another bout of cancer, I probably won't have the energy to be a pest and maybe she'll take mercy on me." She took a sip of her wine. "I wouldn't mind if you put in a good word for me when you have the chance. I think they respect your opinion."

"Sure," Helen said. "Meanwhile, when do you start treatment? And where?"

"In a couple of weeks. Mayo, of course."

"There are a lot of Mayo Clinics," Helen said.

"I've given some thought to having my records transferred to the Mayo in Arizona.

I could use a little sun. Minneapolis is freezing in the winter! And the snow . . ."

"But will you keep your little duplex?"

"Yes, if possible. Mayo has a small residence inn on the property. If they have room for me there, I'll be all set. Oh, Helen, I've had to survive some very tough times in my life. If I can get through this, I might have a grandson in my future. Maybe not right away but even if it's in a few years . . . It's something to look forward to."

Helen was thinking, *She stole my wallet and she lied about being in the hospital. She's got something up her sleeve.*

Victoria's phone chirped in her purse. She pulled it out and looked at it. "Oh, no! I don't want to answer it. It's my son. I told him I don't want to have anything to do with him anymore."

"Then don't answer," Helen said. "Does he know where you are?"

"He might guess I'm in Colorado," Victoria said, but she let the call go to voice mail. Then she listened to the message and her face went white. "He says I have to call him immediately, that it's about the boy, Noah."

"Then call him!" Helen said. "Put it on speaker!"

But Victoria didn't put the call on speaker.

She pressed it to her ear as she slid out of their booth and paced toward the door. In seconds she was back. "Helen!" she said in a stricken whisper. "My son has kidnapped Noah! He thinks he did it for me!"

"For you? How? Why?"

"I don't know. My son and I — we have a troubled relationship but we have yet to part ways entirely. But he's crazy, I'm telling you. And he's dangerous. I have to go to Hannah immediately."

Helen gasped, dug around in her purse and tossed a loose twenty on the table. "I'm going with you!" Helen said and followed.

Victoria jumped in her car and sped away, driving a bit too fast. Helen followed, her heart hammering. Of all the things she worried about, that Victoria was a grifter, a scam artist, she had never in her wildest imagination thought she would put an adorable little child such as Noah in danger.

When Victoria pulled up to the house, she was pleased to note they had immediately called the police. She had been counting on that. She had this all worked out in her head. She was going to save the day and it would lead to a major payday. After all was well and Roger was arrested, Hannah would realize that Victoria was inherently good down to her toes and they would fund her cancer treatment, probably out of money that had been her daughter's anyway.

She nearly sprinted up the steps to the deck and right in the front door without knocking. "My son called me!" she exclaimed.

Owen slowly stood to his great height and Hannah did the same. The police officer stood, as well. "Who is this?" the officer asked.

"This is Noah's biological grandmother," Hannah said. "And, as it happens, Roger Addison's mother."

"I'm Chief Stan Bronoski," he said. "I was called because Noah's gone missing and you, it seems, could be a suspect. You've been trying to see the boy, is that right?"

"But I came to help!"

Helen came in the door and stood inside, right behind Victoria.

"My son called me and said he had the boy! I don't know what he could be thinking, but even as unstable and dangerous as Roger is, he listens to me. I think I can find out where he is and I think he'll give the boy over to me if try to get through to him. He can be defiant but he also tries to please me."

"Where were you at the time the boy was

441

taken? A couple of hours ago?" Stan asked.

"We were having a glass of wine in Leadville," Victoria said. She glanced over her shoulder at Helen, who nodded. "We're friends and get together for an afternoon glass of wine quite often. When I'm in town, that is. I've been away — at the Mayo Clinic. I have cancer. I was having tests and now . . . Never mind all that, the most important thing is Noah. Do you want me to see if I can locate him?"

"Not just yet," Stan said. "Let's back up a little bit. So, you're the grandmother? The same one who sued for custody? Why would you do that?"

"Don't be so melodramatic — it was the best way I could get at least some visitation with the boy, my only daughter's only child. That was on the advice of my lawyer and it's all been settled. I don't see as much of my grandson as I'd like but at least I see him. I think down the road, when Hannah understands I'm sincere and well-meaning, I'll see more of him."

"Why on earth would your son take him?" Owen asked.

Victoria shrugged. "Maybe in his twisted mind he thought that might please me, which it would not. Or maybe he was hoping for some kind of ransom. Really, I won't know until I ask him. But he rarely does a good thing . . ."

"I think we're going to have to get a little more backup before we try to flush him out," Stan told Owen. "Let me make a call." He used his own cell phone to call and separated himself from the people in the room. Then he was back, facing Victoria. "And now," he said to Victoria, "please tell me how you've come to all these conclusions about Roger Addison."

"Well, no one knows him better than I do."

"Is he likely to hurt Noah?" Hannah asked nervously.

"Probably not if that gets in the way of him profiting."

"Your son has been in a lot of trouble, has he?" Stan asked.

"Oh, he can find trouble anywhere. He shouldn't even be here! He's on parole and isn't supposed to leave Minnesota!"

"But you assume he's in Colorado . . . ?"

"How long ago did Noah go missing?" she asked. "Because I just got the call from Roger twenty or thirty minutes ago. He certainly couldn't have done that from out of state!"

Stan's face tightened up a little bit. He gave Victoria a nod. "Why don't you go ahead and ring him up, see if he'll tell you where he is?"

With a heavy sigh, Victoria pulled out her phone, turned away and hit the number. The distant sound of a cell phone chirping could be heard and Victoria turned back to Stan, confused.

Roger stepped out of the hallway that led to the master bedroom. Behind him were Bruce Wilhelm and two federal marshals. Behind them, Cal Jones observed.

Victoria's lips pulled away from her teeth and she hissed.

"That's right, Victoria. You're caught. Roger wore a wire while you gave him instructions on how to kidnap Noah," Wilhelm said. "Your own grandchild, yet. You're sinking lower every year."

"You don't have anything on me," she said. "Hearsay, that's all."

"No, we have a warrant. The testimony of your partners on the seniors' services scam and the guardianship fiasco got us an extradition warrant, and we had a warrant to wire young Roger here . . ."

"You're an idiot," she spat at her son.

"Nah," he said. "I'm just done. And if someone doesn't stop you, you'll end up really hurting someone. Like Noah. I never thought you'd go that far. But then, what's the difference between helpless kids and helpless old people?"

"And then there's the matter of your cancer," Wilhelm said. "How many people have you ripped off with that one?"

"I've been lucky! I've gotten better! I have medical records!"

"I know," Wilhelm said. "We've been collecting them. Pure art, I'll give you that, but the doctors whose letterheads you used don't have you registered as a patient." One of the marshals pulled out handcuffs.

"You can't be serious," she said. "You're going to cuff a little old lady for some fancy paperwork?"

"With your reputation, we should put you in leg irons," he said.

Helen sidled up to Hannah. "Where is Noah?" she whispered.

Hannah smiled. "Noah and Romeo are with Sully. Time to go get them, I think."

Hannah wanted to go to Noah at once while Owen was waiting around with the police until Victoria was taken away. Helen offered to drive Hannah to the Crossing, and Owen agreed to catch up with them when business at the house was settled. Noah and Sully were sitting at a table on the porch, playing checkers. The dogs made perfect bookends, lazily reclining on either side of them. Hannah leaped from the car the moment it stopped in front of Sully's house. She ran across the yard and up the porch steps, wrapping her arms around Noah and pulling him right out of his chair.

"Noah, Noah," she said, nuzzling his neck.

"Wow, you might be overhugging, Hannah. I can't hardly breathe."

She loosened her grip a little. "Sorry. I guess I was missing you."

"I'm right here," Noah said. "Hey, you crying?"

"I'm just a little emotional today," she said.

"Women do that, Noah. Might as well get used to it," Sully said.

"That's okay, Hannah. Sometimes that happens to me. Is Owen coming?"

"He's coming in the SUV so we can take Romeo home. He's just finishing up a couple of things. He should be here soon. And then we should figure out dinner."

"Sounds like you should relax while I figure out dinner," Sully said.

Helen caught up. "I think once we dig around in the freezer, we'll be ready to serve. I know there's marinated chicken and salmon in there. Hannah, tonight you and Owen should sit back and let us cook. I'm sure Cal and his crew will show up. It's time to relax."

"I won't be fully relaxed until certain people leave the state," Hannah said.

Roger Addison had permission from a judge to accompany Detective Wilhelm to Colorado to participate in a sting that would corner his mother. He went with the detective back to Minneapolis on a commercial flight. Victoria was escorted back on a different flight by two US marshals two days later. The marshals were involved because some of her guardianship scams crossed state lines and drove into federal territory, as did some of her cancer fund-raisers, promoted on social media. Previous partners in the short-lived seniors' benefit business had agreed to testify against her; she had waited too long to turn against them. And once the story hit the papers, a number of landlords recognized her picture and called the police, offering their own testimonies about failure to pay rent and unpaid loans.

A successful career in conning people was finally cut off. She'd be facing a grand jury but it was impossible to know what charges she might stand trial for. Undoubtedly there would be a lot of fraud, which was her main career. But any good grifter knew you could never go back to a mark who has found you out, which made Hannah, Owen and Noah pretty much out of the target area. Still, Cal vowed to keep in touch with Bruce Wilhelm for a long time, keeping track of Victoria Addison and, though he had not been charged with any crime, Roger Addison.

On a perfectly and blessedly normal evening at the Abrams household, Noah and Hannah were finishing up their evening reading. They were almost done with *Treasure Island* and looking to start a new book on another day. Owen came to the room carrying a brandy and sat close to Hannah.

"Don't let me interrupt," he said.

"We're just about done for the day," she said. "We've been talking about what we should read next."

"I'm thinking about *Swiss Family Robinson,*" Noah said.

"That's a good one," Owen said.

"And I been thinking about something else. That thing you told me to think about. Like when I feel ready for us all to have the same name. I'm just about ready."

"How would you like to keep your last name, as well? That's very easy," Owen said. "Your name can be Noah Waters Abrams, son of Hannah and Owen Abrams by adoption. Your mom is pretty important to everyone, not only you."

"That's a good way to do it," he said. "I think it will make her happy. But are you ready?"

Hannah held him tight. "We're ready when you are. I think we're already a family — it just needs the paperwork."

Motherhood:
All love begins and ends there.
— ROBERT BROWNING

EPILOGUE

The first Saturday in November, there had already been snowfall in the higher elevations and a generous dusting in the lower elevations, like Owen's house and the Crossing. The aspens had lost their leaves and the pines had snow gathered on their limbs. Court in Leadville was not open on Saturday, but the judge who had presided over their custody hearing opened his chambers and the clerk came in to work.

Hannah, Owen, Noah, Cal and Maggie arrived to meet him there at two in the afternoon. Judge Vincente was not wearing robes today. He met them, invited them in with hugs and handshakes.

"This is the happiest of days," he said. When he was standing, he hunched a little but not much. He was a small man with a big personality. And he was so pleased. "Come in, come in, this is such a pleasure. You know, in family court, I have to attend to so many sad matters and this is such a joy for me." He bent at the waist and spoke to Noah. "Young man, I believe you brought this family together. You must be so proud of yourself."

"I guess I am," he said, smiling.

"Will there be a celebration?" the judge asked.

"A giant party!" Noah said. "They're all getting it ready at our house. Half the town is there. You can come. You want to come?"

"Maybe I will if my wife doesn't have chores for me," the judge said.

"You can bring her. It's okay. There's food!"

The judge chuckled. "A compelling invitation. I'll be sure to extend it to Mrs. Vincente. Now, the business at hand is a marriage and adoption. We will accomplish the marriage first before Mr. and Mrs. Abrams formally adopt Noah . . . Ah . . . do I see a name change here?"

"Yes, sir," Hannah said. "Noah wants to carry his mother's name into the future and we completely agree. Noah Waters will be Noah Waters Abrams. If you approve."

"Fantastic!" the judge said. "First things first. Owen Thomas Abrams and Hannah Marie Russell, do you pledge to honor the covenants of marriage, to be faithful and to support and love each other through the good times and bad? In sickness and health? Work mutually to hold your family together in safety and affection?"

"We do," they said in unison.

"Let me tell you what I know about marriage," he said. "I've been married over fifty years and it wasn't all fun and games, but there were times I couldn't believe the happiness I felt. I saw right away there would be a lot of compromise involved and that's not just for one of you, it's always and forever for both of you. The ratio of giving — it's very important that you both strive to give one hundred percent. And the most important thing — honor and respect each other even when that seems impossible. In fact, it's even more important when it seems impossible. Having made your promises to each other, witnessed by this court, I pronounce you husband and wife. Go ahead and kiss now. We have more business at hand and papers to sign."

Hannah and Owen kissed, then pulled Noah between them.

"As for you, Noah, I think you've made a very wise choice, deciding to make these two your parents. I believe they will teach you, protect you, support you, guide you and demonstrate wonderful life lessons, like the Golden Rule. Do you know about the Golden Rule?"

"Uh-huh. Treat other people the way you would like to be treated. My mom told me that one."

"I'm sorry about your mother, Noah. But not many people are lucky enough to have two wonderful mothers in their lifetimes, and I see you have indeed been lucky. I knew I would approve this adoption before you even walked in the door — the three of you make a very wonderful family. I hope you have only good fortune from this moment forward. And I hope you have a magnificent party!"

After signing and witnessing a marriage license and adoption documents, the adults and Noah piled into the SUV and went back to Owen's house on the lake. Cars lined the drive and were double-parked in front of the workshop and house.

When the Abrams family walked into the house, a wild cheer went up. Champagne was pressed into their hands. Noah was given a champagne glass as well, though his sparkly drink was apple cider.

Sully stepped forward from the group of friends and family. "Hardly anyone can think of a more romantic story than I have with Helen, but you three come mighty close. On this wonderful day when three have become one family, I toast the Abrams family. Here's to dreams coming true."

And the crowd cheered again.

Owen leaned down to whisper in Hannah's ear. "On this wonderful day when three lost souls find their way and come together. I love you, Hannah."

"And you are my dream come true, Owen."

ABOUT THE AUTHOR

Robyn Carr is a RITA® Award-winning, #1 *New York Times* bestselling author of more than forty novels, including the critically acclaimed Virgin River series. Robyn and her husband live in Las Vegas, Nevada. You can visit Robyn Carr's website at www.RobynCarr.com.

The employees of Thorndike Press hope you have enjoyed this Large Print book. All our Thorndike, Wheeler, and Kennebec Large Print titles are designed for easy reading, and all our books are made to last. Other Thorndike Press Large Print books are available at your library, through selected bookstores, or directly from us.

For information about titles, please call:
(800) 223-1244

or visit our website at:
gale.com/thorndike

To share your comments, please write:
Publisher
Thorndike Press
10 Water St., Suite 310
Waterville, ME 04901